DEALING WITH DEBT

International Financial
Negotiations
and Adjustment Bargaining

Titles in This Series

Case Studies in International Affairs
Series Editor: Martin Staniland, University of Pittsburgh

The case-study approach to teaching and learning is on the rise in foreign policy and international studies classrooms. Westview Press is pleased to promote this trend by publishing a series of casebooks for a variety of college courses.

Innovative educators are using case studies to:

- Develop critical thinking skills
- Engage students in decisionmaking and role playing
- Transform lecture courses into interactive courses
- Encourage students to apply theoretical concepts using practical experience and knowledge
- Exercise skills in negotiation, management, and leadership

Each book includes theoretical and historical background material, four to eight case studies from all regions of the world, material introducing and connecting the cases, and discussion questions. Teaching notes are provided to adopting professors, and to encourage the use of several different books and themes within a single class, the casebooks are short, inexpensive paperbacks of approximately 150 pages.

The individual case studies making up the heart of each volume were developed in conjunction with seven institutions—University of Pittsburgh, Harvard University, Georgetown University, Columbia University, Johns Hopkins University, University of Southern California, and the International Peace Academy—under the auspices of The Pew Charitable Trusts. From over 140 case studies developed by leading scholars, the editors have selected those studies that thematically and substantively offer the best classroom examples for each topic in the series.

DEALING WITH DEBT

International Financial Negotiations and Adjustment Bargaining

edited by

THOMAS J. BIERSTEKER

Brown University

Westview Press

BOULDER ■ SAN FRANCISCO ■ OXFORD

Case Studies in International Affairs

This volume, as compiled, copyright © 1993 by Westview Press, Inc. The following case studies have been edited and are reprinted here with permission: "The International Monetary Fund" by Melissa H. Birch, copyright © by the Darden Graduate Business School Sponsors; "The World Bank" by Melissa H. Birch with Casey S. Opitz, copyright © by the Darden Graduate Business School Sponsors; "The 1982 Mexican Debt Negotiations" by Roger S. Leeds and Gale Thompson (Pew case study no. 201) copyright © by The Pew Charitable Trusts; "The Mexican Debt Crisis, 1982" by Adhip Chaudhuri (Pew case study no. 204) copyright © by The Pew Charitable Trusts; "Restructuring Zaire's Debt" by Thomas M. Callaghy (Pew case study no. 206) copyright © by The Pew Charitable Trusts; "Nigeria, 1983–1986: Reaching Agreement with the Fund" by Thomas J. Biersteker (Pew case study no. 205) copyright © by The Pew Charitable Trusts; "The Philippines: Political Crisis and Debt Negotiations" by Penelope A. Walker (Pew case study no. 133) copyright © by The Pew Charitable Trusts.

Published in 1993 in the United States of America by Westview Press, Inc., 5500 Central Avenue, Boulder, Colorado 80301-2877, and in the United Kingdom by Westview Press, 36 Lonsdale Road, Summertown, Oxford OX2 7EW

Library of Congress Cataloging-in-Publication Data
Dealing with debt : international financial negotiations and
   adjustment bargaining / edited by Thomas J. Biersteker.
      p.   cm. — (Case studies in international affairs)
   Includes bibliographical references.
   ISBN 0-8133-1282-5 — ISBN 0-8133-1283-3 (pbk.)
   1. Debt relief—Developing countries.   2. Loans, Foreign—
Developing countries.   3. Debt relief—Developing countries—Case
studies.   I. Biersteker, Thomas J.   II. Series.
HJ8899.D384   1993
336.3'435'091724—dc20   93-19689
                                                                                    CIP

Printed and bound in the United States of America

The paper used in this publication meets the requirements of the American National Standard for Permanence of Paper for Printed Library Materials Z39.48-1984.

10   9   8   7   6   5   4   3   2   1

CONTENTS

PART TWO:
THE POLITICAL ECONOMY OF
INTERNATIONAL FINANCIAL NEGOTIATIONS

FOREWORD

The Westview series Case Studies in International Affairs stems from a major project of The Pew Charitable Trusts entitled "The Pew Diplomatic Initiative." Launched in 1985, this project has sought to improve the teaching and practice of negotiation through adoption of the case method of teaching, principally in professional schools of international affairs in the United States.

By 1989, authors associated with the seven institutions involved in the Diplomatic Initiative had written over 140 case studies in international negotiation for classroom use.[1] In considering a second phase of the program, The Pew Charitable Trusts determined that its emphasis should shift from writing cases to encouraging their adoption in courses taught through the case method.

One aspect of this phase has been the establishment of a clearinghouse at the Graduate School of Public and International Affairs, University of Pittsburgh, to distribute and promote the cases. During the first two years of the clearinghouse's operation, it quickly became clear that a sizable market for the case studies (and a considerable interest in case-method teaching) existed in the larger community of university and college undergraduate instruction. By October 1990, over 15,000 single copies of cases had been sold, and the circle of customers had widened to include instructors in such countries as India, Bulgaria, and the former Soviet Union.

It also became clear that although a classroom use for individual cases would always exist, there was instructional potential in sets of cases selected to illustrate particular issues in negotiation as well as negotiations over particular policy matters. Hence the Westview series, which offers students and instructors the opportunity to examine and discuss specific themes, including themes (such as foreign policymaking) that fall outside of the ambit of international negotiation. Each volume presents a selection of cases, some short, others long, some essentially unchanged, others extensively edited or rewritten. Each volume also contains an introductory chapter, identifying the characteristic features and dilemmas of the kind of negotiation or issue exemplified by the cases. Each volume contains questions for discussion and suggestions for simulation and further reading.

Case-method teaching typically involves two elements. The first (and essential) element is careful reading of a case document by students. The second is one or more classroom sessions in which an instructor, using sustained Socratic questioning, tries to get students to explore the meaning of events that are described, but deliberately not interpreted or explained, in the case document.

Like all teaching, case-method teaching depends on a contract, however implicit. The contract here is framed by two norms: The first is that the material within the case provides a common stock of evidence and a obligatory point of reference. If this norm is broken by the introduction of extraneous or privileged information, the case will cease to serve as a common focus, the assumption of equal information (however artificial and fictitious it may be) will break down, and some students will feel discouraged from participating.

The second norm is one of judgmental equality—that for purposes of the discussion, the instructor willingly suspends his or her authority for the sake of encouraging students to develop and express their own interpretations of events. Although the instructor may (indeed, should) organize discussions so as to lead students into specific questions, he or she will undermine the exploratory and interactive character of the discussions if students have the impression that they are required to discover "the right answers." This does not mean that instructors have to say (much less to believe) that they have no opinions or that one person's opinion is as good as another's. It simply means that they should be prepared to retreat, temporarily, to the roles of agenda-setter and discussion leader, rather than assuming those of decisionmaker and interpreter.

Although obviously there are some important premises regarding educational philosophy and psychology underpinning belief in case-method teaching, the case for instructors holding back is essentially pragmatic—that discussion is a good educational vehicle and that students will only climb onto it if they are allowed to share in the driving.

Case-method teaching is, then, a tool, supplementing the conventional tools of exposition. Cases can be used to follow up lectures; they can (as this series implies) be used comparatively; they can be used for discussion or for simulation. They can be used with or without accompanying writing assignments. They can be used to illustrate theoretical concepts (such as power) or to require students to enter into the agonies of political choice ("What would you have done if you were President Carter?"). But what they invariably do is to enable—and to force—students to take responsibility for their own political and academic education. The faint burning smell of hard thinking hangs in the air after a good case discussion has taken place. Surely anything that produces that smell should be welcome.

The format of this volume is slightly different from that of earlier volumes in the series. Initially, it had been expected that each chapter in a volume would consist of heavily edited case studies and that the texts would therefore differ considerably from those to which the original authors had lent their names. This and some other volumes have, however, used texts very close to the originals commissioned under The Pew Diplomatic Initiative.

Martin Staniland
Series Editor

NOTES

1. The institutions concerned were the School of International Relations, University of Southern California; the School of International and Public Affairs, Columbia University; the Edmund A. Walsh School of Foreign Service, Georgetown University; the John F. Kennedy School of Government, Harvard University; the International Peace Academy (of the United Nations); the Paul H. Nitze School of Advanced International Studies, Johns Hopkins University; and the Graduate School of Public and International Affairs, University of Pittsburgh.

ACKNOWLEDGMENTS

The idea for this book grew out of the first phase of The Pew Diplomatic Initiative, a project launched in a number of the leading professional schools of international affairs in the United States during the latter half of the 1980s. When my fellow project directors and I first met in planning meetings in Philadelphia (and occasionally elsewhere), our principal concern was with the training of our colleagues in the case method of teaching, the mastery of the art of case writing, the initial production of cases concerned with international negotiations, and the search for the answer to the perennial question, "Just what is a case?" After several years of experimentation with case writing and the rewarding experience of case teaching in the classroom, we became increasingly concerned with finding the most effective way of disseminating the rich variety of case materials developed during the project. This book, and the series of which it is a part, is an outgrowth of our efforts.

None of this would have been produced without the pioneering support of The Pew Charitable Trusts, whose trustees and staff boldly demonstrated that a foundation can make a difference. Special thanks are due to James McGann of The Pew Charitable Trusts, who played a critical role representing the foundation during the early years of the program—from his frequent site visits to his patient, informed counsel. I would also like to thank Cecilia Cicchinelli, assistant director of the Center for International Studies at the University of Southern California, who played such a critical role in launching both the Pew project (and the center) in their early years. Steven Lamy and the staff of the Center for Public Education in International Affairs at USC adeptly carried the project forward during the second phase (of integrating case teaching into the classroom and the curriculum). I would also like to thank the students of International Relations 499, who classroom-tested every one of the cases included in this volume (as well as my own teaching method) during our seminar together at USC's School of International Relations during spring 1991.

Each of the cases included in the text was revised and edited (some of them substantially) especially for this volume. Pamela Starr, a Ph.D. candidate in the School of International Relations at USC, audited the IR 499 seminar and discussed each of the cases with me after I taught them in the classroom. She made an initial edit of several of the cases and prepared the first draft of the glossary of terms. A more extensive editing of five of the nine chapters was undertaken by Christine Kearney, a Ph.D. student in the Department of Political Science at Brown University. Chris writes (and edits) with skill and clarity and has provided invaluable assistance in the final manuscript preparation. Kathy Matthes computer-scanned untranslatable texts and prepared disk copies of many of the original case manuscripts. Mary Lhowe of the Thomas J. Watson Jr. Institute for International Studies at Brown University skillfully and cheerfully typeset the entire manuscript, saving me considerable editorial trauma and making it possible to include so many fine cases in a single volume. Additional assistance provided toward the very end of the production process by Peter Biersteker and Nancy Gilgosch is also gratefully acknowledged.

Finally, I would like to thank the series editor, Martin Staniland, for taking on such a good idea, and the Westview editors, Jennifer Knerr and Rachel Quenk, for demonstrating so much patience for a manuscript long promised.

Thomas J. Biersteker

1

International Financial Negotiations and Adjustment Bargaining: An Overview

Thomas J. Biersteker

International financial negotiations between heavily indebted developing countries and their international creditors have dominated the economic policy agenda in most of the developing world since the early 1980s. In 1992, the International Monetary Fund (IMF) was managing arrangements with fifty-six countries worldwide, twenty-eight of which were on the continent of Africa alone. The total number of agreements under negotiation worldwide was far higher.

A growing amount of recent scholarly attention has been devoted to the timing, the scope, and the probability of the success or failure of these negotiations.[1] The conditions and domestic policy changes required for most international financial agreements cut to the core of fundamental questions about the appropriate role of the state in the economy, the division of labor within countries, and the role and place of developing countries in a changing world economy. Accordingly, the prospect for the continuation or renegotiation of many of these agreements continues to dominate policy agendas and debates throughout the developing world.

International financial negotiations are extraordinarily complex. They involve a large number of widely disparate actors, each with elaborate and often contradictory objectives on issues of critical concern. Multilateral debt rescheduling and adjustment agreements routinely involve negotiations among individual debtor countries, international financial institutions (the IMF, the World Bank, the creditor clubs in Paris and London), a wide variety of transnational banks, and the official aid agencies of the major creditor countries. Although some scholars have tried,[2] it is difficult to capture the variation in bargaining strategies and outcomes with simplified two-actor (debtor and creditor) models. Although final agreements may be signed by representatives of debtors and creditors, they are undertaken in a context of simultaneous negotiations under way within each of the principals (i.e., within the bureaucracy of the debtor countries and within individual creditors, whether they be the international financial institutions, creditor countries, or transnational banks). At the very least, a two-level bargaining framework is needed for a comprehension of the nesting of the different bargaining games involved.[3]

To complicate matters further, however, there is also simultaneous bargaining under way among different creditors and different debtors. Transnational banks have attempted to coordinate their strategies with the formation of bankers' committees, but they retain strong differences of interest among themselves and pursue a set of objectives different from those of many official creditors (who are often pursuing complicated foreign policy objectives in addition to the objective of repayment of interest and principal). Among the debtor countries, there have been occasional efforts to negotiate comprehensive multilateral debt relief arrangements or even form a debtors' cartel. Thus, the bargaining relationship should be viewed as a complex, multilayered, nested game, with simultaneous negotiations under way between creditors and debtors, within creditors and debtors, and among creditors and among debtors.

There is also a wide variation among debtor countries in terms of the basic nature of their debt. Most Latin American debtor countries have borrowed extensively from private, transnational banks, whereas the vast majority of African countries have borrowed largely from official, bilateral and multilateral agencies. The qualitative nature of the debt problem of different countries also varies considerably. For some countries, the debt problem has been essentially one of short-term financial liquidity; for others it has become more a question of basic financial solvency. The sequence and timing of debt problems diverge widely as well, further rendering generalization about debt and international financial negotiations difficult.[4]

A GLOBAL DEBT REGIME

Despite the complexity of international financial negotiations (the large number of actors involved, with a plethora of different interests and conditions), it is possible to sketch the broad outlines of the global debt regime that emerged to manage the debt problem during the 1980s. It is a specific (not a diffuse) regime, one that involves a mix of formal and informal instruments (but tending increasingly toward the former); an evolutionary regime with a clear distributive bias, one directed principally against the developing countries.[5]

In a highly informative description of the Bretton Woods balance-of-payments regime written just prior to the outbreak of the debt crisis in 1982, Benjamin Cohen described the 1970s as a period in which a breakdown of the postwar Bretton Woods regime took place, "a change of degree so profound that it appears to border on a transformation of kind."[6] In retrospect, however, it appears that the petrodollar recycling undertaken by the commercial banks during the 1970s was more of an interruption in the postwar balance-of-payments regime than an indication of its profound transformation.

Cohen argued that countries confronting severe balance-of-payments disequilibria face basically two choices: They can either finance the disequilibrium (essentially postponing the costs) or adjust to it (bearing the costs immediately). Not surprisingly, the vast majority of countries prefer the former choice, postponing difficult decisions.[7] The Bretton Woods financing regime was developed historically to ensure that countries would have an adequate supply of international liquidity to facilitate international trade and commercial transactions. Access to liquidity, however, was not intended to be unlimited: "it has long been felt, on principle, [that] governments ought not to enjoy unlimited access to balance-of-payments financing."[8] Although the term *conditionality* does not appear in the original IMF articles of agreement, several critical policy decisions between 1948 and 1952 codified it as a defining principle of the regime.[9]

The postwar financing regime was based on the principle that "nations should be assured of an adequate but not unlimited supply of supplementary financing for balance-of-payments purposes."[10] It has involved norms of formally articulated rights and obligations accepted by each member of the IMF, and it has operated with rules of policy conditionality where access to higher-tranche facilities has been subject to conditions embodied in Fund stabilization agreements, standby arrangements, letters of intent, and mutually agreed-upon performance criteria.[11] Its decisionmaking procedures, based on IMF staff decision routines, include administrative decisionmaking in the secretariat and voting (if necessary) by the Fund executive board.[12]

The global debt regime that emerged in the 1980s is in many ways a reestablishment of many of these components that had fallen into disarray during the 1970s. The basic principle of the regime was reestablished and the primary formal institution of the regime (the IMF) restored to its original position of authority.[13] The foundation upon which the 1980s global debt regime was based was a reinstatement of the principle of conditionality, that is, debtor countries that pursued significant, market-oriented economic reform would be rewarded with some form of relief from their immediate debt burdens. At the outset, this meant balance-of-payments stabilization in exchange for debt rescheduling. After 1985 (under the Baker Plan), medium-term structural adjustment was to be exchanged for fresh new money from commercial banks. In the Brady Plan, launched at the beginning of 1989, continued economic reform was to be rewarded with debt relief. In each of the successive phases of the debt crisis since 1982, debtor countries pursuing significant economic reform were to be rewarded with debt rescheduling

(1982–1985), fresh inflows of new money (under the Baker Plan, 1985–1989), and/or some form of debt relief (under the Brady Plan, 1989 to the present).

The formally articulated rights and obligations of debtors and creditors (the norms of the regime) have been essentially the same as those articulated in the Bretton Woods balance-of-payments regime. Access to new resources (whether from the IMF directly, or indirectly by way of requirements for its approval) has been made contingent upon a serious and continued commitment to pursue market-oriented economic reforms. The rules of the global debt regime of the 1980s have also been broadly similar to those established out of the Bretton Woods system. The IMF created several new facilities to deal with the 1980s debt problem (most notably the structural adjustment facility, or SAF), and it has augmented some of its procedures, such as introducing enhanced surveillance (an increase in the frequency of IMF staff reviews of country compliance with agreed-upon performance criteria). However, the basic rules of the regime have remained largely unchanged.

The IMF did not alter any of its basic decisionmaking procedures during the 1980s. However, creditor clubs such as the Paris Club (for the rescheduling of loans and credits extended by government and official creditors) and the London Club (for non-governmentally insured debts) were used with increasing frequency during the period.[14] The creditor clubs developed decisionmaking procedures to ensure that no Paris Club rescheduling could begin without an IMF agreement in place, that developing country debt would be treated on a case-by-case basis, and that the principle of burden sharing (where heavily indebted countries were expected to seek comparable relief from their different creditors, with the notable exception of the multilateral lending institutions) would be firmly established.

ONE REGIME, MANY ADJUSTMENTS

Despite the emergence of a global regime for the management of debt and the development of a well-established institutionalized framework for the conduct of international financial negotiations, there has been wide variation in the outcome of different negotiations. The IMF has often been criticized for insisting on the same conditions of economic reform for every country requesting financial assistance, that is, for providing the same medicine for all the economic ailments of the developing world.[15] Moreover, both the IMF and the World Bank have been fairly consistent in the general set of policy changes they require for standby agreements, debt reschedulings, and/or debt relief. Nevertheless, within the general guidelines of orthodox stabilization and adjustment, there is room for considerable variation in the specific terms of agreements. It is over the precise nature of this variation that adjustment bargaining is focused in international financial negotiations.

To gain a better idea of the range of choice entailed in international financial negotiations, we should begin by reviewing the key components of "orthodox" stabilization and adjustment. Stabilization and adjustment ordinarily entail a series of measures designed to reduce and transform state economic intervention, with an increased reliance on market mechanisms, more frequent use of monetarist policy instruments, and a shift in public-private relations in the direction of greater support for, and increased reliance on, the private sector. The specific policy measures typically associated with orthodox IMF stabilization programs are short-term measures designed principally to reverse acute balance-of-payments deficits by generating large trade surpluses in relatively short periods of time. Significant devaluations of the national currency are frequently required, along with deliberate efforts to control inflation by limiting consumer demand. Severe restraints on the growth of government spending (or, as a proxy, the size of the government fiscal deficit) are common, as are efforts to limit growth in the supply of money in the economy. Wage demands also tend to be suppressed in an orthodox stabilization package.

Orthodox structural adjustment, ordinarily under the direction of the World Bank, typically includes a collection of policy measures designed to promote longer-term economic recovery, increase economic efficiency, improve resource allocation, and enhance the adaptability of developing country economies to changes in the world economy. It usually involves efforts to institutionalize elements of the reform measures introduced initially as part of shorter-term IMF stabilization efforts. In the most general terms, structural adjustment entails a reduction and redirection of state economic intervention in the economy,[16] in combination with an increased reliance on the market for the allocation of scarce resources and commodities. Specific policy measures common to most orthodox structural adjustment programs (SAPs) include an effort to institutionalize nominal devaluations of the currency in order to generate and sustain real exchange rate adjustment. In some instances a routine currency auction system might be instituted, whereas in others some active form of exchange rate management such as a crawling peg system might be introduced, following the initial devaluation undertaken during the stabilization period.[17] The unification of multiple exchange rates might also be undertaken as part of a structural adjustment effort. Each of these measures entails an institutionalization of exchange rate adjustment in an effort to "get the prices right" (i.e., market-determined) externally.

Another feature common to the majority of orthodox SAPs is the effort to engage in major fiscal policy reform. This usually means that countries reduce (or at least constrain) the rate of growth in government spending, reform the tax structure, rationalize expenditure, phase out or reduce government subsidies, and improve the efficiency of public investment by scaling down and shifting the focus from manufacturing to infrastructure and social sectors.[18] Trade liberalization has also become a central component of virtually every structural adjustment program. Exchange rate flexibility, the elimination of trade licensing systems, the introduction of export incentives, the replacement of quantitative restriction (QRs) by tariffs, and the general lowering of tariff levels are all being pursued (depending to large extent on the policy environment within which the reforms are attempted).

Financial reform is another component associated with the majority of structural adjustment programs. Constraining the rate of growth of the money supply is an objective of many programs, but longer-term financial reform ordinarily entails some institutionalized change as well. Liberalizing foreign exchange controls is a common policy objective, as is the effort to reduce or eliminate subsidized credit, either by removing or simplifying existing ceilings on interest rates and credit.[19] The provision of preferential rates of credit for preferred borrowers unable to service their debts following a major devaluation is also a part of the general financial restructuring involved in most SAPs.[20]

A number of other policy reforms are also typically pursued, depending on the particular country context. Specific measures include reducing price controls, ending or reducing government subsidies, adjusting agricultural pricing policy (introducing new incentive schemes), eliminating state marketing boards, and limiting wage indexation. Privatization has also been routinely prescribed as a component of most World Bank–sponsored structural adjustment programs, at least since the mid-1980s, but many countries are now experimenting with privatization even without World Bank encouragement.

Table 1.1 summarizes the components common to orthodox IMF stabilization and World Bank structural adjustment programs. These are the policy reforms that typically constitute the basis of the initial negotiating position of the international financial institutions in their bargaining with heavily indebted countries. However, the precise terms of the final agreements negotiated by different developing countries can vary significantly. Indeed, this is what international financial negotiations are all about. Some countries will negotiate for an exemption of a key component of orthodox reform (such as the removal of a particular subsidy), whereas others will concentrate principally on the magnitudes of the changes involved (i.e., the size of a currency devaluation or the pace of cutbacks in government spending). In the final analysis, some countries appear to obtain easier terms than others, despite proclamations of universally fair and consistent treatment by the international financial institutions. Just what are the bases of these differences?

BASES OF DEBTOR BARGAINING POWER

The variety in the outcomes of agreements, as well as the appearance of differential treatment by the IMF and the World Bank, suggests that there are major distinctions among the instruments, issues, and interests different debtor countries can bring to the bargaining table in their negotiations with the international financial institutions. Stephan Haggard and Robert Kaufman suggested that the difference in the bargaining outcomes of different countries is best explained by three factors: the size of the country's debt, its strategic significance, and its access to other, nonconditional resources.[21]

Large debtor countries like Brazil, Mexico, and Argentina have tended to receive lower interest rates, longer maturities, and a longer grace period in their debt reschedulings than countries with a relatively smaller debt burden.[22] They have also pioneered more unorthodox rescheduling agreements and been more successful in securing additional forms of relief.[23] Large debtors have tended to fare better at least in part because they have been in a position to threaten the international financial system as a whole (largely through the potential of their unilateral action) and have to be given more attention and taken more seriously as a result. Large debtor countries also tend to be larger countries and hence capable of sustaining relatively autarkic policy measures, at least for a time. Thus, the credibility of their threats to resist orthodox policy reform is greater than the credibility of smaller countries.

Even more important, however, may be the strategic significance of debtor countries. As Haggard and Kaufman suggested, "Strategic and political concerns have...led creditor governments to use their influence on the boards of the IMF and the World Bank to press for greater leniency and to lobby bank advisory groups for expeditious settlement of rescheduling negotiations."[24] Both geography and history have played an important role in the definition of what is strategic; hence the United States has been relatively more concerned with relief for Latin American countries, the Germans for central and Eastern Europe and Turkey, the French for their former colonies in Africa, and the British for indebted members of the Commonwealth.[25] Mexico's geographical proximity to the United States has long given it special status in the negotiation of debt rescheduling, new financing, and relief.[26]

However, the definition of *strategic* has also been determined by ideological affinity and the alliance behavior of debtor countries. The beginning of the debt crisis in 1982 coincided with the height of the second cold war, and accordingly there has been a relatively close association historically between favorable terms in international financial negotiations and the strategic relationship of the debtor country with the United States or its allies. There is no other way to explain why countries with poor reputations for meeting performance criteria (such as Zaire or the Philippines) consistently obtained financing from the IMF throughout this period. More recently, with the waning of the cold war, the definition of *strategic* has undergone some important changes. Today, it is far more difficult for a country like Zaire to invoke its anti-Communist credentials (or, more precisely, its role as a conduit for arms to anti-Communist movements in Angola) in a bid for more favorable terms from its creditors.[27] The cold war may be over, but alliance behavior remains important nonetheless, as indicated by the generous debt relief provided to Egypt following its involvement in the allied coalition against Iraq during the Gulf War.

The availability of nonconditional financial resources (that is, petroleum revenues or the proceeds from commodity price booms) also enhances a debtor country's bargaining position and the final terms it is likely to receive.[28] The presence of additional resources can render a country less vulnerable to external pressure from international financial institutions because it will probably have fewer political incentives to make difficult economic adjustments. The credibility of a debtor country bargaining position in international financial negotiations is also likely to increase if its creditors realize it has access to nonconditional financial resources capable of sustaining it without immediate IMF support.

In addition to the three factors Haggard and Kaufman outlined (size, strategic importance, and access to nonconditional resources), a country's internal or domestic bargaining space can also be crucial for an understanding of the terms it receives in international financial negotiations.[29] Robert Putnam referred to this as the size of the domestic "win-set," or the space or room to maneuver negotiators are allowed by their domestic constituencies. The size of the domestic win-set is a function of the distribution of power, preferences, and possible coalitions among domestic constituents, as well as the political institutions and strategies of international negotiators.[30] A number of different domestic factors can influence the outcome of international financial negotiations, including the degree of internal cohesion, the potential for transnational issue linkage, the salience of the issue, or the articulation of an indigenous alternative to orthodox IMF or World Bank conditions. Other factors, such as the reputation of the principal negotiators and/or the cleverness of their bargaining moves, can further influence the likelihood of reaching (or the actual terms of) an agreement.

The cases included in this text illustrate the enormous variation both in the probability of reaching an agreement in international financial negotiations and in the terms of those agreements. The size of debt (and their economies) has been an important consideration for both Mexico and Brazil. Mexico's geographical proximity to the United States has strongly influenced the nature of its specific terms. For an understanding of the agreements Zaire and the Philippines have worked out with the IMF, it is important to consider their strategic significance to the United States, as well as their historical reputations as debtors. Nigeria's agreement with the Fund is a product of its unique domestic conditions (the return to civilian rule) and the critical intervention of other international institutions. In each of these cases, the nature of the domestic win-set has proven to be a critical factor.

REFORM WITHOUT RELIEF

Developing countries have been struggling with their accumulated debt burden since the early 1980s. Creditor banks and the international financial system are no longer in danger of imminent collapse (indeed, they have not been vulnerable since 1985), and from the perspective of the centers of the international financial system, the debt crisis is over. However, the crisis is far from over in the heavily indebted countries, where living standards have declined significantly and there is little significant relief in sight.[31] There have been a number of different attempts to deal with the debt problem since 1982, but no comprehensive solution has been found, and there is growing evidence that it is causing some disturbing long-term consequences. Indeed, it is beginning to appear that development itself may be increasingly threatened by the continuing debt overhang in heavily indebted countries.

Although a global debt regime has emerged and most countries of the developing world have embarked on extensive economic reform programs, it is not entirely clear that the economic reforms are by themselves sufficient for the problems at hand. Ten years of adjustment and reform is long enough to begin to see evidence of a troubling cycle of debt followed by economic reforms and stringent austerity measures, which in turn are followed by more debt and an extension of economic austerity. The long-term implications of the economic reform process are uncertain, and it is unclear whether the reforms, by themselves, have helped or hindered a resumption of productive investment in heavily indebted countries.

There was a major decline in long-term, productive investment in the heavily indebted countries of the developing world during the 1980s. The decline in investment was extremely severe, falling to levels not seen since the early 1950s in some instances, and by the beginning of the 1990s it had only recovered to levels of investment last experienced in the early 1960s. Moreover, the decrease in investment has been sustained for more than ten years by the high debt service obligations facing many countries. The recovery that has taken place thus far has been slight, rendering the decline in investment more than just the product of a temporary cyclical downturn. We may well be in the midst of a major, long-term development crisis in some countries of the world.

In the global debt regime that has emerged in response to the problem, major economic reforms have been prescribed for the debtor countries by private commercial banks, creditor country governments, and the international financial institutions. Creditors contend that significant economic reforms are a prerequisite for economic recovery, and with the "right" signals, new funds will once again begin to flow into the developing countries, the private sector will begin to invest, and flight capital will return. However, the empirical evidence linking reform to investment recovery in the heavily indebted countries is not very encouraging to date. Perhaps over a much longer term, another ten to fifteen years, reforms will be sufficient to produce an investment recovery. However, that is well beyond the mandate of the economic stabilization and adjustment programs negotiated by either the IMF or the World Bank and raises some important questions about the political sustainability of the reforms over such an extended period. Although economic reforms may be a necessary condition for investment, growth, and long-term development, the empirical evidence about their effects suggests that (by themselves) reforms may not be sufficient to accomplish those objectives.

Conventional arguments about the beneficial effects of reforms have been based on evidence about reforms in countries not faced with the burden of a debt overhang. Accordingly, there have been generous assumptions made about the likely response of commercial bank creditors and multinational corporations. However, as Sebastian Edwards argued, "The behavior of investment has also been very different during the current crisis adjustment period when compared to the historical episodes. In a detailed study of 39 historical episodes of structural adjustment programs between 1962 and 1982 the investment ratio did not experience a significant decline in any of the four years following the implementation of the programs."[32] There is also a discrepancy between the set of deflationary policy measures ordinarily prescribed for short-term stabilization of an economy and the structural adjustment measures prescribed for longer-term development.

Furthermore, as several of the cases included in this volume suggest, there may be a point at which it becomes counterproductive to continue core components of the economic reform process (such as major restraints on government spending), when the debt overhang inhibits both foreign and domestic businesses from resuming investment. Indeed, it is easy to construct a scenario in which a high debt service would force major cutbacks in government investment; the reduction of government investment would not necessarily create space for the private sector but rather accelerate the private sector's decline in investment (especially if there were an historically high degree of interdependence between the two sectors); meanwhile, the expectation of continued debt service requirements would inhibit foreign investors from expanding their foreign investment, further contributing to the decline in total investment. Economic reforms may be able to assist with some of these problems but by themselves may not be sufficient in the presence of a major debt overhang.

Thus, there is an increasingly compelling argument for significant debt relief for the moderately and heavily indebted countries of the developing world. Historically, some form of debt relief has been involved in the resolution of other global debt crises. As Jeffrey Sachs argued, "To get out of a debt crisis, countries have almost always required a sustained period of time in which the debt-servicing burden is sharply reduced or eliminated."[33] Peter Lindert and Peter Morton made very much the same point in their survey of nineteenth- and twentieth-century crises and repayment patterns.[34]

Debt relief may also be required for countries to continue servicing their existing level of debts. Many heavily indebted countries need a recovery of investment to expand the capacity (or improve the efficiency) of their existing production facilities before they can expand exports to service their debts (assuming they are already operating at full capacity). However, their current debt service obligations make it impossible for them to find the resources to invest in those facilities. Thus, debt relief may be required to increase debt repayment prospects.[35] Without it, creditors may be caught in a self-reinforcing trap that prevents highly indebted countries (even the reforming ones) from escaping their predicament and continuing to participate in the international financial regime.

Major debt relief may also be required to save the economic reforms the debt crisis has brought in its wake. Advocates of economic reform have made significant advances in getting their ideas accepted as policy throughout the developing world during the 1980s.[36] For these major changes in macroeconomic policy to be sustained over the longer term, though, some of the theoretical benefits of economic reforms will have to be realized in material terms. A strong-willed (and insulated) leadership with a unified technocratic elite may be able to introduce reforms and sustain the austerity that accompanies them for several years. However, effectively implementing and sustaining major economic reforms will be extremely difficult over the longer term, unless investment and growth can be resumed (or the perception of some benefits can be created).[37] In the final analysis, the macroeconomic conditions that were necessary to introduce sweeping economic reforms (i.e., government fiscal deficits and the rapid increase in debt service requirements) in the first place may undermine the ability of countries to sustain their commitment to reform over the longer term.

The Brady Plan is widely viewed as a move in the right direction, but it remains seriously underfunded, has thus far benefited only a small number of countries, and provided its major beneficiary (Mexico) with only a modest amount of relief. Private commercial banks have continued to increase their loan loss reserves and signaled their intent to limit their sovereign lending to heavily indebted countries in the developing world.[38] Multinational corporations appear no more eager than the commercial banks to expand their position in countries with a major debt overhang, and they are also likely to concentrate their attention on East Asia and Eastern and central Europe. Finally, although the debt service requirements of the heavily indebted countries undergoing reform show little sign of declining, the same ratios for countries previously included among the least indebted in the world (e.g., Ghana, India, Thailand) have recently moved them into the category of moderately and/or heavily indebted countries.[39] The global debt and development problem may be getting worse, not better.

The current approach to the problems of the highly indebted countries—using international financial negotiations to ensure reform, without providing adequate relief—may be flawed. The general approach is not sufficiently attentive to the depth of the economic crisis confronting heavily indebted countries, and it is not attuned to the difficulty of pursuing long-term economic reform in the midst of a major debt overhang. The distribution of global burden sharing has fallen disproportionately on the debtor countries, not on their creditors. At the same time, the distribution of domestic burden sharing within the debtor countries has fallen principally on the poorest and most marginal. Thus, reform without relief (and without domestic compensatory measures) may not contribute to the economic performance objectives of the heavily indebted countries (either for their creditors or for their own populations) and accordingly may be increasingly difficult to sustain.

CASES ON INTERNATIONAL FINANCIAL NEGOTIATIONS AND ADJUSTMENT BARGAINING

The cases selected for inclusion in this volume illustrate well the complexity of international financial negotiations, the operating mechanisms of the global debt regime, the variety of different country adjustments, and the bases of debtor bargaining power. They also draw attention to the ongoing nature of the debt problem and the difficulty of sustaining reform without relief. In Part 1, separate cases on the IMF (Chapter 2), the World Bank (Chapter 3), and the Paris and London clubs (Chapter 4) describe the institutional history and operations of each of the major international financial institutions involved in debt and adjustment bargaining. In Part 2, cases of five different national experiences with international financial negotiations (Mexico, Zaire, Nigeria, the Philippines, and Brazil) illustrate the processes of negotiation, the simultaneity of bargaining within and between creditors and debtors, the different bases of debtor bargaining power, as well as which strategies have worked historically and which have not.

The Mexican case (Chapter 5) describes the origins of the global debt problem, the costs and benefits of Mexico's special relationship with the United States, and the process of iterated negotiations. The Zairian case (Chapter 6) illustrates the importance of strategic significance, the tactic of playing creditors off against each other, and the process of engaging in a Paris Club negotiation (without much sincerity). The Nigerian case (Chapter 7) demonstrates two-level bargaining, third-party mediation, traditional arguments for and against orthodox conditionality, and the enduring consequences of commodity dependence. The Philippine case (Chapter 8) shows how the IMF responds to domestic regime change, how a country's strategic significance can dissipate, and the importance of domestic political cohesion. Finally, the Brazilian case (Chapter 9) focuses on domestic bargaining, the origins of heterodoxy, and the politics and consequences of declaring a payments moratorium. A Glossary of frequently used technical terms and concepts accompanies the volume, along with a Bibliography of materials for further reading and study.

TABLE 1.1 Principal Components of Economic Reform:
Stabilization and Structural Adjustment

Typical IMF stabilization measures:

1. Devalue currency
2. Restrict money supply
3. Pursue fiscal adjustment
   (in particular, cut government spending)
4. Pursue liberalization
   a. of trade regime
   b. of exchange regime
5. Adjust incomes policy
   (in particular, restrain wages)

Typical World Bank structural adjustment measures:

1. Institutionalize real exchange rate adjustment
   a. establish currency auction
   b. introduce crawling peg
   c. unify multiple rates
2. Pursue fiscal policy reform
   a. reduce or constrain the rate of growth of government spending
   b. reform the tax structure
   c. rationalize expenditures
   d. phase out or reduce government subsidies
   e. improve the efficiency of public investment
3. Liberalize trade
   a. maintain exchange rate flexibility (1 above)
   b. eliminate trade licensing
   c. replace quantitative restrictions with tariffs
   d. gradually lower tariff levels
4. Pursue financial reform
   a. liberalize foreign exchange controls
   b. reduce or eliminate subsidized credit
5. Proceed with other policy reform measures
   a. reduce price controls
   b. end or reduce price subsidies
   c. adjust agricultural prices
   d. eliminate state marketing boards
   e. limit wage indexation
   f. pursue privatization

NOTES

1. See especially Joan Nelson (ed.), *Economic Crisis and Policy Choice: The Politics of Adjustment in the Third World* (Princeton, N.J.: Princeton University Press, 1990), and Paul Moseley, Jane Harrigan, and John Toye, *Aid and Power: The World Bank and Policy-Based Lending* (London: Routledge, 1991).

2. Vinod K. Aggarwal, *International Debt Threat: Bargaining Among Creditors and Debtors in the 1980s* (Berkeley: Institute of International Studies, 1987).

3. Robert Putnam, "Diplomacy and Domestic Politics: The Logic of Two-Level Games," *International Organization* 42, 3 (Summer 1988), pp. 427–460.

4. Sebastian Edwards, "Structural Adjustment Policies in Highly Indebted Countries," in Jeffrey D. Sachs (ed.), *Developing Country Debt and Economic Performance: The International Financial System* (Chicago: University of Chicago Press, 1989).

5. The list of regime characteristics is derived from Donald J. Puchala and Raymond F. Hopkins, "International Regimes: Lessons from Inductive Analysis," *International Organization* 36, 2 (Spring 1982), pp. 248–251, although they do not apply them specifically to the 1980s global debt regime.

6. Benjamin J. Cohen, "Balance-of-Payments Financing: Evolution of a Regime," *International Organization* 36, 2 (Spring 1982), p. 458.

7. Ibid., pp. 460–461.

8. Ibid., pp. 461.

9. Ibid., p. 463, and John Ruggie, "International Regimes, Transactions, and Change: Embedded Liberalism in the Postwar Economic Order," *International Organization* 36, 2 (Spring 1982), p. 407, footnote 90.

10. Cohen, "Balance of Payments Financing," p. 465.

11. The operating mechanisms and procedures of the IMF are elaborated more fully in the case by Melissa Birch in Chapter 2

12. Cohen, "Balance of Payments Financing," p. 465.

13. Some might be more inclined to suggest that it was raised to new heights. It is interesting to recall that commercial bankers tended to make light of the international financial institutions during the heyday of commercial bank lending, and there was growing talk of the "irrelevance" of the IMF and the World Bank during the late 1970s.

14. The operations of the creditor clubs are described more fully in the case by Christine Kearney in Chapter 4.

15. Sidney Dell, "Stabilization: The Political Economy of Overkill," in John Williamson (ed.), *IMF Conditionality* (Cambridge: MIT Press, 1983).

16. Thomas J. Biersteker, "Reducing the Role of the State in the Economy: A Conceptual Exploration of IMF and World Bank Prescriptions," *International Studies Quarterly* 34 (1990), pp. 477–492.

17. Edwards, "Structural Adjustment Policies."

18. World Bank, Adjustment Lending: An Evaluation of Ten Years of Experience, Policy and Research Series, Number 1 (Washington, D.C.: World Bank, 1988), pp. 38–41.

19. Ibid., p. 47.

20. Ibid.

21. Stephan Haggard and Robert Kaufman, "The Politics of Stabilization and

Structural Adjustment," in Jeffrey D. Sachs (ed.), *Developing Country Debt and Economic Performance: The International Financial System* (Chicago: University of Chicago Press, 1989), pp. 210–220.

22. Maxwell Watson, Russell Kincaid, Caroline Atkinson, Eliot Kalter, and David Folkerts-Landau, *International Capital Markets: Developments and Prospects* (Washington, D.C.: International Monetary Fund, 1986).

23. Haggard and Kaufman, "The Politics of Stabilization," p. 212.

24. Ibid., p. 215.

25. This is reflected in each of the country cases included in this volume.

26. Indeed, every major U.S. initiative during the course of the global debt problem has been prompted by concern with Mexico—from the realization of the crisis (described in the case on Mexico in Chapter 5) to the initiation of the Baker Plan in 1985 and its successor, the Brady Plan, in 1989.

27. See especially the Zaire case by Thomas Callaghy in Chapter 6 of this volume.

28. Haggard and Kaufman, "The Politics of Stabilization," pp. 216–217.

29. Putnam, "Diplomacy and Domestic Politics."

30. Ibid.

31. Even the celebrated Mexican debt relief agreement (the terms of which are not likely to be obtained by the rest of the heavily indebted countries) appears to have had only a modest (and potentially limited) success. See especially Shafiqal Islam, "It's a Bad Deal for the Model Debtor," in the *New York Times*, August 6, 1989, and John Evans, "Few Regard Mexican Accord as a Model," in the *American Banker*, July 25, 1989.

32. Sebastian Edwards, "Structural Adjustment Policies," p.178.

33. Jeffrey D. Sachs, "Introduction," in Sachs (ed.), *Developing Country Debt and Economic Performance: The International Financial System* (Chicago: University of Chicago Press, 1989), p. 23.

34. Peter H. Lindert and Peter J. Morton, "How Sovereign Debt Has Worked," in Jeffrey D. Sachs (ed.), *Developing Country Debt and Economic Performance: The International Financial System* (Chicago: University of Chicago Press, 1989).

35. Sachs, "Introduction," pp. 20–21.

36. Thomas J. Biersteker, "The 'Triumph' of Neoclassical Economics in the Developing World: Policy Convergence and the Bases of Governance in the International Economic Order," in James N. Rosenau (ed.), *Governance Without Government: Order and Change in World Politics* (Cambridge: Cambridge University Press, 1992).

37. The transitions to democratic rule and the competitive elections that will accompany them over the next few years in countries like Argentina, Brazil, Chile, Nigeria, and Uruguay will tell us a great deal about the potential trade-offs involved in this process.

38. The only exception to this appears to be the export-oriented regimes of East Asia, countries that lack a major debt burden. The opening of Eastern and central Europe is likely to draw further capital away from the heavily indebted countries.

39. This is based on the data contained in the World Bank *World Development Report* (Washington, D.C.: World Bank, 1992), table 24. The latest debt-to-export ratios for the countries listed in the text (for the year 1990) were: Ghana 34.9 percent, India 28.8 percent, and Thailand 17.2 percent. Each of them maintained an average debt-to-export ratio of under 15 percent over the 1982–1987 period.

Part One

INTERNATIONAL INSTITUTIONAL ACTORS

2

The International Monetary Fund

Melissa H. Birch

In July 1944, toward the end of World War II, delegates from forty-five countries meeting at Bretton Woods, New Hampshire, voted to create two international financial institutions, the International Monetary Fund and the World Bank,[1] with complementary purposes but different modes of operation. The IMF was established to restore exchange rate stability in the countries that had been in the war, and then to promote international monetary cooperation and the expansion of world trade.

The Fund extended to its members balance-of-payments assistance; development assistance was left to the World Bank, which provided long-term financing for specific development projects. The IMF was established to provide short- to medium-term monetary assistance to member states experiencing balance-of-payments deficits and to prescribe appropriate means of adjustment to help ensure that recipient countries would be able to overcome their deficit positions.

The Fund's administration of monetary order and exchange rate stability was based on a compact among its member nations: "The Fund's primary financial purpose is 'to give confidence to members by making the general resources of the Fund temporarily available to them under adequate safeguards, thus providing them with opportunity to correct maladjustments in their balance of payments

The original version of this case note was prepared by Casey S. Opitz, research assistant to Professor Melissa H. Birch of the Darden Graduate School of Business Administration, University of Virginia. The case note has been edited slightly and updated for this edition. It is reprinted with permission of the Darden Graduate Business School Sponsors.

without resorting to measures destructive of national or international prosperity'
and 'to shorten the duration and lessen the degree of disequilibrium in the
international balances of payments of members ' "(Article 1, v and vi).[2]

The IMF is composed of a professional staff overseen by a board of governors,
an executive board, and a managing director. The board of governors, the highest
authority in the Fund, consists of a governor (representative) and an alternate from
each member country (156 as of January 1992). These persons are typically
ministers of finance or central bank governors in their countries. The board of
governors meets annually and can also vote on issues by mail throughout the year.

The board of governors delegated to the executive board the responsibility for
conducting the day-to-day business of the Fund. The twenty-two-member (six
appointed, sixteen elected) executive board remains in permanent session in
Washington, D.C., and is headed by a managing director, appointed by and
responsible to the board of governors. In 1988, Michel Camdessus, former director
of the French treasury, was appointed to a five-year term at this post.
Traditionally, the managing director of the IMF has been European, whereas the
president of the World Bank has been American.

SOURCES OF FUNDS

The Fund was created as a pool of currencies of its member nations. Each
country maintains a specified monetary quota, one quarter in reserve assets
(originally gold) and the remainder in its own currency, in a Fund account. The
size of the quota reflects the country's economic size and importance in the world
economy when it first joined the Fund. The quotas also determine the distribution
of voting rights within the Fund; a breakdown of 1991 quotas by country is
provided in Table 2.1. Table 2.2 lists the executive board members and their
voting power. The United States' quota (voting) power in 1991 was just under 19
percent of the total.

When the IMF was established, each country's quota was assumed to be
enough to cover any balance-of-payments deficits it might incur, but the expansion
of world trade throughout the 1960s and the growing number of convertible
currencies increased pressure on member countries' foreign reserves. As a result,
in 1966, as it had done occasionally before, the IMF increased member quotas.
More importantly, the IMF also decided to use a broader range of currencies in its
transactions. The special drawing right (SDR), instituted in 1970, grew out of this
decision.

The SDR was to act as an international currency to supplement gold, dollars,
and other convertible currencies already in use in the international financial system
and thereby increase international liquidity. According to Henry Hazlitt, "These
SDRs were created out of thin air, by a stroke of the pen. They were created,
according to the Fund, 'to meet a widespread concern that the growth of

international liquidity might be inadequate.' These SDRs were allocated to members in proportion to their quotas over specified periods."[3]

The value of the SDR was first pegged to gold; then, between 1976 and 1981, the value was based on a weighted basket of sixteen currencies. In 1981, the basket was reduced to five currencies, which in 1992 were weighted as shown in Table 2.3. The SDR thus became, in effect, the currency of the IMF and is used in the majority of its transactions as well as the determination of member quotas. The SDR's value in relation to other nations' currencies is determined daily by the exchange rates of the five currencies that compose it; it is usually worth more than one dollar. The SDR has gradually come to replace gold as a reserve asset within the Fund. There are 21.4 billion SDRs in existence today, worth about $30 billion.

The IMF can also enhance its liquidity by selling gold for profit (as of April 1985, the IMF held 3,217,341 kilograms of gold), charging service fees, and borrowing from member countries. The Fund undertook most of its borrowings from member states under the General Arrangements to Borrow (GAB), which were first ratified in 1962 and have been revised and renewed every four or five years since. Under the GAB, the IMF can match the maturities of its borrowing and lending by borrowing specific amounts from ten industrial member countries for periods averaging five years at rates of interest identical to those charged for IMF loans. Until the mid-1970s, the IMF's sources of funds were limited to the ten industrialized countries, but then two programs designed to help finance the purchase of oil were instituted with funding coming primarily from oil-exporting nations. In 1983, the total credit available to the Fund through the GAB was increased from the equivalent of about SDR 6.4 billion to SDR 17 billion, plus an associated SDR 1.5 billion facility available from Saudi Arabia.[4]

USES OF FUNDS

The IMF provides financial assistance to its member countries through three broad sets of programs: the unconditional reserve tranche; the conditional credit tranches; and special compensatory, extended financing, and structural adjustment facilities (see Table 2.4). Under the unconditional facility, a country can draw on its reserve tranche (that is, a "slice," or portion, of its country quota) without restriction. A country has a reserve tranche—a reserve position with the Fund—"to the extent that the Fund's holdings of its currency, excluding holdings which reflect the member's use of Fund credit, are less than the member's quota."[5]

The conditional facilities are also based on the tranche concept. Under the first credit tranche, a country can purchase (with its own currency) other currencies or SDRs in an amount up to one quarter of its quota. "A member requesting a drawing limited to the first credit tranche was expected to have in place a program representing reasonable efforts to overcome its balance of payments difficulties, but what constitutes reasonable efforts is in practice left to the borrower's discretion, since a country applying for such a drawing is given the overwhelming benefit of the doubt in any difference of view between the member and the Fund."[6] A particularly important low-conditionality facility, the compensatory financing facility, was introduced in 1963 to assist member countries with temporary export shortfalls that occurred for reasons beyond their control. In 1981, this facility was expanded to cover temporary excesses in the cost of purchasing cereal imports.

In order to draw from the upper or high-conditionality tranches, a country must adopt specific economic adjustment policies designed in coordination with the IMF. In exchange for a concerted effort to meet IMF conditions, a member can draw (purchase) additional tranches (tranches 2, 3, and 4) of other currencies or SDRs, each equal to 25 percent of the country's quota. As a result, a country can draw up to 100 percent of its quota from the low- and high-conditionality facilities.

High-conditionality drawings are usually provided in the form of a standby agreement; that is, a country receives the right to purchase foreign currencies and SDRs in installments over a given period of time—typically one to three years. The installments are made available as long as the country adheres to the terms and conditions of the agreement it made with the IMF when first requesting the facility. Table 2.5 lists, by country, the standby arrangements current at the end of February 1992.

In addition to the high-conditionality credit tranches, several other high-conditionality financing facilities are available: including the extended fund facility (EFF) and the enlarged access policy. The extended fund facility was established in 1974 (after the first oil crisis) to provide assistance to (1) countries with severe structural maladjustment in their trade because of cost and price distortions and (2) countries with slow-growth economies and weak balances of payments. Initially, the program provided medium-term financing up to three years, but ten-year terms were later made available.

In 1981, the enlarged access policy replaced an older program called the supplementary financing facility. Under the enlarged access policy, loans beyond the four tranches can be made to countries with severe balance-of-payments difficulties. As of 1985, guidelines specified annual borrowing limits of 95 to 115 percent of the country's quota, or 280 to 345 percent over a three-year period. The IMF borrowed the necessary funds for this facility from other member countries, as allowed by the GAB.

Although rare, the IMF also provides emergency assistance in the form of immediate first- and second-tranche drawings to countries hit by natural disasters. This financing is provided more liberally than under normal circumstances, but the country requesting emergency assistance has to agree, as usual, to comply with various economic conditions.

In response to the deep and continuing economic crises in the poorest developing countries and a growing sense that traditional sources of concessional lending were insufficient for the task, the IMF created two new facilities for structural adjustment—the structural adjustment facility (SAF) in March 1986 and the enhanced structural adjustment facility (ESAF) in December 1987. Sixty-one of the Fund's poorest members are eligible to use the facilities, although the two largest, China and India, have indicated that they do not intend to draw on the resources.

Each of these new facilities involves the preparation of policy framework papers, basic documents that describe in broad terms the specific measures recipient countries agree to undertake over the medium term. The papers are intended to facilitate consensus formation on adjustment policies both within the recipient country and among the international lending and donor communities and to provide a focus for the mobilization of additional funds. Up to SDR 8.7 billion of concessional resources has been made available for the two facilities (SDR 2.7 billion for the SAF and SDR 6 billion for the ESAF).

With the exception of the enlarged access policy and the structural adjustment facilities, none of these transactions is technically a loan because each is part of a country's quota. A country purchases foreign currencies and SDRs with its own currency and then, over time, has to repurchase its currency with foreign currencies or SDRs:[7] "When making a purchase, a member pays an equivalent amount in its own currency, which it is required to repurchase after specified periods of time since Fund resources are available only for temporary use. Consequently, the transactions are not legally or operationally loans, which also explains why the Articles avoid the terminology of loans and repayments and refer instead to purchases and repurchases."[8] However, because these purchases—often called drawings—and repurchases are similar to loans and repayments, lending parlance is often applied to the transactions, and they are often, either mistakenly or out of convenience, referred to as loans.

Since one currency is exchanged for another, "the Fund's assistance to any member does not reduce the combined total of the Fund's holdings of SDRs and currencies, although it changes its composition. From this angle the Fund can be viewed as an asset warehouse that transfers one asset in exchange for another."[9] Table 2.6 provides a breakdown of the repurchase and repayment schedules by type of financing facility. The installment specifications are actually a general guideline; alternative schedules can be worked out and applied to different countries, depending on their situations.

CONDITIONALITY

Drawing on the reserve tranche, as noted previously, is unconditional. For other facilities, however, the IMF requires that certain terms and conditions be met in order to help ensure that a country that asks to purchase or borrow foreign currencies and SDRs will be able to overcome its balance-of-payments difficulties and repurchase its currency (or repay the loan) on schedule. To purchase the first credit tranche, the country has to demonstrate that it is attempting to overcome its balance-of-payments deficit. Granting of a high-conditionality standby facility necessitates that the country's minister of finance send to the IMF a letter of intent that outlines the terms and conditions (the performance criteria and policy understandings) that the country and the IMF have agreed upon. To draw on the standby facility, the country has to demonstrate that it is attempting to live within the conditions set forth in the letter.

The IMF decides what should be included in the terms and conditions by determining (1) how large the current account balance improvement should be, (2) how much output can be increased without sparking or accelerating inflation within the country, and (3) the appropriate exchange rate for the country's currency. If the IMF decides that the currency should be devalued, it will then determine whether devaluation should be carried out in conjunction with some restraint on wages. If the IMF believes that the currency is overvalued but that a devaluation is not in order, it asks the country to reduce its inflation rate below the world rate.[10]

The IMF rarely requests that a country impose import restrictions because it considers such a step not to be in the country's best interest. In addition, in keeping with its liberal orientation, the IMF argues that restricting imports also harms the abilities of other countries to export. Instead, the IMF will request the country to cut back domestic demand to free up goods for export and decrease demand for imports. This cutback can be effected by some combination of (1) tax increases, (2) reductions in government spending, or (3) more monetarist macroeconomic policies, estimating the demand for money and then controlling credit (typical of the Fund). The IMF will also often request that the country liberalize its trade restrictions, so that the allocation of domestic resources might be better rationalized.

The IMF next monitors the country's adherence to the letter of intent. Some of the terms are actually preconditions that have to be kept before the standby facility will be approved. Such terms might include a devaluation, an increase in taxes, or an increase in interest rates. The other provisions could be considered either performance criteria or policy understandings. The continued disbursement of installments under the standby facility depends on the ability of the country to demonstrate that it is meeting the performance criteria. "Performance criteria are undertakings given by the country which, if violated, involve suspension of further disbursements by the Fund until new understandings are reached."[11] These criteria can include quantitative measures, such as ceilings on credit and floors on reserves, as well as qualitative measures, such as a commitment to reduce trade restrictions. By contrast, "policy understandings are actions that the country agrees to take, but which do not have any explicit sanction associated with nonfulfillment. Because failure to take policy understandings seriously would also predispose the Fund to take an uncharitable view of any breach of the performance criteria, they are not without importance."[12]

PROBLEMS AND CRITICISMS

Even a cursory review of the purpose and methods of the IMF would be incomplete without a brief summary of some of the charges leveled against the Fund. Most critics do not believe that the IMF is inherently bad or that the idea behind its existence is misguided; instead, they argue against specific aspects of the Fund's mode of operation.

One of the charges commonly leveled against the IMF is that it imposes inflexible and onerous conditions on individual countries, with little consideration for differences in types of economies. Another criticism is that some of the stabilization programs offer no hope of permanent adjustment; the Fund is too interested in short-term "shock treatments"—painful, quick-fix adjustments that fail to address underlying structural probìlems. Therefore, it is argued, the IMF perpetuates economic dependency through its terms and conditions. Some critics suggest that the IMF should, at a minimum, modify its methods: "The Fund also sought to adapt to new problems created by the oil shocks and the world recession in a number of ways: increasing its lending power; making increased use of the extended fund facility; reducing insistence on rigorous conditionality. But it experienced difficulties in altering programmes to accommodate the changed forms of adjustment required in response to exogenously-generated payments deficits. It is hopefully not unfair to characterize the Fund's 1982 policy conditionality as trying to tackle present-day problems with the policies of the 1960s."[13]

The Fund replies that because it is providing the financing or loans, the IMF has the right to assure that the money is repaid as it sees fit. It also argues, although perhaps less convincingly, that conditionality does in fact vary with the country and its economy. The IMF maintains that history does not bear out the allegation that conditionality has a negative impact on economic growth.

Critics also charge that the IMF is biased against socialism and favors the free market approach exclusively. The Fund's response could be summed up thus: A stabilization program "is nonideological: it seeks to promote economic rationality, and it just happens that under a wide range of circumstances the readiest means to that end involves harnessing, instead of fighting, market forces."[14] In addition, the Fund also points out that some socialist countries are members of the IMF, and their governments have received economic assistance.

Ohers argue that the IMF takes too doctrinaire a monetarist approach by frequently ordering the imposition of credit ceilings and minimizing the role of fiscal policy, except to shrink the public-sector deficit. These critics contend that a country should be able to decide for itself how best to adjust its balance of payments. The IMF insists that the imposition of a credit ceiling is simply a shorthand approach to decreasing public spending.[15]

The austerity measures the IMF imposes tend to affect directly personal incomes within the countries, primarily as a result of the frequent condition that government expenditures and subsidies be decreased. "The Fund has often been criticized for the distributional impact of austerity programs adopted under its guidance. It has tended to reply that it has no business interesting itself in the distributional consequences of member's programs, and (somewhat inconsistently) that in any event, the improvement in the rural-urban terms of trade that usually results from a more outward orientation and price liberalization is distributionally progressive rather than regressive."[16]

The Fund's detractors also complain that the IMF overstepped its bounds by overextending itself into intermediation that should have been handled by commercial banks during the 1980s. Specifically, the IMF is accused of becoming the strong-arm agent of the banks by requesting repayment of (or at least interest payments on) private bank loans as a condition for financing. This approach, it has been said, supersedes the Fund's original (actual or perceived) function as the international lender of last resort. In the words of one analyst, "The IMF conditions impose austerity on the debtor countries—people widely perceived to be poor—in order to pay many billions of dollars in interest to New York banks—widely perceived to be rich. The IMF soon found itself portrayed as a tool of the Yankee banks, and domestic politics in debtor countries elevated those who resisted the IMF conditions and pulled down those who cooperated with the Fund's recommendations."[17]

Almost all the criticisms of the Fund have been aimed at rectifying perceived deficiencies in its methods; few have been made with the express intent of encouraging its dissolution. The IMF attempts to bring order to an ever-changing world economy by increasing countries' international liquidity. Over the past forty-eight years, the world has experienced relative prosperity and general liberalization of the financial markets, as well as unprecedented growth in international trade and investment. The IMF was not solely responsible for these developments, but it has clearly played an important role in facilitating the growth of the world economy.

TABLE 2.1   IMF Quotas, 1991 (million SDRs)

Member	Quota	Member	Quota
Afghanistan	86.7	El Salvador	89.0
Algeria	623.1	Equatorial Guinea	18.4
Angola	145.0	Ethiopia	70.6
Antigua & Barbuda	5.0	Fiji	36.5
Argentina	1,113.0	Finland	574.9
Australia	1,619.2	France	4,482.8
Austria	775.6	Gabon	73.1
Bahamas, The	66.4	Gambia, The	17.1
Bahrain	48.9	Germany	5,403.7
Bangladesh	287.5	Ghana	204.5
Barbados	34.1	Greece	399.9
Belgium	2,080.4	Grenada	6.0
Belize	9.5	Guatemala	108.0
Benin	31.3	Guinea	57.9
Bhutan	2.5	Guinea-Bissau	7.5
Bolivia	90.7	Guyana	49.2
Botswana	22.1	Haiti	44.1
Brazil	1,461.3	Honduras	67.8
Bulgaria	310.0	Hungary	530.7
Burkina Faso	31.6	Iceland	59.6
Burundi	42.7	India	2,207.7
Cambodia	25.0	Indonesia	1,009.7
Cameroon	92.7	Iran	660.0
Canada	2,941.0	Iraq	504.0
Cape Verde	4.5	Ireland	343.4
Central African Rep.	30.4	Israel	446.6
Chad	30.6	Italy	2,909.1
Chile	440.5	Jamaica	145.5
China	2,390.9	Japan	4,223.3
Colombia	394.2	Jordan	73.9
Comoros	4.5	Kenya	142.0
Congo, People's Rep. of	37.3	Kinibati, Rep. of	2.5
Costa Rica	84.1	Korea	462.8
Cote d'Ivoire	165.5	Kuwait	635.3
Cyprus	69.7	Lao People's Dem. Rep.	29.3
Czechoslovakia	590.0	Lebanon	78.7
Denmark	711.0	Lesotho	15.1
Djibouti	8.0	Liberia	71.3
Dominica	4.0	Libya	515.7
Dominican Rep.	112.1	Luxembourg	77.0
Ecuador	150.7	Madagascar	66.4
Egypt	463.4	Malawi	37.2

(continues)

TABLE 2.1 *(continued)*

Member	Quota	Member	Quota
Malaysia	550.6	Senegal	85.1
Maldives	2.0	Seychelles	3.0
Mali	50.8	Sierra Leone	57.9
Malta	45.1	Singapore	92.4
Mauritania	33.9	Solomon Islands	5.0
Mauritius	53.6	Somalia	44.2
Mexico	1,165.5	South Africa	915.7
Mongolia	25.0	Spain	1,286.0
Morocco	306.6	Sri Lanka	223.1
Mozambique	61.0	Sudan	169.7
Myanmar	137.0	Suriname	49.3
Namibia	70.0	Swaziland	24.7
Nepal	37.3	Sweden	1,064.3
Netherlands	2,264.8	Syrian Arab Rep.	139.1
New Zealand	461.6	Tanzania	107.0
Nicaragua	68.2	Thailand	386.6
Niger	33.7	Togo	38.4
Nigeria	849.5	Tonga	3.25
Norway	699.0	Trinidad and Tobago	170.1
Oman	63.1	Tunisia	138.2
Pakistan	546.3	Turkey	429.1
Panama	102.2	Uganda	99.6
Papua New Guinea	65.9	United Arab Emirates	202.6
Paraguay	48.4	United Kingdom	6,194.0
Peru	330.9	United States	17,918.3
Philippines	440.4	Uruguay	163.8
Poland	680.0	Vanuatu	9.0
Portugal	376.6	Venezuela	1,371.5
Qatar	114.9	Viet Nam	176.8
Romania	523.4	Western Samoa	6.0
Rwanda	43.8	Yemen, Rep. of	120.5
St. Kitts & Nevis	4.5	Yugoslavia	613.0
St. Lucia	7.5	Zaire	291.0
St. Vincent & Grenadines	4.0	Zambia	270.3
Sao Tome & Principe	4.0	Zimbabwe	191.0
Saudi Arabia	3,202.4	TOTAL	91,127.55

Note: Countries that became members after May 30, 1990, are not eligible for consent to quota increase.
Source: IMF, *Annual Report* 1991. Reprinted with permission.

TABLE 2.2   IMF Executive Directors and Voting Power (as of April 30, 1991)

DIRECTOR	ELECTED	
Alternate Casting Votes of Votes in the General Department and the SDR Department (percent of Fund total)	Jacques De Groote (Belgium) Johann Prader (Austria) Austria Belgium Czechoslovakia Hungary Luxembourg Turkey (46,328-4.88 percent)	Mohamed Finaish (Libya) Azizali Mohammed (Pakistan) Bahrain Egypt Iraq Jordan Kuwait Lebanon Libya Maldives Oman Pakistan Qatar Somalia Syrian Arab Republic United Arab Emirates Yemen, Republic of (32,276 - 4.13percent)
APPOINTED		
Thomas C. Dawson II (Vacant) United States[a] (179,433-18.89 percent[b])	Renato Filosa (Italy) Nikos Kyriazidis (Greece) Greece Italy Malta Poland Portugal (45,357-4.77 percent)	C. Scott Clark (Canada) Gabriel C. Noonan (Ireland) Antigua and Barbuda Bahamas, The Barbados
David Peretz Paul Wright United Kingdom (62,190-6.55 percent)		Belize Canada Domenica Grenada
Bernd Goos Bernd Esdar Germany (54,287-5.71 percent)	Angel Torres (Spain) Roberto Marino (Mexico) Costa Rica El Salvador Guatemala	Ireland Jamaica St. Kitts and Nevis St. Lucia St. Vincent (38,709-4.07 percent)
Jean-Pierre Landau Jean-Francois Cirelli France (45,078-4.74 percent)	Honduras Mexico Nicaragua Spain Venezula (44,401-4.67 percent)	
Koji Yamazaki Naoki Tabata Japan (42,483-4.47 percent)	G. A. Posthumus (Netherlands) G.P.J. Hogeweg (Netherlands) Bulgaria	E. A. Evans (Australia) Grant H. Spencer (New Zealand) Australia Kiribati Korea New Zealand
Muhammad Al-Jasser Abdulrahman Al-Tuwaijri Saudi Arabia (32,274-3.40 percent)	Cyprus Israel Netherlands Romania Yugoslavia (43,775-4.61 percent)	Papua New Guinea Philippines Seychelles Soloman Islands Vanuatu Westem Samoa (33,254-3.50 percent)

TABLE 2.2 (*continued*)

LB. Monyake (Lesotho)	Alexandre Kafka (Brazil)	Abbas Mirakhor
LJ. Mwananshiku (Zambia)	Juan Carlos Jaramillo	(Islamic Republic of Iran)

Angola	Botswana	(Colombia)		Omer Kabbaj (Morocco)	
Burundi	Ethiopia	Brazil	Colombia	Afghanistan	Algeria
Gambia	Kenya	Dominican Republic		Ghana	Tunisia
Lesotho	Liberia	Ecuador	Guyana	Iran, Islamic Rep. of	
Malawi		Haiti	Panama	Morocco	
Mozambique		Suriname		(21,691-2.28 percent)	
Namibia	Nigeria	Trinidad & Tobego			
Sierra Leone		(27,582-2.90 percent)		Corentino V. Santos	
Sudan	Swaziland			(Cape Verde)	
Tanzania	Uganda	J. E. Ismael (Indonesia)		Yves-Marie T. Koissy	
Zambia	Zimbabwe	Tanya Sirivedhin		(Cote d'Ivoire)	
(29,388-3.09 percent)		(Thailand)		Benin	
		Fiji	Indonesia	Burkina Faso	
Markus Fogelholm		Lao People's Dem. Rep.		Cameroon	
(Finland)		Malaysia		Cape Verde	
Ingimundur Fridriksson		Myanmar	Nepal	Central African Republic	
(Iceland)		Singapore	Thailand	Chad	Comoros
Denmark	Finland	Tonga	Viet Nam	Congo	Cote d'Ivoire
Iceland	Norway	(27,094-2.85 percent)		Djibouti	
Sweden				Equatorial Guinea	
(32,338-3.40 percent)		Dai Qianding (China)		Gabon	
		Zhang Zhixiang (China)		Guinea	
G. K. Arora (India)		China		Gunea-Bissau	
L. Eustace N. Fernando		(24,159-2.54 percent)		Madagascar	
(Sri Lanka)				Mali	Mauritania
Bangladesh		Alejandro Vegh (Uruguay)		Mauritius	Niger
Bhutan		A. Guillermo Zoccali		Rwanda	
India		(Argentina)		Sao Tome and Principe	
Sri Lanka		Argentina	Bolivia	Senegal	Togo
(28,208-2.97 percent)		Chile	Paraguay	Zaire	
		Peru	Uruguay	(18,940-1.99 percent)	
		(23,373-2.46 percent)			
				Total	939,618[c]

[a] Voting power varies on certain matters pertaining to the General Department with use of the Fund's resources in that department.

[b] Percentages of total votes (950,025) in the General Department and the SDR Department.

[c] This total does not include the votes of Cambodia, Mongolia, and South Africa, which did not participate in the 1990 Regular Election of Executive Directors. the combined votes of those members total 10,407, which is 1.10 percent of those in the General Department and the SDR Department.

Source: IMF, *Annual Report,* 1991. Reprinted with permission.

TABLE 2.3 Special Drawing Rights Composition

Currencies	Valuation (in percent)	Equivalent (1 SDR =), April 30, 1993
U.S. dollar	42	$1.43
Deutsche mark	19	2.25 DM
Japanese yen	15	158. Y
French franc	12	7.75 F
Pound sterling	12	0.90 £

Source: IMF Survey 22, no. 11, May 31, 1993, p. 174.

TABLE 2.4 IMF Fund Facilities and Policies (September 1991)

The facilities and policies through which the Fund provides financial support to its member countries differ, depending on the nature of the macroeconomic and structural problems they seek to address and the terms and degree of conditionality attached to them. They consist of the following:

Standby arrangements, which typically cover periods of one to two years, focus on appropriate macroeconomic policies, such as exchange rate and interest rate policies, aimed at overcoming balance-of-payments difficulties. Performance criteria to assess policy implementation, such as budgetary and credit ceilings, appropriate exchange and interest rate policies, and avoidance of restrictions on current payments and transfers, are applied and purchases (or drawings) are made in installments. Repurchases (or repayments) are made in three to five years, except for purchases made with resources borrowed by the Fund under the enlarged access policy.

Extended arrangements, under which the Fund supports medium-term programs that generally run for three years (or up to four years in exceptional circumstances) and are aimed at overcoming balance-of-

payments difficulties attributable to structural as well as macroeconomic problems. The program states the general objectives and policies for the three-year period and the policies and measures for the first year; policies for subsequent years are spelled out in annual reviews. Performance criteria are applied and repurchases are made in four to ten years, except for purchases made with resources borrowed under the enlarged access policy.

Enlarged access policy, which is used to increase the resources available under stand-by and extended arrangements for programs that need substantial Fund support. Access to the Fund's general resources under the enlarged access policy has been subject to annual limits of 90 percent of 110 percent of quota; three-year limits of 270 percent or 330 percent of quota; and cumulative limits, net of repurchases, of 400 percent of 440 percent of quota, depending on the seriousness of a member's balance-of-payments need and the strength of its adjustment effort. However, the Fund has temporarily (until the end of 1991) suspended the lower annual, three-year, and cumulative limits. The Fund borrowed to help finance purchases under this policy, and

(continues)

TABLE 2.4 *(continued)*

repurchases of purchases financed with borrowed resources are made in three and a half to seven years. In September 1990, the board decided that once borrowed resources had been fully used, ordinary resources would be substituted to meet commitments of borrowed resources in financing purchases made under the enlarged access policy.

Structural adjustment facility (SAF) arrangements, where resources are provided on concessional terms to support medium-term macroeconomic and structural adjustments in low-income countries facing protracted balance-of-payments problems. The member develops and updates, with the assistance of the staffs of the Fund and the World Bank, a medium-term policy framework for a three-year period, which is set out in a policy framework paper (PFP). Within this framework, detailed yearly policy programs are formulated and are supported by SAF arrangements, under which annual loan disbursements are made. The programs include quarterly benchmarks to assess performance. The rate of interest on SAF loans is 0.5 percent and repayments are made in five and a half to ten years.

Enhanced structural adjustment facility (ESAF) arrangements, whose objective, conditions for eligibility, and program features are similar to those of SAF arrangements, but which differ in the scope and strength of structural policies, and in terms of access levels, monitoring procedures, and sources of funding. In November 1990, the board endorsed the possibility of a fourth annual ESAF arrangement, provided it is approved before the end of November 1992, and so long as resources are available.

The compensatory and contingency financing facility (CCFF), which serves two purposes. The compensatory element provides resources to members to cover export shortfalls and excesses in cereal import costs and in oil import costs that are temporary and arise from events beyond their control; the contingency element helps members with Fund arrangements to maintain the momentum of adjustment when faced with a broad range of unforeseen, adverse external shocks, such as declines in export prices or increases in import prices and fluctuations in interest rates. Repurchases are made in three and a quarter to five years. In November 1990, the board agreed to introduce an oil import element in the CCFF temporarily (up to the end of 1991) to compensate members for sharp increases in import costs for crude petroleum, petroleum products, and natural gas.

The buffer stock financing facility (BSFF), under which the Fund provides resources to help finance members' contributions to approved buffer stocks. Repayments are made within three and a quarter to five years or earlier. Currently, the BSFF may be used to finance eligible members' contributions to the 1987 International Natural Rubber Agreement.

Sources: IMF, *Annual Report* 1991 (Washington, D.C.: International Monetary Fund, 1991), pp. 44-45.

TABLE 2.5 The International Monetary Fund—Fund Standby, Extended, Structural Adjustment Facility (SAF) and Enhanced Structural Adjustment Facility (ESAF) Arrangements as of February 29, 1992 (million SDRs)

Member	Date of Arrangement	Expiration Date	Amount Agreed	Undrawn Balance
Stand-by arrangements			**7,214.43**	**4,883.08**
Algeria	June 3, 1991	March 31, 1992	300.00	75.00
Argentina	July 29, 1991	June 30, 1992	780.00	487.50
Barbados	Feb. 7, 1992	May 31, 1992	23.89	15.36
Brazil	Jan. 29, 1992	Aug. 31, 1993	1,500.00	1,372.50
Bulgaria	March 15, 1991	March 14, 1992	279.00	50.38
Cameroon	Dec. 20, 1991	Sept. 19, 1992	28.00	20.00
Congo	Aug. 27, 1990	May 26, 1992	27.98	23.98
Costa Rica	April 8, 1991	April 7, 1992	33.64	12.00
Cote d'Ivoire	Sept. 20, 1991	Sept. 19, 1992	82.75	66.20
Czechoslovakia	Jan. 7, 1991	April 3, 1992	619.50	99.56
Dominican Rep.	Aug. 28, 1991	March 27, 1993	39.24	39.24
Ecuador	Dec. 11, 1991	Dec. 10, 1992	75.00	56.44
Egypt	May 17, 1991	Nov. 20, 1992	278.00	174.40
El Salvador	Jan. 6, 1992	March 5, 1993	41.50	41.50
Gabon	Sept. 30, 1991	March 23, 1993	28.00	24.00
India	Oct. 31, 1991	June 30, 1993	1,656.00	1,386.00
Jamaica	June 28, 1991	June 30, 1992	43.65	32.75
Jordan	Feb. 26, 1992	Aug. 25, 1993	44.40	44.40
Mongolia	Oct. 4, 1991	Oct. 3, 1992	22.50	11.25
Morocco	Jan. 31, 1992	March 31, 1993	91.98	73.58
Nicaragua	Sept. 18, 1991	March 17, 1993	40.86	23.83
Nigeria	Jan. 9, 1991	April 8, 1992	319.00	319.00
Panama	Feb. 24, 1992	Dec. 23, 1993	93.68	68.63
Papua New Guinea	July 31, 1991	Sept. 30, 1992	26.36	26.36
Philippines	Feb. 20, 1991	Aug. 19, 1992	264.20	207.58
Romania	April 11, 1991	April 10, 1992	380.50	62.40
Uruguay	Dec. 12, 1990	March 15, 1992	94.80	85.80
Extended arrangements			**10,009.60**	**4,192.90**
Hungary	Feb. 20, 1991	Feb. 19, 1994	1,114.00	636.37
Mexico	May 26, 1989	May 25, 1992	3,263.40	233.10
Poland	April 18, 1991	April 17, 1994	1,224.00	1,147.50
Tunisia	July 25, 1988	July 24, 1992	207.30	51.83
Venezuela	June 23, 1989	March 22, 1993	3,857.10	1,851.50
Zimbabwe	Jan. 24, 1992	Jan. 23, 1995	343.80	272.60

(*continues*)

TABLE 2.5 (*continued*)

Member	Date of Arrangement	Expiration Date	Amount Agreed	Undrawn Balance
SAF arrangements			**101.15**	**54.07**
Benin	June 16, 1989	June 15, 1992	21.91	6.26
Burkina Faso	March 13, 1991	March 12, 1994	22.12	15.80
Comoros	June 21, 1991	June 20, 1994	3.15	2.25
Lao P.D.R.	Sept. 18, 1989	Sept. 17, 1992	20.51	5.86
Rwanda	April 24, 1991	April 23, 1994	30.66	21.90
Sao Tome & Principe	June 2, 1989	June 1, 1992	2.80	2.00
ESAF arrangements			**2,499.28**	**899.62**
Bangladesh	Aug. 10, 1990	Aug. 9, 1993	345.00	115.00
Bolivia	July 27, 1988	July 2, 1992	136.05	22.68
Burundi	Nov. 13, 1991	Nov. 12, 1994	42.70	38.43
Ghana	Nov. 9, 1988	March 5, 1992	388.55	---
Guinea	Nov. 6, 1991	Nov. 5, 1994	57.90	49.22
Guyana	July 13, 1990	July 12, 1993	81.52	26.57
Kenya	May 15, 1989	Aug. 1, 1992	261.40	45.23
Lesotho	May 22,1991	May 21, 1994	18.12	15.86
Madagascar	May 15, 1989	May 14, 1992	76.90	25.63
Malawi	July 15, 1988	Sept. 29, 1992	66.96	5.58
Mauritania	May 24, 1989	May 23, 1992	50.85	33.90
Mozambique	June 1, 1990	May 31, 1993	85.40	45.75
Senegal	Nov. 21, 1988	June 2, 1992	144.67	---
Sri Lanka	Sept. 13, 1991	Sept. 12, 1994	336.00	280.00
Tanzania	July 29, 1991	July 28, 1994	181.90	160.50
Togo	May 31, 1989	May 30, 1992	46.08	15.36
Uganda	April 17, 1989	April 16, 1992	179.28	19.92
TOTAL			19,824.45	10,029.67

Note: Figures may not add to totals because of rounding.
Data: IMF Treasurer's Department.
Source: *IMF Survey*, April 13, 1992. (Reprinted with permission.)

TABLE 2.6 Repurchase and Repayment Periods Under Fund Facilities

Facility	Repurchase Periods	Installments
Credit tranches and compensatory financing	3 to 5 years	8 quarterly
Extended fund facility (EFF)	4 to 10 years	12 semi-annual
Enlarged access policy (supplementary financing facility)	3.5 to 7 years	8 semi-annual
Structural adjustment facility (SAF)	5.5 to 10 years	3 annual
Enhanced structural adjustment facility (ESAF)	5.5 to 10 years	6 semi-annual

NOTES

1. For more information on the World Bank, see Chapter 3.

2. Anand G. Chandavarkar, *The International Monetary Fund: Its Financial Organization and Activities* (Washington, D.C.: International Monetary Fund, 1984), p. 1.

3. Henry Hazlitt, *From Bretton Woods to World Inflation* (Chicago: Regnery Gateway Press, 1984), p. 15.

4. Chandavarkar, *The International Monetary Fund*, pp. 18–23.

5. Ibid., p. 38.

6. John Williamson, *The Lending Policies of the International Monetary Fund* (Washington, D.C.: Institute for International Economics, August 1982), p. 65.

7. The IMF levies an 0.5 percent service charge, to be paid upon disbursement, on all but reserve tranche transactions. A commitment fee of 0.25 percent per year is charged on the unused portions of standby and extended arrangement facilities, but it is refunded if a purchase is made. The IMF also charges 0.2 percent per year, plus Fund borrowing costs, for the enlarged access policy credit. These charges are payable only in SDRs. Williamson, *The Lending Policies*, pp. 56–67.

8. Ibid., p. 41.

9. Chandavarkar, *The International Monetary Fund*, p. 41.

10. Williamson, *The Lending Policies,* p. 26.

11. Ibid., p. 36.

12. Ibid., pp. 36-37.

13. Tony Killick, Graham Bird, Jennifer Sharpley, and Mary Sutton, "IMF Policies in Developing Countries: The Case for Change," *Banker*, April 1984, p. 33.

14. Williamson, *The Lending Policies,* p. 56.

15. Ibid., p. 53.

16. John Williamson, "On Seeking to Improve IMF Conditionality," *American Economic Review*, May 1983, p. 357.

17. Paul Craig Roberts, "World Debt: The IMF Solution Has Become the Problem," *Business Week*, July 9, 1984, p. 12.

3

The World Bank

Melissa H. Birch and Thomas J. Biersteker

The World Bank, more formally known as the International Bank for Reconstruction and Development (or IBRD), was founded as the sister institution of the International Monetary Fund in July 1944 at the Bretton Woods conference. Representatives from forty-five countries approved the formation of the IMF to oversee short-term balance-of-payments and exchange rate adjustments for member states and the creation of the IBRD to provide long-term financing, first for post–World War II reconstruction and development efforts and later for development projects in less economically advanced countries. The IBRD was designed to complement the IMF's short-term focus by taking a longer-term, development perspective. The IBRD's development activities are designed to enhance the IMF's mission of promoting balance-of-payments stability by encouraging the development of productive resources in deficit countries, especially those resources with a good potential for generating reliable foreign exchange earnings. More specifically, the IBRD's articles of agreement state that the Bank is to promote foreign investment for development through loan guarantees and participations; it is also to supplement private investment in projects it deems appropriate, when other sources of funds are insufficient.

The original version of this case note was prepared in 1985 by Professor Melissa H. Birch, with the research assistance of Casey Opitz, both of the Darden Graduate School of Business Administration, University of Virginia. The current version of the case has been updated, revised and expanded by Professor Thomas J. Biersteker, with the assistance of Christine Kearney, both of the Department of Political Science at Brown University. The ordering of the names of the principal authors indicates the weight of their respective contributions to this version of the case note.

The World Bank originally consisted of just the IBRD, but as new needs were encountered, it created additional institutions and became more of an umbrella organization of global development institutions. In 1955, the Economic Development Institute (EDI) was founded for the purpose of training government officials in economic management. The International Finance Corporation (IFC) was formed in 1956, specifically to provide assistance without government guarantee to private enterprises in developing countries that were attempting to promote the private sector. In 1960, the International Development Association (IDA) was founded to provide concessional financing to the poorest countries, those whose abilities to garner foreign exchange with which to repay their loans did not meet the IBRD's stricter commercial standards. In 1988, the Multilateral Investment Guarantee Agency (MIGA) was formed to promote direct investment, especially equity investment, in developing countries. To this end, MIGA provides guarantees against noncommercial (i.e., political) risk. The IBRD remains the largest and most important institution within what has become known as the World Bank Group. This chapter deals primarily with the operations of the IBRD.

As of June 1991, the IBRD was composed of 156 member countries. Each country is represented by a governor (usually either the finance minister or a central bank board member), whose voting power is determined by the country's capital subscription in the Bank. The board of governors exerts ultimate control within the Bank but delegates most of its authority to the twenty-two-member executive board of directors composed of five directors appointed by the countries holding the most shares in the Bank: the United States, Japan, Germany, the United Kingdom, and France. The rest are elected by the board of governors. Each director represents a country or group of countries from the same geographical location and/or with similar economic interests. Table 3.1 lists the current executive directors and their voting rights. In routine practice, formal votes are rarely taken; instead, a general consensus among the directors is ordinarily achieved on each loan and policy decision.

The president of the World Bank serves as the chair of the executive board and is appointed by the board. Traditionally, the president of the World Bank has been an American, just as the managing director of the IMF has been European. In recent years, World Bank presidents have been appointed from the ranks of American business and politics. Robert McNamara, a former president of the Ford Motor Company and secretary of defense, served as Bank president from 1968 through 1981. He was succeeded by A. W. Clausen, a former president of the Bank of America. In 1986, Barber Conable, a former Republican congressman from New York, succeeded Clausen, and in turn was succeeded by Lewis Preston, former chairman of J. P. Morgan and a member of the Federal Reserve Board, in September 1991.

The operational day-to-day core of the Bank, however, is its staff of nearly 6,000 economists, financial analysts, engineers, and technical specialists who work with member country officials on the formulation of development projects suitable for IBRD financing and who supervise and monitor the progress of those projects. As a result of their activities, the IBRD has become the recognized leader in development lending and typically takes the lead in aid consortia or jointly funded development projects. The Bank's headquarters is located in Washington, D.C., but each country to which the IBRD provides financing is visited two or three times each year by members of the staff, primarily to oversee the progress of the projects being financed, as well as to analyze the general state of the economy. The Bank also maintains residential representatives in forty-seven developing countries in which it has extensive, ongoing development activities. The residential representatives and their expatriate staffs have diplomatic status, interact routinely with high-ranking government officials responsible for economic policy, and occasionally play an influential role in the domestic economic policy dialogue. They also gather statistical information on the performance of the local economy and conduct economic analyses for the Bank as well as for IMF missions and creditor club reschedulings (see Chapters 2 and 4).

SOURCES OF FUNDS

The IBRD obtains funds from four sources: capital subscriptions of its member countries, capital market borrowing, loan repayments, and retained earnings. Each country's subscription, based on the country's economic size and importance in the world economy, consists of paid-in and callable capital. Subscriptions totaled $139.1 billion in fiscal 1991. Approximately 10 percent of paid-in capital would be payable in dollars or gold; the remainder would be paid in the currencies of each member country. Each country is expected to maintain the dollar value of its balance in the event of exchange rate fluctuations.[1] Paid-in capital represented just under 7 percent of total capital in 1991. The remaining callable portion acts as collateral against which the Bank borrows in financial markets around the world. As of 1991, there had been no need to request that countries submit any portion of their callable subscriptions.

The IBRD borrowed $10.9 billion on international capital markets during fiscal 1991. Borrowing on international capital markets has been the source of most IBRD financing, and as of June 30, 1991, outstanding debt in some forty-two currencies totaled more than $90 billion. The Bank attempts to fit its own debt repayments to its expected receipts from loans, so the maturities of its public offerings in bond markets throughout the world have averaged eight to ten years, generally at fixed interest rates comparable to those of government issues. The Bank's bonds have a triple-A rating, reflecting the financial strength of the institution.

The terms of IBRD borrowing reflect the sound financial practices of the Bank and the excellent performance history it has achieved. The IBRD has earned a profit every year since 1948. In fiscal year 1991, the Bank earned a net income of nearly $1.2 billion, virtually back to the level of its record earnings in 1986. Most of the 1991 earnings were allocated to the Bank's reserve to increase its total capital. If net income exceeds the amount needed for allocation to the general reserve account, "consideration will first be given to a waiver, beginning July 1, 1991, of up to twenty-five basis points of the interest-rate spread on the borrower's semiannual debt-service payments to the IBRD."[2] Total reserves amounted to $10.0 billion by the end of fiscal 1991, establishing a reserves-to-loan ratio of 11.2 percent. Despite its very solid financial position (Table 3.2), the public often views the IBRD as a foreign aid agency rather than an efficient, profit-making, financial institution. World Bank loans are documented at least as fully as commercial bank loans, with borrowers often having to meet much tougher standards of creditworthiness. The World Bank disburses most of its loans in installments, and the repayment record of World Bank loans is far superior to the recent experience of commercial banks.

LENDING POLICY

Under the IBRD's articles of agreement, the Bank's total outstanding guarantees, participations, and/or direct loans cannot exceed 100 percent of its subscribed capital, reserves, and surplus. This is in sharp contrast to private financial institutions, which typically lend up to twenty times their capital. Thus, the Bank's lending limit, $137 billion in 1990, is statutory and not based on its ability to borrow in financial markets around the world.

Between 1949 and 1985, lending by the World Bank group of institutions grew at an average annual rate of about 10 percent. Although the volume of loans approved continued at that rate between 1986 and 1990, disbursement of loans has been uneven, declining in absolute terms in 1986 and 1989 (Table 3.3). Net disbursements were even more erratic during the second half of the 1980s, declining in 1988 and 1989, before jumping by some 200 percent in 1990.[3] The large increase in net lending in 1990 was due largely to a $2 billion loan to Mexico in support of its debt restructuring and a sharp decline in prepayments. The sluggishness of IBRD lending in the late 1980s has been attributed to an above-average rate of loan cancellations and very slow implementation of some Bank projects as borrowing governments have been unable to provide their portion of project funding.[4]

IBRD loans have an average maturity of seventeen years, with a four-year grace period. The Bank introduced variable interest rate lending in July 1982, and by the end of fiscal 1990, some 30 percent of the Bank's loans had been converted to variable rates. On average, the IBRD finances 30 percent of the total cost of a project; the remaining funds come from sources internal to the country and other external sources (either bilateral lending agencies or other multilateral development institutions). By 1991, India was the largest World Bank borrower, at $15.6 billion, followed by Mexico at $14.4 billion, Indonesia at $14.1 billion, Brazil at $12.7 billion, and Turkey at $8.8 billion.[5] Loans outstanding were $90.6 billion, or 63 percent of total loans.

The Bank's early loans were directed toward rebuilding a war-torn Europe, but by the early 1950s, attention began to shift to the needs of less-developed countries. Latin America had historically been the recipient of more IBRD financing than any other geographic region, but South and East Asia have received increasing shares. Until the early 1960s, development of electrical power infrastructure and transportation systems received the most financing. Later, agriculture and rural development became the focus of IBRD lending. In recent years, lending for energy projects has grown most rapidly, accounting for some 20 percent of the World Bank's loans by 1990. The World Bank's cumulative loans by purpose and region is shown in Table 3.4.

The emphasis and rhetoric of the Bank have also changed substantially over time. During the 1970s, under the presidency of McNamara, the Bank shifted its attention toward the alleviation of absolute levels of poverty. Emphasis was placed on the provision of clean water, the construction of rural infrastructure, redistribution with growth, and the satisfaction of basic human needs. After Clausen succeeded McNamara as Bank president in the early 1980s, focus shifted away from basic needs provision and toward a more neoliberal model of development, stressing the importance of the market, the need to reduce the role of the state in the economy, and the possibilities of privatization of state-owned enterprises.[6] By the end of the 1980s, the Bank muted its attack on the state and began to address other issues, as its annual *World Development Reports* emphasized the role of women in development, governance, human development, the idea of sustainable development, and the environment.

Although there are several different lending facilities at the IBRD, project lending is its hallmark and has been developed and refined into a standard set of procedures that have proven highly successful. First, staff economists meet with country officials to determine which projects would be of greatest development benefit. Those mutually agreed to be of highest priority become part of a five-year lending program to the country. Second, the IBRD and the country (often with IBRD assistance) perform separate technical, institutional, economic, and financial feasibility studies to ensure the individual project's worth. The IBRD staff present the joint conclusions and its own recommendations to the executive board of the World Bank for approval. Finally, if approved, each project is supervised and its progress monitored by members of the IBRD's staff of economists, engineers, and technical specialists. Detailed progress reports are submitted to the Bank, and on-site inspections are conducted at least on an annual basis but usually two or three times a year.[7] The total loan amount is not disbursed at once but over the life of the project. Each disbursement is to be specifically requested by the borrower, and to ensure proper use of the funds, each request is analyzed in light of past progress. This method of loan disbursement allows no room for the refinancing of projects, and typically the size of the undisbursed portion of the project and other World Bank loans would be a sufficient deterrent to default. As a result, the IBRD has experienced virtually no loan losses, write-offs, or nonaccruals from its development lending.

In an effort to improve the general economic environment in which its projects are undertaken, the IBRD expanded its program lending with the launching of structural adjustment lending in 1980. This lending does not finance specific projects but instead provides rapidly disbursing, medium-term financing (one-to-three-year disbursement periods, similar to those of the IMF) to help a country overcome severe balance-of-payments difficulties. It was expected that structural adjustment lending would be limited. Eligible borrowers would be only those countries in which a serious deterioration in the balance of payments had occurred and whose leaders were willing to undertake measures that implied a substantial shift in policy and institutional change.

In the structural adjustment program's first five years of operation, however, thirty-one structural adjustment loans totaling $4.5 billion were approved. In fiscal 1991 alone, structural and sectoral adjustment lending accounted for 26 percent of the Bank's total commitments, valued at $5.7 billion (Table 3.5). As the debt crisis has dragged on (at least from the perspective of many developing countries), it has become evident that the number of countries with the problems that structural adjustment operations are designed to address has been much larger than originally anticipated. By 1990, the Bank noted that

> Structural-adjustment and sectoral-adjustment lending were important activities of the Bank during the decade of the 1980s. Notwithstanding the fact that the Bank continues to rely on investment projects for the majority of its development lending, adjustment operations will likely remain important in the near term. For this reason, the Bank actively seeks ways to increase their effectiveness. During the past year, a second evaluation of adjustment operations reached conclusions that were consistent with those of the first evaluation: that adjustment lending has been moderately successful in improving aggregate economic performance and that, on the average, countries receiving adjustment loans performed better than those that did not.[8]

In many important respects, the operations of the two international financial institutions founded at Bretton Woods (the IMF and the World Bank) began to converge during the 1980s, as they introduced structural adjustment lending and facilities to address the interrelated problems of indebtedness and development.

CONTROVERSIES

Like the IMF, the World Bank has also generated controversy and received a fair amount of criticism. Some policymakers in developing countries have complained that the World Bank and the IMF do not sufficiently coordinate their efforts. They argue that World Bank and Fund programs within a given country often clash or undercut one another. The IMF, on the one hand, is interested primarily in the external account: an improved balance of payments, lower government deficits, and decreased foreign debt, all in the near to medium term. The World Bank, on the other hand, focuses on the timely and efficient completion of large development projects, which often require increased government spending and ordinarily involve increased levels of debt. These development projects are meant to produce an overall improvement in the balance of payments but usually only in the long term.

Moreover, the policy recommendations of Bank and Fund programs can in some instances weaken the fiscal basis of the state. Simultaneously reducing the state's productive and regulatory roles may undercut its ability both to influence the activities of significant economic actors in a country and to provide essential services. In particular, the privatization of successful state enterprises, in conjunction with the reduction of import duties (brought about by trade liberalization), can serve to undermine a country's domestic tax base. Since many developing countries lack the administrative capacity to construct an effective tax-monitoring system to deal with a radically reformed economy (especially in the short term), the consequences for the fiscal basis of the state can be serious. Both the IMF and World Bank have begun to recognize some of these coordination problems and are continually making an effort to improve their collaboration in individual member countries.[9]

Its close coordination with the IMF has increasingly generated controversy over the terms of its adjustment lending or over the World Bank's conditionality. Its general recommendations for policy reform have taken the Bank far beyond the politically neutral and technical role it publicly claims for itself. Its insistence on a change in the role of the state in the economy has far-reaching political implications, some of which cut to the core of critical questions about the nature of the state, the justification for its intervention, and the most appropriate forms of intervention. The Bank is an intergovernmental organization whose officers are specifically proscribed from becoming involved in domestic politics; "its officers shall not interfere in the political affairs of any member; nor shall they be influenced in their decisions by the political character of the member or members concerned."[10] But its policy recommendations are not neutral in their effects and are designed to reorient state intervention away from a particular strategy of development. However unsatisfactory or little realized in practice, import substitution industrialization and redistributive social reform both are under attack by the reform and structural adjustment process.

Furthermore, the Bank has invested a great deal of time and resources in pursuit of the belief that a reduction of the role of the state in the economy will produce greater efficiency and better economic performance. However, even if the Bank were able to succeed in changing the role of the state in the economy as it wishes, critics contend it would be naive to assume that developing countries would have found the path to sustained, noninflationary growth and development. Inefficient and unwise state intervention in the economy have certainly contributed to stabilization and adjustment problems, but they are not the only sources of economic difficulty. Structural features of the world economy (such as producer price declines and import price swings) have combined with cyclical changes (such as interest rate increases and industrial country protectionism) to produce conditions that have been, and continue to remain, central to problems of development.[11]

In both developed and developing countries, there has been a good deal of criticism of the role the World Bank has played in resolving the global debt crisis. Some contend that the Bank should concern itself solely with project lending and leave structural adjustment programs for balance-of-payments purposes to the IMF. The World Bank justifies its creation of structural adjustment lending by noting that structural adjustment is often a long-term process and the IMF does not provide long-term financing of any sort. Furthermore, "even project lending can blur the distinction between the basic tasks of the two organizations. The Bank wants its project loans to promote development and creditworthiness, but the Bank is interested also in an improved balance of payments as a means of promoting development. The Bank's interest in a member's economic and financial policies has been broad enough, therefore, to justify the description of it as 'encyclopedic,' with the result that the policies that the Bank may recommend can include some that fall within the Fund's competence as well."[12]

At the same time, Rimmer de Vries, chief international economist at Morgan Guaranty Trust Company, echoed the sentiments of the administration of Ronald Reagan, calling the Bank's role in resolving the debt crisis "rather disappointing." He criticized the Bank for continuing "to concentrate on project lending even though this has proven inadequate" and for being "slow to improve the attractiveness of commercial bank co-financing and to make use of its guarantee authority."[13]   Critics like de Vries have pointed to the decline in World Bank lending in the late 1980s as a sign of its failure to meet the needs of both global capital markets and developing countries. They would like to see the Bank play a more active role in attracting private capital back into developing countries and in reducing the risk associated with commercial sovereign lending.

In its defense, the Bank points out that it has been unable to broaden its scope and increase its level of lending activity because of its limited capital. Despite Washington's professed interest in an expanded role for the World Bank in the debt crisis, the United States was reluctant to support World Bank president Clausen's call for an increase in the Bank's capital at the height of the debt crisis in the early 1980s. The United States claimed that its reluctance to increase the bank's capital stemmed from a concern that the institution would be unable to expand its lending programs effectively.[14]   The Bank also noted that its efforts to leverage its limited capital by increasing private lending in the Third World through cofinancing and guarantees met with resistance from commercial bankers who had no interest in increasing their new lending to developing countries. Although the Bank was constrained to operate within its traditional limits, "the reasons for this lower [lending] figure went beyond the difficulties associated with program design and domestic-resource mobilization. Creditworthiness and performance problems in several major borrowing countries required the IBRD to limit temporarily its exposure in them."[15]

Some observers, especially in developing countries, find this defense inadequate. They argue that, in view of the magnitude of the crisis at hand and the adjustment efforts very poor countries were forced to make, the Bank should have been more flexible. Long-term development lending would have been welcome relief to many developing countries suffering from economic decline. In response, the IBRD has pointed out that its hallmark conservatism and its strong lending record have established its reputation and allowed it to borrow at low cost in international financial markets.

Despite the increasing controversy over World Bank practices during the 1980s, it may be useful to recall the broader objectives of the Bank and the wide range of services it continues to provide. As one observer has pointed out, "I think it is fair to say the borrowers trust the World Bank. They trust its objectivity and its commitment simply to do the right thing. Borrowers want to maintain a relationship with an institution that does not attach political strings to loans and that has a competent body of professionals whose role is to make decisions strictly on economic and financial grounds. I have no doubt that, for some borrowers, it is that pool of intelligence and the objectivity of the Bank's technical advice that are as important as the actual transfer of monetary resources."[16]

TABLE 3.1 Executive Directors and Voting Rights—June 30, 1991

Executive Director	Alternate	Casting Votes of	IBRD Total	IBRD % of	IDA Total	IDA % of
Appointed						
E. Patrick Coady	Mark T. Cox, IV	United States	206,507	17.59	1,269,436	16.71
Masaki Shiraton	(vacant)[a]	Japan	94,020	8.01	746,192	9.82
Gerhard Boehmer[b]	Harald Rehm	Germany	72,649	6.19	525,122	6.91
Jean-Pierre Landau	Philippe de Fontaine Vive	France	69,647	5.93	299,850	3.95
David Peretz	Robert Graham-Harrison	United Kingdom	69,647	5.93	420,870	5.54
Elected						
Jacques de Groote (Belgium)	Walter Rill (Austria)	Austria, Belgium, Czechoslovakia, Hungary Luxembourg, Turkey	59,685	5.08	303,987	4.00
Rosario Bonavoglia (Italy)	Fernando S. Carneiro (Portugal)	Greece, Italy, Malta,* Poland, Portugal*	59,350	5.06	407,040	5.36
Frank Potter (Canada)	Clarence Ellis (Guyana)	Antigua and Barbuda,* The Bahamas,* Barbados,* Belize, Canada, Dominica, Grenada, Guyana, Ireland, Jamaica,* St. Kitts, Nevis, St. Lucia, St. Vincent, the Grenadines	51,854	4.42	329,035	4.33
Eveline Herfkens (Netherlands)	Boris Skapin (Yugoslavia)	Bulgaria,* Cyprus, Israel, Netherlands, Romania,* Yugoslavia	50,048	4.26	229,065	3.02

Director	Alternate	Casting the votes of				
Moises Nam (Venezuela)	Sivia Charpentier[c] (Costa Rica)	Costa Rica, El Salvador, Guatemala, Honduras, Mexico, Nicaragua, Panama, Spain, Venezuela*	46,866	3.99	221,235	2.91
J.S. Baijar (India)	M. A. Syed (Bangladesh)	Bangladesh, Bhutan, India, Sri Lanka	45,384	3.87	326,693	4.30
Jonas H. Haratz[d] (Iceland)	Jorunn Maehlum (Norway)	Denmark, Finland, Iceland, Norway, Sweden	44,772	3.81	370,510	4.88
John H. Cosgrove (Australia)	A. John Wilson (New Zealand)	Australia, Kiribati, Korea (Rep. of), New Zealand, Papua New Guinea, Solomon Islands, Vanuatu, Western Samoa	39,580	3.37	200,099	2.63
Wang Liansheng (China)	Jin Liqun (China)	China	35,221	3.00	154,320	2.03
Mohamed Benhocine (Algeria)	Salem Mohamed Omeish (Libya)	Afghanistan, Algeria, Ghana, Iran (Islamic Rep. of), Libya, Morocco, Tunisia	32,741	2.79	115,741	1.52
Vibul Aunsnunta (Thailand)	Aung Pe (Myanmar)	Fiji, Indonesia, Lao People's Democratic Rep., Malaysia, Myanmar, Nepal, Singapore,* Thailand, Tonga, Viet Nam	31,804	2.71	228,329	3.01
Ernest Leung (Philippines)	Paulo C. Ximenes-Ferreira (Brazil)	Brazil, Colombia, Dominican Rep., Ecuador, Haiti, Philippines, Suriname,* Trinidad and Tobago	31,428	2.68	230,036	3.03

(continues)

TABLE 3.1 *(continued)*

Executive Director	Alternate	Casting Votes of	IBRD		IDA	
			Total	% of	Total	% of
Fawzi Hamad Al-Sultan (Kuwait)	Mohamed W. Hosny (Arab Rep. of Egypt)	Bahrain,* Egypt (Arab Rep. of), Jordan, Kuwait, Lebanon, Maldives, Oman, Pakistan, Qatar,* Syrian Arab Rep., United Arab Emirates, Yemen (Rep. of)........ 30,767		2.62	269,900	3.55
J. Ayo Langley (The Gambia)	O. K. Matambo (Botswana)	Angola, Botswana, Burundi, Ethiopia, The Gambia, Guinea, Kenya, Lesotho, Liberia, Malawi, Mozambique, Namibia,* Nigeria, Seychelles,* Sierra Leone, Sudan, Swaziland, Tanzania, Uganda, Zambia, Zimbabwe........ 30,083		2.56	308,951	4.07
Ibrahim A. Al-Assaf (Saudi Arabia)	Ahmed M. Al-Ghannam (Saudi Arabia)	Saudi Arabia............ 25,390		2.16	254,722	3.35
Felix Alberto Camarasa (Argentina)	Nicolas Flano (Chile)	Argentina, Bolivia, Chile, Paraguay, Peru, Uruguay*.... 24,745		2.11	143,701	1.89
Jean-Pierre Le Bouder (Central African Rep.)	Ali Bourhane (Comoros)	Benin, Burkina Faso, Cameroon, Cape Verde, Central African Rep., Chad, Comoros, Congo (People's Rep. of the), Cote d'Ivoire,				

Djibouti, Equatorial Guinea, Gabon,
Guinea-Bissau, Madagascar, Mali,
Mauritania, Mauritius, Niger, Rwanda,
Sao Tome and Principe, Senegal,
Somalia, Togo, Zaire........21,843   1.86   241,707   3.18

In addition to the executive directors and alternates shown in the foregoing list, the following also served after October 31, 1990:

Executive Director	End of Period of Service	Alternate Director	End of Period of Service
Cesare Caranza (Italy)	February 11, 1991	Abdulaziz Al-Sehail (Saudi Arabia)	December 21, 1990
Chang-Yuel Lim (Rep. of Korea)	May 31, 1991	Robert G. Carling (Australia)	February 28, 1991
		Bernd Esdar (Germany)	January 31, 1991
		M. Mustafizur Rahman (Bangladesh)	April 30, 1991
		Yukio Yoshimura (Japan)	June 7, 1991

Note: Iraq (3,058 votes in the IBRD and 9,407 votes in IDA), Democratic Kampuchea (464 votes in the IBRD and 7,826 votes in IDA), Mongolia (716 votes in the IBRD and 546 votes in IDA), and South Africa (13,712 votes in the IBRD and 24,592 votes in IDA) did not participate in the 1990 regular election of executive directors.
*Member of the IBRD only.
[a] Kiyoshi Kodera (Japan) was appointed effective July 8, 1991.
[b] To be succeeded by Fritz Fischer (Germany) as of July 1, 1991.
[c] To be succeeded by Gabriel Castellanos (Guatemala) as of July 1, 1991.
[d] To be succeeded by Einar Magnussen (Norway) as of August 1, 1991.
Source: World Bank, *Annual Report 1991.* Reprinted with permission.

TABLE 3.2 IBRD Average Costs, Profitability, and Return
(percentages based on average balances during fiscal year)

	Fiscal Year	
	1985	1989
Fiscal year costs		
Average cost of:		
New borrowings	7.98	7.73
Total debt outstanding	8.67	7.38
Total funds (debt and equity[a])	7.44	6.31
Fiscal year returns		
Average returns on:		
Loans disbursed and outstanding[b]	9.04	7.86
Liquid investments[c]	12.63	8.20
Total earning assets	10.10	8.20
Profitability measures		
Spreads (difference between)		
Loans:		
Return on loans outstanding and cost of total debt	0.37	
Return on loans outstanding and cost of total funds	1.60	1.89
Liquidity:		
Return on liquid investments and cost of total debt	3.96	
Return on liquid investments and cost of total funds	5.19	
Earning assets:		
Return on total earning assets and cost of total funds	2.66	
Net income		
Return on average equity[a]	14.90	7.29
Return on average liquid investments and loans		
(earning assets)	2.09	1.09
Leverage and returns on capital		
Ratio of reserves to loans (%)	8.5:1[e]	10.2
Ratio of outstanding loans to equity[d]	4.0:1	5.30:1
Ratio of outstanding debt to equity[d]	4.9:1	5.46:1

[a] Equity defined as usable paid-in capital, reserves, and accumulated net income.

[b] Interest on loans, commitment charges, and front-end fees as a percentage of average disbursed loans outstanding.

[c] Book return includes realized capital gains (losses). Financial return, including unrealized capital gains (losses), was 16.15 percent for fiscal 1985 and 9.20 percent for fiscal 1984.

[d] Equity defined as total paid-in capital, reserves, and accumulated net income.

[e] Data from 1986.

Source: World Bank, *Annual Report* (Washington, D.C.: World Bank, 1985 and 1990).

TABLE 3.3 IBRD and IDA Loans and Disbursements, 1980-1989

| | Fiscal Year | | | | | | | | | |
	1980	1981	1982	1983	1984	1985	1986	1987	1988	1989
IBRD										
	Millions of US Dollars									
Loans approved[a]	7,644	8,809	10,330	11,138	11,947	11,356	13,179	14,188	14,762	16,433
Disbursements[b]	4,363	5,063	6,326	6,817	8,580	8,645	8,263	11,383	11,636	11,310
Total income	2,800	2,999	3,372	4,232	4,655	5,529	6,815	7,689	8,549	8,274
Net income	588	610	598	752	600	1,137	1,243	1,113	1,004	1,094
General reserve	2,600	2,567	2,772	3,052	3,337	3,586	4,896	6,284	7,242	7,576
New borrowings	5,173	5,069	8,521	10,292	9,831	11,086	10,500[c]	9,321[d]	10,832	9,286
Subscribed capital	39,959	36,614	43,165	52,089	56,011	58,846	77,526	85,231	91,436	115,668
	Number									
Operations approved	144	140	150	136	129	131	131	127	118	119
Borrowing countries	48	50	43	43	43	44	41	39	37	38
Member countries	135	139	142	144	146	148	150	151	151	151
Higher level staff[e] (number)	2,463	2,552	2,689	2,703	2,735	2,805	3,617[f]	3,616	3,358	3,398

(continues)

TABLE 3.3 (continued)

	Fiscal Year									
	1980	1981	1982	1983	1984	1985	1986	1987	1988	1989
IDA										
	Millions of US Dollars									
Credit amounts	3,838	3,482	2,686	3,341	3,575	3,028	3,140	3,486	4,459	4,934
Disbursements	1,411	1,878	2,067	2,596	2,524	2,491	3,155	3,088	3,397	3,597
Usable resources, cumulative	20,773	22,331	25,280	27,967	30,910	33,295	39,167	43,614	48,665	53,097
	Number									
Operations approved[g]	103	106	97	107	106	105	97	108	99	106
Borrowing countries	40	40	42	44	43	45	37	39	36	42
Member countries	121	125	130	131	131	133	134	135	137	137

[a] Excludes loans to IFC of $100 million in FY 1981, $390 in FY 1982, $145 million in FY 1983, $100 million in FY 1984, $400 million in FY 1985, $150 million in FY 1986, $200 million in FY 1987, $200 million in FY 1988, and $179 million in FY 1989.

[b] Excludes disbursements on loans to IFC.

[c] Excludes $109 million in borrowings approved in FY 1986 and settled in FY 1987.

[d] FY 1987 amount is as of the date of settlement. Amounts in prior years are as of date of executive board approval.

[e] Higher-level staff on regular and fixed-term appointments held against authorized budget positions.

[f] In FY 1986, as a result of an institutionwide job-grading exercise, the Bank's grade structure changed, and the definition of what constituted higher-lever staff expanded considerably.

[g] Joint IBRD/IDA operations are counted only once as IBRD operations.

Source: World Bank, Annual Report (Washington, D.C.: World Bank, 1989).

TABLE 3.4 IBRD and IDA Cumulative Lending Operations, by Purpose and Region, June 30, 1991 (millions of US dollars)

| Purpose[b] | IBRD Loans to Borrowers, by Region[a] | | | | |
	Africa	Asia	Europe, Middle East, and N. Africa	Latin America and the Caribbean	Total
Agriculture and Rural Development					
Agricultural credit	319.8	1,568.4	2,898.8	2,660.9	7,447.9
Agricultural sector loan	16.8	585.3	1,332.0	2,507.1	4,441.2
Agroindustry	30.0	325.2	1,149.7	1,228.4	2,733.3
Area development	1,628.6	1,756.1	996.5	3,385.4	7,766.6
Fisheries	0.0	106.7	48.0	16.2	170.9
Forestry	349.5	78.0	317.5	116.0	861.0
Irrigation and drainage	110.2	4,110.8	2,713.1	2,274.5	9,208.6
Livestock	170.7	318.0	236.0	1,042.0	1,766.7
Perennial crops	634.5	1,410.8	108.0	123.0	2,276.3
Research and extension	111.7	448.4	207.4	585.0	1,352.5
Total	3,371.8	10707.7	10,007.0	13938.5	38,025.0
Development Finance Companies	1,059.0	5,377.8	6,843.7	7,311.1	20,591.6
Education	392.1	3,390.2	2,592.5	1,795.4	8,170.2
Energy					
Oil, gas, and coal	385.2	4,614.8	2,522.8	1,382.2	8,905.0
Power	1,782.1	14,747.7	6,707.2	11,239.7	34,476.7
Total	2,167.3	19,362.5	9,230.0	12,621.9	43,381.7

(continues)

TABLE 3.4 (continued)

IBRD Loans to Borrowers, by Region[a]

Purpose[b]	Africa	Asia	Europe, Middle East, and N. Africa	Latin America and the Caribbean	Total
Industry					
Engineering	27.7	10.0	11.0	9.5	58.2
Fertilizer and other chemicals	0.0	2,167.8	791.4	848.5	3,807.7
Industry sector loan	15.6	2,770.1	2,802.9	1,359.5	6,948.1
Iron and steel	20.0	189.0	512.8	1,067.0	1,788.8
Mining, other extractive	533.5	0.0	237.2	747.5	1,518.2
Paper and pulp	48.4	105.5	263.3	20.0	437.2
Textiles	63.0	157.4	307.3	0.0	527.7
Tourism sector loan	54.5	25.0	96.6	187.5	363.6
Total	762.7	5,424.8	5,022.5	4,239.5	15,449.5
Nonproject	1,943.6	3,829.3	6,085.9[c]	5,215.6	17,074.4
Population, Health, and Nutrition	289.4	618.8	335.2	1,105.8	2,349.2
Public-sector Management	0.0	32.0	130.0	1,454.0	1,616.0
Small-scale Enterprises	440.7	1,431.5	834.0	1,985.6	4,691.8
Technical Assistance	138.8	53.0	254.8	286.8	733.4
Telecommunications	510.2	1,348.2	1,091.8	508.3	3,458.5
Transportation					
Airlines and airports	59.0	14.8	7.0	218.5	299.3
Highways	1,817.8	5,096.7	3,640.3	5,828.3	16,383.1
Pipelines	0.0	0.0	94.5	23.3	117.8

	Africa	Asia	Europe, Middle East, and N. Africa	Latin America and the Caribbean	Total
Ports and waterways	285.9	1,722.5	1,716.0	523.7	4,248.1
Railways	733.5	3,013.8	1,483.9	1,938.5	7,169.7
Transportation sector loan	61.6	377.2	556.0	188.6	1,183.4
Total	2,957.8	10,225.0	7,497.7	8,720.9	29,401.4
Urban Development	933.7	3,159.4	981.3	3,853.1	8,927.5
Water Supply and Sewerage	1,059.8	1,685.4	3,064.8	3,373.7	9,183.7
Grand total	16,026.9	66,645.6	53,971.2	66,410.2	203,053.9

IDA Credits to Borrowers, by Region[c]

	Africa	Asia	Europe, Middle East, and N. Africa	Latin America and the Caribbean	Total	Total IBRD and IDA
Agriculture and Rural Development						
Agricultural credit	385.6	2,559.3	305.5	23.5	3,273.9	10,721.8
Agriculture sector loan	848.3	393.7	40.0	1.4	1,283.4	5,724.6
Agroindustry	361.4	676.9	138.0	16.5	1,192.8	3,926.1
Area development	1,602.1	1,983.7	200.6	86.1	3,872.5	11,639.1
Fisheries	55.7	192.3	67.3	0.0	315.3	486.2
Forestry	358.6	1,010.0	1.7	12.8	1,383.1	2,244.1
Irrigation and drainage	855.6	5,619.5	1,281.5	18.5	7,775.1	16,983.7
Livestock	457.2	331.2	49.5	67.5	905.4	2,672.1
Perennial crops	488.9	491.5	15.0	3.2	998.6	3,274.9
Research and extension	562.3	735.1	159.2	21.0	1,477.6	2,830.1
Total	5,975.7	13,993.2	2,258.3	250.5	22,477.7	60,502.7

(continues)

TABLE 3.4 (*continued*)

	IDA Credits to Borrowers, by Region[c]					
	Africa	Asia	Europe, Middle East, and N. Africa	Latin America and the Caribbean	Total	Total IBRD and IDA
velopment Finance Companies	1,281.2	578.6	273.7	144.1	2,277.6	22,869.2
Education	2,045.2	2,393.5	730.5	86.2	5,255.4	13,425.6
Energy						
Oil, gas, and coal	427.5	407.4	111.0	33.0	978.9	9,883.9
Power	1,130.1	3,635.3	393.6	189.7	5,348.7	39,825.4
Total	1,577.6	4,042.7	504.6	222.7	6,327.6	49,709.3
Industry						
Engineering	16.7	0.0	0.0	0.0	16.7	74.9
Fertilizer and other chemicals	35.0	884.0	76.4	0.0	995.4	4,803.1
Industry sector loan	302.7	335.8	29.5	0.0	668.0	7,616.1
Iron and steel	40.0	0.0	0.0	0.0	40.0	1,828.8
Mining, other extractive	13.9	16.0	0.0	49.5	79.4	1,597.6
Paper and pulp	50.0	0.0	0.0	0.0	50.0	487.2
Textiles	20.0	104.7	7.0	0.0	131.7	659.4
Tourism sector loan	18.0	20.2	48.5	0.0	86.7	450.3
Total	496.3	1,360.7	161.4	49.5	2,067.9	17,517.4
Nonproject	3,127.5	3,070.5	395.0	287.4	6,880.4	23,954.8
Population, Health, and Nutrition	842.1	1,337.3	313.2	99.5	2,592.1	4,941.3
Public-sector Management	307.7	0.0	0.0	0.0	307.7	1,923.7
Small-scale Enterprises	228.7	281.5	88.8	27.5	626.5	5,318.3

Technical Assistance	737.3	155.2	44.6	38.5	975.6	1,709.0
Telecommunications	352.1	869.3	142.7	0.0	1,364.1	4,822.6
Transportation						
Airlines and airports	14.0	7.5	2.5	0.0	24.0	323.3
Highways	2,716.1	1,183.1	282.3	167.3	4,348.8	20,731.9
Pipelines	0.0	0.0	0.0	0.0	0.0	117.8
Ports and waterways	413.9	372.7	44.7	16.0	847.3	5,095.4
Railways	587.6	1,124.2	138.5	45.0	1,895.3	9,065.0
Transportation sector loan	392.2	348.5	30.0	0.0	770.7	1,954.1
Total	4,123.8	3,036.0	498.0	228.3	7,886.1	37,287.5
Urban Development	868.5	1,448.7	251.3	127.0	2,695.5	11,623.0
Water Supply and Sewerage	675.5	1,453.2	573.6	78.8	2,781.1	11,964.8
Grand total	22,619.2	34,020.4	6,235.7	1,640.0	64,515.3	267,569.2[d]

[a] Except for the total amount shown in footnote d, no account is taken of cancellations subsequent to original commitment. IBRD loans to the IFC are excluded.
[b] Operations have been classified by the major purpose they finance. Many projects include activity in more than one sector or subsector.
[c] Includes $497 million in European reconstruction loans made before 1952.
[d] Cancellations amount to $14,080.12 million for the IBRD and $2,191.09 million for IDA, totaling $16,271.21 million.
Source: World Bank *Annual Report 1991.* Reprinted with permission.

TABLE 3.5 World Bank Adjustment Operations, Fiscal Year 1991 (millions of US dollars)

		World Bank Financing		
Country	Project	IBRD	IDA	Total
Sector-adjustment loans				
Algeria	Enterprise and financial-sector restructuring	350.0	---	350.0
Argentina	Public-enterprise reform adjustment	300.0	---	300.0
Bangladesh	Financial-sector adjustment (supplement)	---	3.5	3.5
Bolivia	Financial-sector adjustment III (supplement)	---	14.5	14.5
Colombia	Public-sector reform	304.0	---	304.0
Comoros	Macroeconomic reform and capacity building	---	8.0	8.0
Indonesia	Private-sector development II	250.0	---	250.0
Jamaica	Trade and financial-sector adjustment II	30.0	---	30.0
Kenya	Agricultural-sector adjustment II	---	75.0	75.0
Kenya	Export development	---	100.0	100.0
Kenya	Financial-sector adjustment	---	67.3	67.3
Madagascar	Public-sector adjustment (supplement)	---	1.7	1.7
Malawi	Industry and trade adjustment (supplement)	---	7.2	7.2
Mauritania	Public-enterprise sector adjustment (supplement)	---	4.0	4.0
Mexico	Agricultural-sector adjustment II	400.0	---	400.0
Mexico	Export-sector loan	300.0	---	300.0
Morocco	Financial-sector development	235.0	---	235.0
Pakistan	Energy-sector loan II (supplement)	28.0	---	28.0
Philippines	Environment and natural-resources management	158.0	66.0	224.0
Poland	Restructuring and privatization	280.0	---	280.0
Poland	Financial-instutions development	200.0	---	200.0
Sri Lanka	Public manufacturing-enterprises adjustment	---	120.0	120.0
Tanzania	Agricultural adjustment (supplement)	---	16.1	16.1

Togo	Population/health adjustment	--	14.2	14.2
Uganda		--	100.0	100.0
Total	Agricultural-sector adjustment	2,835.0	597.5	3,432.5
Structural-adjustment loans				
Benin	Structural adjustment II	--	55.0	55.0
Burkina Faso	Structural adjustment I	--	80.0	80.0
Czechoslovakia	Structural adjustment I	450.0	--	450.0
Egypt	Structural adjustment I	300.0	--	300.0
El Salvador	Structural adjustment I	75.0	--	75.0
Ghana	Structural adjustment II (supplement)	--	8.3	8.3
Ghana	Private-investment promotion	--	120.0	120.0
Guyana	Structural adjustment II (supplement)	--	18.0	18.0
Guyana	Structural adjustment II (supplement)	--	4.3	4.3
Honduras	Structural adjustment I (supplement)	--	20.0	20.0
Honduras	Structural adjustment II	90.0	--	90.0
Hungary	Structural adjustment II	250.0	--	250.0
Mali	Structural adjustment I	--	70.0	70.0
Poland	Structural adjustment I	300.0	--	300.0
Rwanda	Structural adjustment I	--	90.0	90.0
Senegal	Structural adjustment IV (supplement)	--	7.1	7.1
Sri Lanka	Economic restructuring (supplement)	--	7.0	7.0
Togo	Structural adjustment IV	--	55.0	55.0
Uganda	Economic recovery program II (supplement)	--	2.0	2.0
Zambia	Economic recovery program	--	210.0	210.0
Zambia	Economic recovery program (supplement)	--	27.2	27.2
Total		1,465.0	773.9	2,238.9
Grand total		4,300.0	1,371.4	5,671.4

Note: Table does not include $150 million interest support to Venezula and $65 million to Uruguay for debt and debt-service reduction.
Source: World Bank *Annual Report 1991.* Reprinted with permission.

NOTES

1. World Bank, *Annual Report 1985* (Washington, D.C.: World Bank, 1985), p. 205.

2. World Bank, *Annual Report 1991* (Washington, D.C.: World Bank, 1991), p. 71.

3. World Bank, *Annual Report 1990* (Washington, D.C.: World Bank, 1990), p. 74.

4. World Bank, *Annual Report 1986* (Washington, D.C.: World Bank, 1986), p. 22.

5. World Bank, *Annual Report 1991*, pp. 192–193.

6. Robert L. Ayres, *Banking on the Poor: The World Bank and World Poverty* (Cambridge: MIT Press, 1983), p. 74.

7. For more information, see Warren C. Baum, *The Project Cycle* (Washington, D.C.: World Bank, 1982).

8. World Bank, *Annual Report 1990*, p. 54.

9. For more on IMF-World Bank collaboration efforts, see Joseph Gold, *The IMF and the World Bank* (Washington, D.C.: International Monetary Fund, 1982), pp. 511–521, and David D. Driscoll, *The IMF and the World Bank: How Do They Differ?* (Washington, D.C.: International Monetary Fund, 1992).

10. International Bank for Reconstruction and Development, *Articles of Agreement*, Article 4, Section 10 (Washington, D.C.: World Bank, 1989), p. 13.

11. See especially Gerald K. Helleiner, "The Question of Conditionality," in Carol Lancaster and John Williamson (eds.), *African Debt Financing* (Washington, D.C.: Institute for International Economics, 1986).

12. Gold, *The IMF*, pp. 511–512.

13. "World Bank Is Under Pressure from U.S. to Expand Its Role in Global Debt Crisis," *Wall Street Journal*, October 1, 1985.

14. Eugene H. Rotberg, *The World Bank: A Financial Appraisal* (Washington, D.C.: World Bank, 1981), pp. 11–12.

15. World Bank, *Annual Report 1985*, p. 15.

16. Rotberg, *World Bank*, pp. 11–12.

4

The Creditor Clubs: Paris and London

Christine A. Kearney

Multilateral external debt reschedulings are often conducted under the auspices of creditor clubs, quasi-institutional arenas for refinancing accumulated debts, the most prominent of which are the Paris and London clubs. The forum for a given rescheduling is determined by the characteristics of the creditors. Loans and credits extended by government or official creditors are renegotiated in the Paris Club regardless of the borrower's status (public sector or private sector). Nongovernmentally insured debts owed to commercial banks are restructured in the London Club. Neither club has a formal or permanent institutional structure. There are no charters or formal mandates, and precise memberships vary with each rescheduling. Nevertheless, a distinct set of rules and procedures is associated with each club.

THE PARIS CLUB—BACKGROUND

The first Paris Club was convened in 1956 in response to Argentina's request for official debt relief. Argentina had accumulated substantial arrears on export credits that were extended or insured by several European governments. As these governments had not, for the most part, established the convertibility of their national currencies, a series of bilateral reschedulings would have been complicated and time-consuming. To avert these problems and to ensure uniformity of treatment among creditors, a multilateral rescheduling forum, the Paris Club, was conceived.[1]

The traditional participants in Paris Club debt reschedulings include the debtor country government and the governments of its major official creditors. The debtor is usually a developing country, and the creditors are ordinarily major industrial countries, usually members of the Organization for Economic Cooperation and Development (OECD). In recent years, however, developing countries (Brazil, Argentina, and Mexico, for instance) have occasionally participated as creditors. The IMF, World Bank, UN Conference on Trade and Development (UNCTAD), and, where relevant, regional development banks are also represented at Paris Club negotiations. Although in theory all official creditors can attend a given debtor country's rescheduling, in practice only the largest creditors participate. Some former Eastern bloc countries, China, and some Middle Eastern countries also have not taken part in Paris Club reschedulings, and there have been cases where developing countries chose not to participate as creditors, even when the debt owed to them was significant.[2]

In addition to membership, the pattern and frequency of Paris Club reschedulings have varied over the past three decades. Prior to 1976, the Paris Club had concluded approximately twenty-six separate rescheduling agreements with only twelve countries.[3] By contrast, 150 reschedulings, many of them repeat rescheduling agreements, were negotiated with fifty debtor countries between 1976 and 1990.[4] Developments in this latter period are summarized in Table 4.1 and Figure 4.1.

CHARACTERISTICS OF PARIS CLUB RESCHEDULINGS

Four interrelated attributes or principles have come to characterize Paris Club negotiations: imminent default, short-term relief, conditionality, and burden sharing.

The first principle refers to the practice of reserving the Paris Club mechanism almost exclusively for cases of imminent default. That is, creditor governments will not entertain a request for debt rescheduling unless there is evidence (the existence of substantial payments arrears for instance) that the debtor country will default on its external debt without relief. As Chandra Hardy observed, "The response of official creditors is delayed until the debtor's situation has deteriorated to the point where the suspension of all debt service payments appears imminent. The meeting takes place not to avoid a liquidity crisis but in response to one."[5] The rationale behind this practice is often attributed to creditors' desire to limit the frequency of requests for debt relief.

The strength of the imminent default principle is evident in the handling of the 1981 Pakistan rescheduling. Western creditors were anxious to bolster Pakistan's faltering economy following the Soviet invasion of Afghanistan. Although some creditors were prepared to participate in a Paris Club negotiation despite the absence of imminent default, "others (including the United States) argued successfully that a different venue should be found to preserve the integrity of the Paris Club process."[6] To avoid setting a precedent, then, debt relief for Pakistan was eventually coordinated through a World Bank aid consortium.

Closely related to the imminent default principle is the Paris Club creditors' premise that the debtor country's difficulties are essentially short-term problems caused by inappropriate domestic policies. As a result, the Paris Club has seen its purpose as providing temporary relief to restore debtor country creditworthiness and encourage the resumption of bank lending and official financial flows.[7] This attitude is reflected in the short (usually one-year) consolidation periods, the maximum ten-year maturity periods, and the average six-year grace periods specified in typical rescheduling agreements.[8]

Some have argued that this short-term focus, both in terms of amount consolidated and length of repayment schedule, is a deliberate creditor strategy to control debtor policies. They contend that the imminent default and short-term relief principles ensure that debtor countries are kept on a "short leash." Thus Chris Carvounis noted that "the short-term focus of the Paris Club's rescheduling provides lenders with [a] means of controlling debtor policies, because the debtor nation will need the further cooperation of the Club if [that nation] encounters future debt-servicing obstacles."[9]

Others, however, point to several developments in the 1980s as evidence of increasing creditor sensitivity to debtor countries' difficulties. For example, to alleviate the pattern of chronically indebted countries' returning year after year, the Paris Club introduced multiyear rescheduling agreements (MYRAs) in 1985. In addition, the menu approach to rescheduling, which includes partial debt forgiveness, lower interest rates, and extended maturity periods, was instituted in 1988 for heavily indebted low-income countries. In general, the 1980s witnessed a lengthening of average consolidation and repayment periods for all types of debtors.[10]

Because the Paris Club assumes that debtor country balance-of-payments difficulties are the result of inappropriate domestic policies, it is not surprising that the third major characteristic of Club reschedulings is conditionality. As a prerequisite to Paris Club negotiations, creditors insist that debtor countries conclude an agreement, usually an upper credit tranche arrangement, with the IMF. The centrality of Fund programs to the rescheduling process is reflected in the following assessment by Michael Kuhn and Jorge Guzman: "The single most important factor in determining the frequency of Paris Club reschedulings remained the rate at which Fund-supported programs were concluded...The unprecedented number of rescheduling agreements in 1989 is thus largely a reflection of the record number of countries whose programs are supported by the Fund."[11]

IMF programs serve a dual purpose. They both assure creditors that the debtor country will enact policies that improve its ability to service debts, and they provide a monitoring mechanism through which requests for subsequent reschedulings can be evaluated. The introduction of MYRAs has further increased the IMF's surveillance role, as the annual renewal of these agreements is often contingent on a debtor country's continued successful implementation of a Fund-sponsored economic reform program.[12] In some cases, of course, IMF conditionality was not possible because the debtor country was not a member of the IMF. In such instances, creditors have generally formed a task force of experts to negotiate policy reforms directly with the debtor country. Variants of this procedure have been used for reschedulings with Poland (prior to 1987), Mozambique (prior to 1984), and Cuba.[13]

The fourth principle of Paris Club reschedulings is burden sharing, which in essence means that debtor countries are expected to seek comparable relief from all of their various creditors (with the notable exception of the multinational lending institutions, which are given priority in repayment). Four provisions generally included in the Agreed Minutes of Paris Club meetings translate this burden-sharing principle into concrete terms. First, the access clause commits all participating creditors to report the contents of bilateral agreements to the Paris Club chairperson. Second, the initiative clause requires that debtors negotiate comparable rescheduling arrangements with nonparticipating official creditors and private creditors. Third, the most-favored-nation clause commits debtors to give creditors not participating in the Agreed Minutes no more preferential treatment than that accorded to Paris Club creditors. Finally, Agreed Minutes usually contain a provision in which the debtor country agrees to inform the chairperson of the contents of agreements reached with other creditors. The burden-sharing principle is particularly significant, as repeat reschedulings and MYRAs are often conditioned on debtor country progress with other creditors.[14]

A TYPICAL PARIS CLUB RESCHEDULING SCENARIO

A debtor country typically initiates the rescheduling exercise by sending a formal request for a meeting to the chairperson of the Paris Club, who is usually an official of the French treasury. At the time of the formal request, or shortly thereafter, the debtor provides the Club with a summary of its external debt service payments, broken down according to official creditor. Using this information, and with supplemental data provided by the IMF and other multilateral institutions, the chairperson determines the debtor's eligibility for rescheduling (the debtor must be facing imminent default) and then decides which creditor country governments should participate. If the debtor already has a standby agreement with the IMF covering the period for which relief is requested, then the chairperson can set the meeting date. Otherwise the debtor is informed of the conditionality requirements. During the course of these preliminaries, the creditors review the information provided by the IMF concerning its arrangements with the debtor and acquaint one another with the status of their credits to the debtor.

The rescheduling meeting itself usually spans one or two days. Before 1983, standard Paris Club practice allowed two days for negotiations, but in subsequent years, as the number of debt relief requests increased, negotiations were sometimes limited to one day. Regardless of duration, however, rescheduling negotiations display a consistent pattern. First, the chairperson invites the debtor country, often represented by its finance minister, to explain the request for relief. Second, observers from multilateral institutions make presentations. The IMF usually begins and is followed in succession by the World Bank, the regional development bank (if relevant), and UNCTAD. Finally, the creditors ask questions of the debtor country delegation and the institutional observers.[15]

After these preliminaries, the creditors, accompanied by the IMF representative, meet without the debtor to negotiate an initial rescheduling package. The IMF representative is included for his or her expertise regarding the standby arrangement on which rescheduling packages are premised. The initial package generally represents the hardest terms requested by any creditor. Once it is formulated, the chairman relates this offer informally to the debtor country delegation, which ordinarily rejects it. What follows thereafter is a series of negotiations whose length varies from case to case depending primarily on the ability of the creditors to construct subsequent offers. Although debtors can in theory continue to reject creditors' rescheduling offers (and thus prolong the negotiations), in practice they generally do not, "and by lunchtime of the second day it is usually possible to reach agreement on a package of terms."[16]

The final agreed scheduling terms are embodied in the Agreed Minute, which is then signed *ad referendum* by all participating creditors. By signing this document, the heads of creditor delegations agree to "recommend to their respective governments" the terms set forth in the Agreed Minute.[17] Formal implementation, however, requires revision of the payment obligations specified in the various loan contracts concerned. Therefore, the debtor country must then conclude a bilateral agreement with each creditor country. The agreed minute generally specifies a deadline for completing these separate bilateral agreements.

PARIS CLUB RESCHEDULING TERMS

The terms included in a typical Agreed Minute can be divided into five components. First, the type of credits eligible for rescheduling are specified. Usually medium-term and long-term debt service, encompassing both interest and principal, are covered, whereas short-term debt and obligations to multilateral institutions are excluded. Second, the Agreed Minute contains a cutoff date before which loans must have been contracted in order for their debt service to be covered by the rescheduling agreement. Cutoff dates are generally six to twelve months before the date of the Paris Club agreement, but there have been cases where creditors accepted cutoff dates as late as the day before the consolidation period. In successive reschedulings with the same country, Paris Club creditors strongly resist moving the cutoff date forward.[18]

The third component of Paris Club terms is the consolidation period, or the time frame in which the debt service payments to be consolidated or rescheduled have fallen or will fall due. Creditors have traditionally preferred to limit the period to one year, but since the 1980s there has been a lengthening of the average consolidation period mainly because of the advent of MYRAs.[19] Although creditors favor short consolidation periods, debtors almost invariably prefer multiyear consolidation periods.

Paris Club creditors rarely reschedule 100 percent of the debt service payments falling within a given consolidation period, and thus the fourth component specified in an Agreed Minute is nonconsolidated debt. That is, the Agreed Minute indicates the portion of obligations falling within the consolidation period that the debtor is to meet on schedule. This distinction between consolidated and nonconsolidated debt, however, has lost some meaning of late, because creditors have frequently rescheduled the supposedly "nonconsolidated" portion, albeit on less generous terms than the "consolidated" portion.[20]

The fifth and final component of rescheduling agreements is the repayment schedule, which generally consists of a grace period followed by a repayment period. Together, the grace and repayment periods constitute the arrangement's overall maturity. Although the average maturity period is ten years, since 1987, creditors have accepted the principle of extending maturity periods to between fifteen and twenty years for heavily indebted countries.[21]

THE LONDON CLUB—A PARALLEL FRAMEWORK

The Paris and London clubs are fundamentally similar in that "they are both ad hoc groups of creditors without any formal mandate or rules of procedure."[22] The key difference between the two clubs, as mentioned previously, is that London Club creditors are commercial banks rather than official lenders. However, London Club procedures and practices also diverge from Paris Club reschedulings in several additional respects.

First, the scope and type of debt rescheduled by the London Club differ significantly from typical Paris Club terms, mainly because London Club creditors are more concerned than official creditors with profit margins. The Paris Club generally negotiates only credits already in force, whereas the London Club is willing to negotiate new credits. And though the Paris Club usually reschedules both principal and interest debt service payments, the London Club almost never reschedules interest obligations, and it charges current market interest rates on the principal payments rescheduled. In this regard, the interest rates in Paris Club reschedulings are generally lower (overall) because Paris Club creditors normally preserve the concessionality inherent in the original loans they reschedule. In addition, the Paris Club tries to avoid consolidation periods longer than one year, whereas the London Club is generally open to multiyear consolidation periods when extended relief is deemed necessary.[23]

The second area of divergence concerns participation and the length and cost of rescheduling negotiations. As mentioned, Paris Club negotiations are theoretically open to all official creditors who accept Paris Club procedures, though in practice only creditors holding a specified amount of the applicant country's debt participate in rescheduling negotiations. By contrast, London Club reschedulings must include all commercial banks with exposure to the debtor country, regardless of the amount. Banks holding small amounts of debt, however, tend to be represented by their country's largest international banks on an international steering committee (or bankers' committee) which actually negotiates the rescheduling package.

Because London Club reschedulings involve a greater number of participants than Paris Club negotiations, they are generally longer and thus more costly. In addition, whereas the Paris Club negotiates a framework for rescheduling (the Agreed Minute) that is then legally implemented through a series of bilateral agreements, the London Club negotiates one comprehensive agreement that is legally binding once formulated. For these reasons, London Club rescheduling discussions tend to be drawn out over several months. Alexis Rieffel summarized these differences as follows: "The Paris Club is capable of completing a rescheduling agreement involving billions of dollars of obligations in eight to twelve hours of negotiations at no cost to the debtor other than plane fare to Paris and two days' lodging for its delegation. The contrast with the London Club is dramatic and certainly not lost on the debtors."[24]

A third and final category of differences between the Paris and London clubs involves prerequisites for rescheduling. As discussed above, the Paris Club requires a debtor country to be in a position of imminent default and to have an agreement with the IMF in place before undertaking rescheduling negotiations. The London Club, by contrast, is far more likely to engage in "preemptive" rescheduling and to restructure debt service payments in the absence of an IMF arrangement.[25]

Although these differences may be substantial, they should not obscure the links and cooperation between the London and Paris clubs. Both creditor groups share the common purpose of rescheduling developing country debt in the most timely and efficient manner possible. Furthermore, as both clubs also place a good deal of emphasis on comparability of treatment among creditors, the rescheduling exercise for a given country often necessitates some degree of coordination between the Paris and London clubs.

TABLE 4.1   Multilateral Official Debt Reschedulings, 1976–July 1990[a]

Debtor Country[b]	Date of Agreement	Forum	Number of Participating Creditors	Amount Consolidated (millions of US dollars)	Maturity (years)[c]
1976					
Zaire I	June 16	Paris Club	11	270	9
1977					
Zaire II	July 7	Paris Club	11	170	9
Sierra Leone I	Sept. 15	Paris Club	6	39	11
Zaire III	Dec. 1	Paris Club	10	40	10
1978					
Turkey I	May 20	OECD	14	1,300	7
Gabon I	June 20	Special task force	5	63	--
Peru I	Nov. 3	Paris Club	14	420	7
1979					
Togo I	June 15	Paris Club	9	260	10
Turkey II	July 25	OECD	17	1,200	8
Sudan I	Nov. 13	Paris Club	11	487	10
Zaire IV	Dec. 11	Paris Club	14	1,040	10
1980					
Sierra Leone II	Feb. 8	Paris Club	7	37	10
Turkey III	July 23	OECD	17	3,000	10
Liberia I	Dec. 19	Paris Club	8	35	9
1981					
Togo II	Feb. 20	Paris Club	11	232	9
Poland I	April 27	Creditor Group	15	2,110	8
Madagascar I	April 30	Paris Club	11	140	9
Central African Republic I	June 12	Paris Club	6	72	9
Zaire V	July 9	Paris Club	12	500	10
Senegal I	Oct. 12	Paris Club	13	75	9
Uganda I	Nov. 18	Paris Club	6	30	10
Liberia II	Dec. 16	Paris Club	8	25	9
1982					
Sudan II	March 18	Paris Club	13	203	10
Madagascar II	July 13	Paris Club	11	107	9
Romania I	July 28	Paris Club	15	234	6
Malawi I	Sept. 22	Paris Club	6	25	8
Senegal II	Nov. 29	Paris Club	12	74	9
Uganda II	Dec. 1	Paris Club	4	19	9

TABLE 4.1 (*continued*)

Debtor Country[b]	Date of Agreement	Forum	Number of Participating Creditors	Amount Consolidated (millions of US dollars)	Maturity (years)[c]
1983					
Costa Rica I	Jan. 11	Paris Club	10	136	9
Sudan III	Feb. 4	Paris Club	15	518	16
Togo III	April 12	Paris Club	11	300	10
Zambia I	May 16	Paris Club	12	375	10
Romania II	May 18	Paris Club	11	736	7
Mexico	June 22	Creditor Group	15	1,199	6
Central African Republic II	July 8	Paris Club	5	13	10
Peru II	July 26	Paris Club	20	466	8
Ecuador I	July 28	Paris Club	13	142	8
Morocco I	Oct. 25	Paris Club	12	1,152	8
Malawi II	Oct. 27	Paris Club	5	26	8
Niger I	Nov. 14	Paris Club	5	36	9
Brazil I	Nov. 23	Paris Club	16	2,337	8
Zaire VI	Dec. 20	Paris Club	13	1,497	11
Senegal III	Dec. 21	Paris Club	11	72	9
Liberia III	Dec. 22	Paris Club	8	17	9
1984					
Sierra Leone III	Feb. 8	Paris Club	11	25	10
Madagascar III	March 23	Paris Club	13	89	11
Sudan IV	May 3	Paris Club	15	249	16
Cote d'lvoire I	May 4	Paris Club	12	230	9
Yugoslavia I	May 22	Creditor Group	15	500	7
Peru III	June 5	Paris Club	18	704	9
Togo IV	June 6	Paris Club	11	75	10
Jamaica I	July 16	Paris Club	10	105	9
Zambia II	July 20	Paris Club	13	253	10
Mozambique I	Oct. 25	Paris Club	12	283	11
Niger II	Nov. 30	Paris Club	5	26	10
Liberia IV	Dec. 17	Paris Club	7	17	10
Philippines I	Dec. 20	Paris Club	15	757	10
1985					
Argentina I	Jan. 16	Paris Club	16	2,040	10
Senegal IV	Jan. 18	Paris Club	11	122	9
Somalia I	March 6	Paris Club	5	127	10
Costa Rica II	April 22	Paris Club	10	166	10
Ecuador II[d]	April 24	Paris Club	13	450	8
Mauritania I	April 27	Paris Club	8	68	9

(*continues*)

TABLE 4.1 *(continued)*

Debtor Country[b]	Date of Agreement	Forum	Number of Participating Creditors	Amount Consolidated (millions of US dollars)	Maturity (years)[c]
Dominican					
Republic I	May 21	Paris Club	7	290	10
Madagascar IV	May 22	Paris Club	13	128	11
Yugoslavia II	May 24	Creditor Group	16	812	8
Togo V	June 24	Paris Club	8	27	11
Cote d'Ivoire II	June 25	Paris Club	12	213	9
Poland II	July 15	Creditor Group	17	10,930	12
Chile I	July 17	Creditor Group	7	146	7
Jamaica II	July 19	Paris Club	6	62	10
Equatorial					
Guinea I	July 22	Paris Club	3	38	10
Morocco II	Sept. 17	Paris Club	11	1,124	9
Zaire VII	Sept. 18	Paris Club	11	408	10
Panama I	Sept. 19	Paris Club	7	19	8
Poland III	Nov. 19	Creditor Group	17	1,400	10
Niger III	Nov. 21	Paris Club	4	38	10
Central African					
Republic III	Nov. 22	Paris Club	7	14	10
	1986				
Zambia III	March 4	Paris Club	13	371	10
Guinea I	April 18	Paris Club	12	196	10
Yugoslavia III[e]	May 13	Creditor Group	16	901	8
Zaire VIII	May 15	Paris Club	11	429	10
Mauritania II	May 16	Paris Club	8	27	9
Cote					
d'Ivoire III[d]	June 27	Paris Club	12	370	9
Bolivia I	July 17	Paris Club	12	449	10
Congo I	July 18	Paris Club	10	756	10
Mexico II[f]	Sept. 17	Paris Club	14	1,912	9
Tanzania I	Sept. 18	Paris Club	16	1,046	10
Gambia, The I	Sept. 19	Paris Club	7	17	10
Madagascar V[g]	Oct. 23	Paris Club	12	212	10
Sierra Leone IV	Nov. 19	Paris Club	10	86	10
Niger IV	Nov. 20	Paris Club	4	34	10
Senegal V	Nov. 21	Paris Club	10	65	10
Nigeria I	Dec. 16	Paris Club	19	6,251	10
	1987				
Brazil II[h]	Jan. 21	Paris Club	14	4,178	6

TABLE 4.1 (*continued*)

Debtor Country[b]	Date of Agreement	Forum	Number of Participating Creditors	Amount Consolidated (millions of US dollars)	Maturity (years)[c]
Gabon II	Jan. 21	Paris Club	12	387	10
Philippines II[g]	Jan. 22	Paris Club	14	862	10
Jamaica III	March 5	Paris Club	9	124	10
Morocco III	March 6	Paris Club	11	1,008	10
Chile II	April 2	Paris Club	7	157	7
Zaire IX	May 18	Paris Club	13	671	15
Argentina II	May 20	Paris Club	14	1,260	10
Egypt I	May 22	Paris Club	18	6,350	10
Mauritania III	June 15	Paris Club	9	90	15
Mozambique II	June 16	Paris Club	14	361	20
Uganda III	June 19	Paris Club	5	170	15
Somalia II	July 22	Paris Club	6	153	20
Guinea-Bissau I	Oct. 27	Paris Club	6	25	20
Senegal VI	Nov. 17	Paris Club	7	79	16
Poland IV	Dec. 16	Paris Club	17	9,027	10
Cote d'Ivoire IV	Dec. 18	Paris Club	13	567	10
1988					
Ecuador III	Jan. 20	Paris Club	12	438	10
Gabon III	March 21	Paris Club	12	326	10
Togo VI	March 22	Paris Club	11	139	16
Niger V	April 21	Paris Club	4	37	20
Malawi III	April 22	Paris Club	6	27	20
Yugoslavia IV	July 13	Paris Club	16	1,291	10
Brazil III	July 28	Paris Club	13	4,992	10
Jamaica IV[g]	Oct. 24	Paris Club	9	147	10
Morocco IV	Oct. 26	Paris Club	11	969	10
Mali I	Oct. 27	Paris Club	6	63	Menu
Madagascar V[g]	Oct. 28	Paris Club	12	254	Menu
Bolivia II[g]	Nov. 14	Paris Club	9	226	10
Tanzania II	Dec. 13	Paris Club	15	377	Menu
Central African Republic IV[i]	Dec. 14	Paris Club	8	28	Menu
Niger VI	Dec. 16	Paris Club	4	48	Menu
1989					
Senegal VII	Jan. 24	Paris Club	11	143	Menu
Trinidad & Tobago I	Jan. 25	Paris Club	9	209	10
Uganda IV[g]	Jan. 26	Paris Club	5	89	Menu

(*continues*)

TABLE 4.1 *(continued)*

Debtor Country[b]	Date of Agreement	Forum	Number of Participating Creditors	Amount Consolidated (millions of US dollars)	Maturity (years)[c]
Equatorial Guinea II	March 2[j]	Paris Club	2	10	Menu
Nigeria II	March 3	Paris Club	17	5,600	10
Guinea II	April 12	Paris Club	11	123	Menu
Guyana I	May 24	Paris Club	9	195	20
Cameroon I	May 24	Paris Club	13	535	10
Philippines III[i]	May 26	Paris Club	13	1,850	10
Costa Rica III	May 26	Paris Club	8	182	10
Mexico III[k]	May 30	Paris Club	14	2,400	10
Mauritania IV	June 19	Paris Club	9	52	Menu
Togo VII	June 20	Paris Club	11	76	Menu
Benin I	June 22	Paris Club	8	193	Menu
Zaire X	June 23	Paris Club	13	1,530	Menu
Jordan I	July 19	Paris Club	14	587	10
Angola I	July 20	Paris Club	11	446	10
Gabon IV	Sept. 19	Paris Club	11	545	10
Ecuador IV[j]	Oct. 24	Paris Club	12	397	10
Chad I	Oct. 24 [j]	Paris Club	3	38	Menu
Guinea-Bissau II[g]	Oct. 26	Paris Club	5	21	Menu
Mali II[k]	Nov. 22	Paris Club	5	44	Menu
Cote d'Ivoire V[g]	Dec. 18	Paris Club	13	881	14
Argentina III	Dec. 21	Paris Club	16	2,450	10
1990					
Senegal VIII	Feb. 12	Paris Club	11	107	Menu
Poland V	Feb. 16	Paris Club	17	9,350	14
Bolivia III[j]	March 15	Paris Club	10	276	Menu
Tanzania III	March 16	Paris Club	15	199	Menu
Jamaica V	April 26	Paris Club	9	179	10
Trinidad and Tobago II	April 27	Paris Club	8	110	10
Mozambique III[i]	June 14	Paris Club	12	707	Menu
Central African Republic V	June 15	Paris Club	4	4	Menu
Togo VIII[i]	July 9	Paris Club	10	90	Menu
Madagascar VII	July 10	Paris Club	12	181	Menu
Zambia IV	July 12	Paris Club	12	965	Menu

TABLE 4.1 (*continued*)

Sources: Agreed Minutes of debt reschedulings and Fund staff estimates; Michael G. Kuhn and Jorge P. Guzman, *Multilateral Official Debt Rescheduling: Recent Experience* (Washington, D.C.: International Monetary Fund, 1990), pp. 2-4. Reprinted with permission.

[a] The reschedulings exclude both debt restructurings conducted under the auspices of aid consortia and official debt reschedulings for countries not members of the Fund, but include agreements with Poland signed prior to its date of membership in the Fund (June 12, 1986) and the agreement with Angola signed prior its date of membership in the Fund (September 19, 1989).

[b] Roman numerals indicate the number of debt reschedulings for that country since 1976.

[c] "Menu" refers to reschedulings on Toronto terms (see Appendix II). Agreed Minutes specify first and last payment dates for different categories of debts consolidated rather than maturity and grace periods. The maturities generally refer to the period from the middle of the consolidation period to the last payment date for previously non-rescheduled current maturities on medium- and long-term debt as indicated in communiques of the rescheduling agreements.

[d] Includes three separate one-year consolidation periods of the multiyear restructuring agreement.

[e] The conditional second tranche of the consolidation took effect after a further meeting with creditors in 1987.

[f] Includes two separate consolidation periods.

[g] Includes conditional extension.

[h] Includes two separate consolidation periods; however, the second tranche of the consolidation did not become effective.

[i] Includes two separate tranches.

[j] Date of informal meeting of creditors on the terms to be applied in the bilateral reschedulings. Since only two creditors were involved for Equatorial Guinea and three creditors for Chad, creditors did not call for a full Paris Club meeting.

[k] Includes three separate tranches.

Number of Initial and Repeat
Rescheduling Agreements

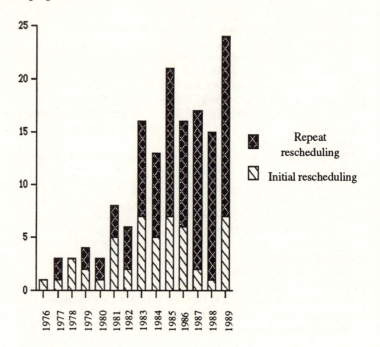

FIGURE 4.1   Multilateral Official Debt Renegotiations
for All Countries, 1976–1989

(continues)

Amounts Rescheduled by
SAF/ESAF-Eligible
and Other Countries

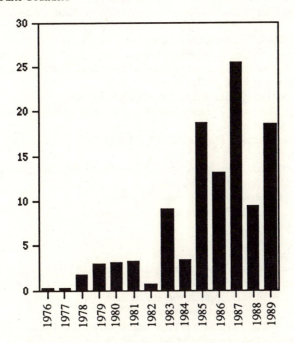

FIGURE 4.1   *(continued)*
Sources: Agreed Minutes and IMF staff estimates.

NOTES

1. Irving S. Friedman, *The World Debt Dilemma: Managing Country Risk* (Washington, D.C.: Council for Banking Studies, 1983), pp. 108–109.

2. Michael G. Kuhn and Jorge P. Guzman, *Multilateral Official Debt Rescheduling: Recent Experience* (Washington, D.C.: International Monetary Fund,1990), p. 18.

3. Alexis Rieffel, *The Role of the Paris Club in Managing Debt Problems* (Princeton, N.J.: Princeton University, Essays in International Finance, no. 161, December 1985), p. 4.

4. Kuhn and Guzman, *Multilateral Official Debt,* p. 1.

5. Chandra Hardy,"Rescheduling Developing Country Debts," *Banker,* July 1981, p. 34.

6. Rieffel, *The Role of the Paris Club,* pp. 5-6.

7. K. Burke Dillon, C. Maxwell Watson, G. Russell Kincaid, and Chanpen Puckahtikom, *Recent Developments in External Debt Restructuring* (Washington, D.C.: International Monetary Fund, 1985).

8. Kuhn and Guzman, *Multilateral Official Debt,* pp. 9–12.

9. Chris C. Carvounis, *The Debt Dilemma of Developing Nations* (Westport, Conn.: Quorum Books, 1984), p. 73.

10. Kuhn and Guzman, *Multilateral Official Debt,* p. 12.

11. Ibid, p. 7.

12. Dillon, Watson, Kincaid, and Puckahtikom, *Recent Developments,* pp. 23–24.

13. Rieffel, *The Role of the Paris Club,* p. 9.

14. Kuhn and Guzman, *Multilateral Official Debt,* p. 17.

15. Rieffel, *The Role of the Paris Club,* pp. 16–18.

16. Ibid, p. 18.

17. Ibid, p. 21.

18. Ibid, pp. 19–20.

19. Kuhn and Guzman, *Multilateral Official Debt,* p. 12.

20. Rieffel, *The Role of the Paris Club,* p. 20.

21. Kuhn and Guzman, *Multilateral Official Debt,* p. 13.

22. Rieffel, *The Role of the Paris Club,* p. 22.

23. Dillon, Watson, Kincaid, and Puckahtikon, *Recent Developments,* pp. 13–18.

24. Rieffel, *The Role of the Paris Club,* pp. 14–15.

25. Ibid, pp. 22–23.

Part Two

THE POLITICAL ECONOMY OF INTERNATIONAL FINANCIAL NEGOTIATIONS

5

Mexico, 1982: Paving the Way with Exceptions

On Friday, August 13, 1982, the Mexican finance minister, Jesus Silva Herzog, arrived in Washington with only one day's advance notice. His country was on the brink of bankruptcy, and he needed U.S. financial assistance. Unless the finance minister could piece together a rescue package in Washington to avoid default on the country's $80 billion external debt, Mexico would be forced to undertake the largest suspension of payments to foreign creditors by any government in the post–World War II period.

The U.S. government was not fully prepared for Silva Herzog's sudden visit or for Mexico's financial crisis. Few formal steps had been taken to get ready for such a serious situation, let alone for the disruptive effects it might have on the international financial system. Thus, the U.S. government was forced to respond to Mexico's crisis, and to a potential international financial crisis, without the benefit of contingency plans and without the time carefully to organize and implement a solution.

This chapter integrates material from two cases originally prepared for The Pew Diplomatic Initiative. Much of the material on the "Washington Weekend" is derived from Roger S. Leeds and Gale Thompson's "The 1982 Mexican Debt Negotiations," produced by the Pew Project at the Johns Hopkins School of Advanced International Studies. Much of the material on the negotiations undertaken following the initial financial arrangement (the BIS, IMF, and commercial bank agreements) is derived from Adhip Chaudhuri's "The Mexican Debt Crisis, 1982," prepared for the Pew Project at Georgetown University's School of Foreign Service. Christine Kearney redrafted much of the original case material and added information from other scholarly studies of the Mexican case. Pamela Starr, a doctoral candidate at the School of International Relations at the University of Southern California, drafted the appendix on Mexican politics.

The objective of the Mexican and U.S. governments was to arrange for interim financing until Mexico could reach agreement both with the IMF on an economic program and with its private creditors on a longer-term financial package. In the course of two days of virtually nonstop negotiations now known as the "Washington weekend," U.S. policymakers assembled a rescue package of short-term funds totaling more than $2 billion. To address longer-term issues, Mexican officials also met with representatives of the U.S. Federal Reserve Board (the Fed) to arrange a medium-term loan under the auspices of the Bank for International Settlements (BIS) and with IMF officials to initiate the protracted process of securing new long-term financing.

This case considers the origins of Mexico's crisis, tells the story of the Washington weekend negotiations (August 13–15, 1982), and relates the events that led to both medium-term loans from the Fed and the BIS and long-term financial agreements between Mexico and the IMF and private international banks. The primary focus, however, is on the complexities of the negotiating process surrounding the origins of the global debt crisis: the strategies and interests that informed the U.S. government, the IMF, the major money center banks, and the Mexican government in responding to an unexpectedly large and threatening international financial crisis.

THE INTERNATIONAL FINANCIAL CLIMATE

Mexico's insolvency would have been extremely serious even if it had been an isolated incident in world affairs. It was not, however, an isolated event. A string of financial upheavals that erupted during summer 1982 caused many people to believe that the international banking system was being subjected to more pressure than at any other time since the early 1930s. A deep international recession contributed to a series of unexpected events that had heightened uncertainty about the stability and suitability of the existing international banking and financial system.

The first omen came in May, when an obscure New Jersey government bond trading company, Drysdale Government Securities, defaulted on a $162 million obligation to Chase Manhattan Bank and abruptly went out of business. It was revealed that Drysdale had been engaging in fraudulent trading activities with a number of banks. Attention thus shifted from the substantial losses ($285 million) incurred by Chase Manhattan and a number of other U.S. banks to the larger question of the safety and stability of the U.S. government securities market, where the daily trading volume was an estimated $30 billion.

The following month, the international financial markets became the focus of concern. On June 18, Roberto Calvi, chairman of Italy's largest commercial bank, Banco Ambrosiano, was found hanging from London's Blackfriars Bridge—an apparent suicide. When Calvi was subsequently linked to approximately $1.6

billion of funds "missing" from his bank, a cloud of suspicion arose over the Italian banking system. Matters worsened in July, when a wholly owned subsidiary of Ambrosiano in Luxembourg declared bankruptcy. The Euromarkets were thrown into confusion when the Bank of Italy disavowed responsibility for the Ambrosiano subsidiary's outstanding debts, claiming that a central bank does not have an obligation to depositors who suffer losses in a subsidiary located in another national jurisdiction.

Meanwhile, in the United States, the Ambrosiano scandal was replaced in the headlines by the July bankruptcy of a small Oklahoma bank, Penn Square, which had sold hundreds of millions of dollars in questionable loans to a number of large money center banks. Penn Square had employed possibly fraudulent banking practices when it originally extended these loans to companies engaged in high-risk oil and gas exploration. However, it also became evident that the larger banks that later purchased the loans had not adequately investigated their reliability. Bank analysts and the financial press began to speculate about how many more Penn Squares and Drysdale Securities were lurking in the financial world, and how much damage incidents of this type would have on the stability of the banking system.

As bankers, regulators, and public-policymakers struggled to cope with one financial impropriety after another, the developing countries' "debt crisis" became the most serious threat of all. Although debt reschedulings were not new phenomena—twenty-two had been undertaken by the commercial banks since 1975[1]—they had been largely limited to small, poor nations. By summer 1982, however, several major international borrowers had shown signs of economic failure. Poland threatened default on $4.8 billion in winter 1981–1982 and Argentina struggled to remain current on its external debt payments after its Falklands-Malvinas war with the United Kingdom. The events in Poland alerted the public and forced bankers to address the possibility of much larger losses than they had previously envisaged, whereas the Argentine situation led bankers to be more cautious about further lending anywhere in Latin America.

Thus, for a variety of domestic and international reasons, the banking system was under stress by 1982. There was a sense of mounting alarm, as uncertainty increased amid heightened speculation about how much strain the system could endure. Then, in mid-August, Mexico emerged as the ultimate test of the financial market's resilience.

THE PATH TO MEXICO'S CRISIS

The grave economic situation that precipitated Finance Minister Silva Herzog's urgent visit to Washington had both external and internal origins. At the international level, Mexico faced a new environment in the early 1980s: rising real interest rates, a recession in the United States, and a collapse in the world price of Mexico's chief export, oil. These developments, caused in large part by the contractionary monetary policy of the U.S. Federal Reserve Board, had several adverse consequences for Mexico. First, the rise in real interest rates sharply increased Mexico's debt service payments (Figure 5.1 and Table 5.1). Loans that had been contracted on variable interest rates in the 1970s now entailed heavy interest costs. Second, the recession in the United States, which also spread to Europe, reduced demand in Mexico's principal export markets and thus lowered the volume of Mexican exports. Finally, the drop in world demand for petroleum products and the subsequent weakening of oil prices drastically reduced Mexico's export earnings. In short, Mexico's debt burden increased significantly at a time when its ability to pay with export earnings (specifically from petroleum) was weakened significantly.

In addition to these difficult international economic conditions, certain domestic economic decisions made by the Mexican government also contributed to Mexico's problems in 1982. In particular, Mexican leaders chose in the mid- to late- 1970s to spend heavily on social welfare programs and the development of the petroleum industry (see the Appendix to this chapter), even though government revenues were not growing rapidly enough to meet the costs of such policies. The large fiscal deficits that resulted were then treated as temporary problems that would be overcome once new oil production took effect. In the meantime, the deficits were financed with commercial bank loans, which were relatively easy to obtain, given the international banks' highly liquid position[2] and Mexico's history of high growth rates and projected oil export earnings.

This strategy seemed to work well for Mexico until changes occurred in the international environment (described above) in the early 1980s. Although confronted with declining oil receipts and rising debt service payments, the Mexican government continued to spend. Between 1980 and 1982, the central government's deficit, as a percentage of gross domestic product (GDP), tripled. At the same time, Mexico's trade was suffering. Both the one-sided focus on the energy sector in the late 1970s and the declining U.S. and European demand for Mexican exports during the recession of the early 1980s had weakened Mexico's nonoil export performance. The decrease in petroleum prices and Mexican oil export earnings was therefore a particularly serious blow. Meanwhile, imports continued to increase rapidly, and by 1981 Mexico had a current account deficit of $13.9 billion, as compared with $1.9 billion in 1977 (Table 5.2).

With the public deficit rising and the balance of payments deteriorating, the Mexican government accelerated its foreign borrowing. Total external debt jumped from $20.6 billion in 1979 to $42.7 billion in 1981 (see Table 5.2). Between 1978 and the end of 1981, U.S. banks alone increased their loans to Mexico from $5.5 billion to $22.4 billion,[3] and lending by non-U.S. banks followed a similar pattern. By 1982, Mexican credits accounted for 41 percent of the total combined capital of the nine largest U.S. banks, making them highly vulnerable in the event that Mexico could not meet its repayment obligations.

It was not until early 1982, however, that the Mexican economic situation began to unravel in earnest. Until then, external borrowing had permitted President Jose Lopez Portillo to sustain high growth rates and the value of the peso, even in the face of increasing trade deficits and accelerating inflation. But Mexican citizens began to doubt the stability of this economic environment and, in anticipation of a peso devaluation, sought shelter for their assets in dollar investments. The ensuing capital flight finally forced a 30 percent devaluation of the peso in February 1982. This measure, though, seemed only to erode confidence further, perhaps because it was not accompanied by any antiinflationary policies and was taken less than two weeks after the president's promise to "defend the peso doggedly." Inflation and capital flight continued unabated,[4] economic growth declined (Table 5.3). In May, Lopez Portillo fired his minister of finance and the central bank president and replaced them with more "orthodox" figures— Silva Herzog and Miguel Mancera. Yet even this new economic team seemed unable to contain Mexico's deteriorating economic situation.

Throughout this period, the United States monitored events closely and even became directly involved. Beginning in March 1982, Mexico's finance minister and central bank president made regular visits to Washington to consult with Federal Reserve Board members and Treasury Department officials and to seek official U.S. funds. First on April 30 and again at the end of June and July 1982, the Mexican central bank was forced to arrange emergency twenty-four-hour currency swaps with the Federal Reserve in order to meet month-end legal reserve requirements.[5] The Bank of Mexico was the only developing country central bank to have an established swap line with the U.S. Federal Reserve system—a testimony to the exceptional importance of Mexico to the U.S. economy. These last-minute swaps, equivalent to short-term loans, were symptomatic of Mexico's increasingly serious financial difficulties.

In early August 1982, Mexico finally hit bottom. On August 4, yet another currency swap had to be arranged with the Fed, but this one was for longer than twenty-four hours and was conditioned on the Mexican government's agreement to enter into discussions with the IMF. In an attempt to curb the public-sector deficit, Silva Herzog also announced domestic price increases on heavily subsidized items. Electricity rates would go up 30 percent, petroleum prices would rise 67 percent, and—most controversially—the price of bread and tortillas would increase 100 percent. These desperate measures further eroded domestic confidence and accelerated capital flight. Pressure on the peso consequently reached untenable levels, and on August 5, the Mexican government imposed a dual exchange rate: an official rate to be used for key imports and foreign debt repayment and a market rate that could be devalued further. When even this action did not bring positive results, and with Mexico's foreign reserves approaching only $200 million (the net outflow from the central bank was $100 million per day),[6] the government took drastic measures. On August 12, President Lopez Portillo closed the foreign exchange markets[7] without providing any official explanation. The same day, Finance Minister Silva Herzog made separate phone calls to U.S. treasury secretary

Donald Regan, Federal Reserve Board chairman Paul Volcker, and IMF managing director Jacques de Larosiere to inform them that he would be arriving in Washington the following day to discuss serious matters with them.

Mexican difficulties of any type are of great concern to the United States. Mexico and the United States share a 1,760-mile border, and thus Mexican internal developments can easily affect North American lives. Not only do millions of legal and illegal immigrants enter the United States from Mexico every year, Mexico is crucial to the U.S. economy. In 1982, Mexico was the third largest trading partner of the United States after Japan and Canada, sold more oil to the United States than Saudi Arabia,[8] and purchased U.S. grain in quantities second only to Japan.[9] The United States provided two-thirds of Mexico's imports.[10] Between 1981 and 1982, however, the U.S. trade balance with Mexico was transformed from a $4 billion surplus to a $4 billion deficit, largely because of Mexico's drastic reduction of imports during the financial crisis. This staggering $8 billion deterioration represented the worst reversal in trade performance by the United States with any country in the world and would have negative consequences for the rest of the U.S. economy. Treasury Secretary Regan testified before Congress that about 192,000 U.S jobs could be lost as a result.[11]

In the financial sector, U.S. transactions with Mexico were also substantial. U.S. commercial banks held an estimated 30 percent of Mexico's external debt,[12] and the debt was equivalent to 46 percent of the capital of the seventeen largest U.S. banks.[13] In addition to U.S. bank loans outstanding to Mexico, the outflow of Mexican capital to the United States was significant. In 1982, it was estimated that Mexicans had deposits in U.S. banks worth $14 billion, and that they owned an additional $30 billion of U.S. real estate.[14]

Thus, Silva Herzog, Regan, Volcker, and the other actors involved in negotiating Mexico's financial rescue understood that regardless of any personal sentiment they might attacha to the situation, Mexico's problems were to some extent the United States' problems as well.

THE WASHINGTON WEEKEND:
PRELUDE TO THE GLOBAL DEBT REGIME

When Silva Herzog arrived in Washington, D.C., on Friday, August 13, 1982, he had no particular plan to propose. He did, however, have objectives. He knew, for instance, that Mexico's grave financial problems would require a big package of help, perhaps as much as $20 billion eventually,[15] that the IMF was good for about $4 billion over a period of three years, and that the private banks would have to help by rescheduling a major portion of Mexico's external debt. He also knew that an IMF agreement and a commercial bank rescheduling would take time—time that Mexico did not have. By the following Monday morning when the banks reopened, Mexico's foreign exchange reserves would have to be replenished in order to reassure the international financial community that Mexico was able and willing to meet its short-term financial obligations. Otherwise, a series of defaults might be triggered that would seriously damage both the international banking system and Mexico's credit reputation. Silva Herzog's Washington trip therefore had a dual purpose: to initiate the lengthy negotiations with the IMF and the private banks and, in the meantime, to secure short-term financing from the U.S. government to prevent a Mexican default on Monday.

The Mexican finance minister's first meeting that Friday morning was with de Larosiere, managing director of the IMF. He arrived at 9 a.m., and the session lasted only one hour. Since 1981, the IMF had been conducting a routine study of Mexican finances, and since July 1982, an IMF team had, at Silva Herzog's invitation, been informally studying Mexico's economic situation. There was thus no need on August 13 for Silva Herzog to make a detailed presentation or to convince de Larosiere of the magnitude of Mexico's problems. Instead, Silva Herzog assured the managing director that Mexico was aware of its grave situation, that President Lopez Portillo was prepared to negotiate an austerity program with the IMF to restore Mexico's finances, and that Mexico therefore wanted the maximum loan it could draw from the Fund, as quickly as possible.

De Larosiere promised the Mexican finance minister SDR 3.4 billion over the 1982–1985 period, contingent upon the successful conclusion of a formal agreement between the Fund and the Mexican government. Out of concern for the stability of the international financial system, he also urged that the Mexican government publicly acknowledge it was seeking IMF assistance and that Silva Herzog integrate all of his crisis management efforts, including any agreement with the private banks, into one large, coherent package. Three days later, on August 16, an IMF mission headed by Sterie Beza arrived in Mexico City to negotiate a letter of intent with Mexican policymakers. Both the IMF and the Mexicans were optimistic that an agreement could by reached by the end of September 1982.

Thus armed with the IMF's blessing, Silva Herzog continued his Friday visitations. His next stop was the U.S. Federal Reserve Board and a meeting with Volcker. Volcker, like de Larosiere, was well informed about the steady deterioration of Mexico's foreign exchange reserves (he arranged the currency swaps described above) and deeply concerned that a Mexican default might seriously damage the international banking system. He was particularly anxious, however, about the effects of a possible Mexican default on U.S. commercial banks, the nine largest of which had loaned 44.4 percent of their capital base to Mexico. It was crucial for the banks' survival that Mexico continue making interest (as distinct from principal) payments on its debt. Finally, Volcker knew that the exposure of U.S. banks to Brazil and Argentina was equally high, and that those two large debtor countries would be watching to see how Mexico and the international financial community managed this crisis.

With these concerns in mind, Volcker took three actions to facilitate resolution of Mexico's crisis. First, he and Silva Herzog estimated that Mexico would need $2 billion to avoid catastrophe on Monday morning, and he suggested that the Mexican finance minister solicit this funding from the U.S. Treasury. Second, Volcker acknowledged Mexico's need for some private bank debt relief and urged Silva Herzog to arrange immediately with the private banks for a meeting at the New York Federal Reserve. To facilitate the process, Volcker gave him a list of private telephone numbers where leading U.S. bankers could be reached, even on their summer vacations. By the end of the weekend, Silva Herzog had contacted several of them.

Finally, Volcker advised Silva Herzog to seek medium-term bridge loans from the central banks of Europe and Japan, so that Mexico could continue functioning while the IMF and private bank agreements were being arranged. He indicated that as much as $1.5 billion might be raised from these central banks and that the United States alone was prepared to furnish half that amount. To arrange this funding, Volcker suggested a session at the BIS in Basel, Switzerland. In fact, after Silva Herzog left that day, Volcker began calling the world's leading central bankers, and by the end of the weekend, he had arranged for a BIS meeting in Basel on August 18.

Having set the wheels of long- and medium-term financial relief in motion, Silva Herzog turned to his remaining, and most pressing objective: securing the estimated $2 billion that Mexico needed by Monday to meet its short-term obligations. After lunch that same day, August 13, he therefore proceeded to the U.S. Treasury Department. There he embarked on a set of negotiations that would last through Sunday evening, August 15, and would involve not only the Treasury but the U.S. Departments of Agriculture, State, Energy, and Defense and the Office of Management and Budget (OMB) as well.

Unlike the IMF and the Fed, the U.S. Treasury was not well prepared to handle either the urgency and scope of Mexico's problems or the complexities of international economic management. Secretary Regan had spent more of his time in office implementing President Reagan's domestic policies than monitoring international financial developments. His deputy secretary, R. T. McNamar, had little international banking experience, and assistant secretary for international affairs, Marc Leland, was in London on other business. Silva Herzog and his team, Angel Gurria of the Mexican treasury and central bank director Mancera, had therefore both to convince U.S. Treasury leaders of the severity of Mexico's crisis and make lengthy, detailed presentations to apprise them of the latest Mexican economic developments.

During some time spent alone with Secretary Regan early that afternoon, Silva Herzog managed to drive home the seriousness of Mexico's financial situation. Regan agreed to help and then turned matters over to Deputy Secretary McNamar. The secretary had a speech on tax legislation to deliver the following day (Saturday, August 14) in New York and a Sunday morning meeting with President Reagan at Camp David. Thus, although Regan remained in contact throughout the weekend, it was McNamar who handled subsequent negotiations from the U.S. side.

After Regan left, the talks turned first to an assessment of Mexico's exact cash flow status. Angel Gurria and several U.S. analysts studied Mexican loan records and identified precisely "what debts were coming due, when, and to whom."[16] In this way, by late Friday, Volcker and Silva Herzog's earlier $2 billion estimate of Mexico's immediate requirements was verified. Discussion subsequently centered on finding the funds and ensuring their availability for Mexican use by Monday.

The first billion was easily procured through the Department of Agriculture. Mexico was a large importer of food, and the United States, a surplus producer, had aided Mexico before with credits for food purchases.[17] The secretary of agriculture, John Brock, told McNamar Saturday morning that surplus U.S. grain and other products were available, and by Saturday afternoon, he had arranged through the Commodity Credit Corporation to extend more than $1 billion of guarantees to U.S. exporters for sales of agricultural commodities to Mexico. Although the large size of the guarantee was "highly irregular," according to one former department official, "there was no debate. Word came down from on high to do it, and we did."[18]

The second billion, by contrast, was raised only after extensive U.S. maneuvering and a significant amount of conflict between U.S. and Mexican negotiators. From the outset, the Americans and Mexicans had agreed that the most practical way to arrange emergency financing for Mexico was through some sort of exchange of U.S. money for Mexican oil. The problem, however, was determining where in the U.S. government this money could be obtained on short notice. McNamar's first thought was to tap the Social Security Fund, but he soon discovered that the legal impediments to such action were insurmountable. He then focused on the Exchange Stabilization Fund (ESF), which had been established in 1934 to stabilize the U.S. dollar against foreign currencies. His general counsel assured him that the $1 billion in funds for Mexico could be obtained from the ESF, but only if they were secured against acceptable Mexican collateral. The solution was obvious. "The principal asset that Mexico had that we could use," McNamar said, "was oil."[19]

However, the ESF funds also had to be repaid within a matter of days. Some entity within the U.S. government would therefore have to purchase the Mexican oil collateral and then use the proceeds to repay the ESF. On August 13, McNamar ascertained from the Department of Energy that the United States could use Mexican crude oil for the Strategic Petroleum Reserve (SPR).[20] Then he gained assurances from the Department of Defense, which handles SPR purchases, that the necessary $1 billion was available in cash to make the proposed Mexican oil purchase. Finally, he had to convince the OMB to approve the complicated transaction. OMB approved it in principle but stipulated that the terms of the oil purchase had to be justifiable to the U.S. Congress as "a prudent use of taxpayers' dollars," when measured against what could be obtained on the private market.

Thus, McNamar would have to cut a hard deal with Silva Herzog and his team.[21]

The first substantive U.S. proposal was to purchase the Mexican oil at about $28 per barrel—a concessionary price considering it was then selling on the world market for $32 per barrel. Silva Herzog was astonished. Not only would this price compromise Mexican relations with other oil producers (who might feel undercut) and customers (who might demand similar terms), but it would also be politically explosive. To sell Mexico's patrimony at bargain prices, especially to the historically domineering United States, could only anger nationalist elements in the Mexican government and further mar Lopez Portillo's already tarnished reputation (given the current crisis). Silva Herzog broke off the negotiations to call the Mexican president. It was 3 a.m. Saturday morning.

As expected, Lopez Portillo was furious at the U.S. proposal. Rather than recall his team, however, he dispatched two additional Mexican officials to Washington: Jose Andres Oteyza, the minister of patrimony (responsible for social programs in Mexico and a prominent figure of the nationalist left), and Julio Rodolfo Montezuma Cid, the director of Mexico's national oil company, PEMEX. Lopez Portillo apparently hoped that Oteyza's participation would legitimize any subsequent oil deal with the national populists in the Mexican ruling party (see Appendix). Thus, when the talks resumed on August 14, both men were present.

Oteyza declared at the outset that Mexico would not accept any oil deal denominated in U.S. dollars per barrel. Instead, he proposed that the agreement take the form of an interest-bearing loan, with Mexican oil as repayment. The U.S. side obliged and returned late Saturday afternoon with an offer for a $1 billion loan, which Mexico would repay over a fifteen-month period with $1.3 billion worth of oil shipments. In effect, the Americans were offering Mexico a 35 percent interest rate. Oteyza, after consulting with a now irate Lopez Portillo, responded that Mexico would not pay more than 20 percent in interest charges, and that even that amount was an outrage. The negotiators recessed Saturday night at an impasse.

On Sunday morning, the American team met alone at the Treasury to discuss ways of restarting the negotiations. Someone suggested disguising the proposed loan's high interest rate by charging a front-end negotiating fee in the range of $100 million. A heated discussion ensued. In the midst of it U.S. ambassador to Mexico John Gavin proposed to McNamar that they leave the meeting. Gavin wanted to present the negotiating fee idea to the Mexicans as soon as possible because he feared that Lopez Portillo might soon suspend the negotiations permanently. The ambassador knew Lopez Portillo, and Mexico's economic problems personally, and he was loath to see U.S.-Mexican relations founder while U.S. policymakers bickered over short-term financial details.

Gavin and McNamar met with Silva Herzog and Oteyza at their hotel in midmorning. McNamar unveiled the idea of the front-end fee, and the two Mexicans accepted it in principle. They were annoyed, however, by the $100 million amount. Silva Herzog called Lopez Portillo and received orders to break off the talks anew. The Mexican finance minister then relayed this message to the two Americans and said that his team would be flying home after a lunch at the Mexican embassy. A Mexican default now seemed inevitable. However, in the course of the discussions, Silva Herzog had registered interest at a suggestion to cut the negotiating fee in half. Gavin and McNamar therefore hurried back to the Treasury to argue this option to their colleagues.

Once there, the OMB representatives flatly refused to accept a $50 million negotiating fee, citing their obligations to Congress and the U.S. taxpayers as justification. Ambassador Gavin countered that it would be a pity to wreck U.S. relations with Mexico over a negotiating fee. Then, at about 4 p.m. Sunday, Treasury Secretary Regan returned from Camp David with instructions from President Reagan to help Mexico if possible. McNamar brought Regan up-to-date on the most recent phase of the talks, and Regan ordered McNamar to offer the $50 million negotiating fee to the Mexican ministers. McNamar called Silva Herzog at the Mexican embassy, and by 8 p.m. Sunday the oil deal was concluded.

The terms of the final agreement, try as the Mexicans would to disguise them, translated to an effective oil price of $27.40 per barrel—lower than the original U.S. offer of $28 per barrel. If this were judged as a pure loan, Mexico would pay over 30 percent in interest charges. Oteyza, among others, felt Mexico had been robbed. Nevertheless, that weekend the Mexican negotiating team obtained a financing package from the U.S. government that included a $1 billion loan linked to oil sales and a $1 billion agricultural loan guarantee. In addition, Volcker had initiated steps to arrange a central bank loan for Mexico through the BIS, and Silva Herzog had begun the discussion process with the IMF and Mexico's private bank creditors.

CONSOLIDATING THE WEEKEND AGREEMENTS: THE BIS, THE IMF, AND THE COMMERCIAL BANKS

The Washington weekend negotiations had averted the most immediate threat to Mexico and the international financial system—a potential Mexican default on Monday, August 16—and had initiated steps toward long-term financial assistance for Mexico. However, resolving Mexico's debt crisis ultimately required the consolidation of these long-term agreements. The possibilities for a BIS loan, an IMF accord, and an agreement with the private commercial banks had to be converted into realities.

The BIS Loan

The Wednesday, August 18, BIS meeting in Switzerland did not go entirely smoothly, even though Federal Reserve chairman Volcker had established a basic agreement by telephone prior to the session. After the Mexican team identified its financial needs and withdrew from the meeting, the negotiations began in earnest. Representatives from the central banks of Belgium and Germany expressed doubts about Lopez Portillo's ultimate willingness to accept IMF conditions in exchange for financial assistance. Moreover, after the recent Polish debt rescheduling, the German banks were hesitant to shoulder the additional monetary responsibility of assisting Mexico. The French representatives were equally reluctant, and the Europeans felt in general that Mexico was essentially an "American problem."

Under pressure from the U.S. Fed and Bank of England representatives, however, the Europeans agreed to provide 50 percent of a $1.5 billion bridge loan to Mexico (a loan that would be repaid as soon as Mexico began receiving funds from the IMF). The United States, in line with a prearranged formula, would supply the other 50 percent. The loan would be disbursed in three parts, and Mexico would have to provide acceptable collateral to receive the first installment (as a hedge against the possible failure of Mexican negotiations with the IMF). A BIS team was subsequently dispatched to Mexico City to arrange the collateral. At the end of the session, Spain, as a gesture of support for its former colony, volunteered an additional $175 million. The United States matched that amount as well, bringing the total BIS loan to $1.85 billion.

The IMF Accord

Meanwhile, in Mexico City, an IMF team had been negotiating an economic reform program with Mexican officials since August 16. Most of the preliminary analysis had been conducted informally prior to the Washington weekend, and by August 28–29, an agreement was essentially completed. In general terms, the IMF program called for fiscal and monetary austerity on the part of the Mexican government in order to limit additional Mexican foreign borrowing and reduce demand in the Mexican economy for imports and foreign exchange. In this way, the IMF hoped to make more resources available for servicing Mexico's external debt.

More specifically, the program stipulated that the Mexican government would reduce its budget deficit from 18 percent of Mexico's GDP (in 1982), to 8.5 percent by 1983, 5.5 percent by 1984, and 3.5 percent by 1985. To achieve these deficit reductions, there would be cuts in government subsidies (for food and other basic items) and tax increases. The agreement also called for monetary restraint and caps on union wage increases to control Mexico's inflation rate, which was then 100 percent. Finally, the plan included market reforms such as abolishing exchange controls and export subsidies.

Although this IMF program was likely to have recessionary consequences for Mexico, Silva Herzog and central bank president Mancera agreed to its terms. It appeared that the agreement could be announced at the annual meetings of the IMF and World Bank, which were scheduled to begin September 5 in Toronto,

Canada. The Mexican and IMF negotiators hoped that announcing the agreement in this forum would dramatically improve confidence in Mexico's economy and thereby assist the rescue effort. Events in Mexico, however, undermined this strategy.

Even before the Washington weekend, a group of officials in the Mexican government had been advocating default, as well as other anti-U.S. and anti-IMF policies, as a way to solve Mexico's financial problems without compromising Mexican economic growth or independence. While Silva Herzog was meeting with the IMF team, this group, which included Oteyza, former planning minister Carlos Tello, and Lopez Portillo's left-leaning son, went to the Mexican president with advice. Rather than criticize the IMF agreement, however, they focused on the issue of capital flight. A major cause of Mexico's current crisis, they asserted, was capital flight undertaken by the nation's upper class—not captains of industry interested in the nation's welfare but speculators seeking pecuniary gains. Furthermore, Mexico's private banks were facilitating this harmful activity. Thus, to stop the speculation and protect the national economy, they urged the president to nationalize the banks and impose strict foreign exchange controls.

On September 1, 1982, Lopez Portillo accepted the advice of Tello and his allies. He announced to the Mexican Congress that he had signed decrees that would nationalize the private banks and establish exchange controls. In the same speech, Lopez Portillo also defended his social programs as the most useful means for achieving income redistribution, and he blamed Mexico's foreign exchange problems almost entirely on speculation and external causes. Finally, he appointed Tello as the new head of Mexico's central bank. Silva Herzog had not been consulted on any of these issues. He left for Toronto as surprised as the members of the international financial community he was going to meet there.

Once in Toronto, the Mexican finance minister met privately with de Larosiere, who assured him that the new Mexican policies would not necessarily block an agreement with the IMF. The IMF director was accustomed to political tirades aimed at his organization and had therefore taken Lopez Portillo's September 1 announcements in stride. Nevertheless, de Larosiere criticized the exchange controls and bank nationalizations. Silva Herzog then asked the managing director to draft a memo to Lopez Portillo outlining all the steps that would now be necessary to conclude Mexico's IMF agreement. De Larosiere complied. The memo was written in terms general enough to give Lopez Portillo an out, but specific enough to resemble the agreement that had already been drafted by IMF and Mexican negotiators (described above). Lopez Portillo approved the memo on September 11, 1982.

When discussions with IMF officials resumed, however, new difficulties emerged. Tello, who was now central bank president, adamantly opposed the policy conditions contained in the proposed IMF standby agreement, but his negotiating position was weakened by two events. First, the BIS had suspended payments on its bridge loan, pending agreement with the IMF. Second, the nationalization of the Mexican banks had caused a run on their New York branches on September 7. U.S. banks that held deposits with the Mexican branches through the interbank market started cashing their deposits, and the Mexican banks began to run out of funds. The Mexican banks paid out more than their reserves could cover, causing a $70 million shortfall in the bank clearinghouse system. Alerted to the pending crisis, Fed Chairman Volcker deposited an advance on Mexico's BIS loan with its New York branch banks. Although the September 7 crisis was averted, the Mexican banks could only look forward to more of the same on the following day. Volcker was not willing to watch Mexico's BIS loan be spent in this manner, and with the support of the European central banks, he pressured Mexican officials to force their banks to place a moratorium on all interbank withdrawals by U.S. banks. Mexico's reputation with American bankers thus suffered significantly.

Tello tried to strengthen his negotiating position during September and October by attempting to form a debtors' cartel with Brazil and Argentina. However, he failed to get enthusiastic support from the leadership of either country. On November 10, Tello (together with Silva Herzog) signed a letter of intent with the IMF containing all of the conditions stipulated by the IMF the previous August. All that remained to activate the Fund program was the approval of the IMF's directors. Tello's victory was a symbolic one, but nevertheless important in the context of Mexican politics: the letter of intent incorporated a statement identifying external factors as the cause of Mexico's debt crisis.

Agreement with the Commercial Banks

On a different but parallel track, negotiations with the private banking community had also begun in earnest soon after the Washington weekend. On August 19, Silva Herzog met informally with senior officials of Mexico's major creditor banks in New York City, followed by a dinner at the New York Federal Reserve Bank attended by Volcker, McNamar of Treasury, and the chairman of the New York Fed, Anthony Solomon. Officials from Citibank, the Bank of America, and other major money center banks did not have to be convinced of the need to come to the assistance of Mexico, but representatives of the multitude of smaller American banks, subscribers in large, syndicated loans to Mexico, would require persuasion to participate in a long-term solution to Mexico's debt problem. A strategy for persuading the smaller banks was worked out at the dinner meeting, and the major banks formed an advisory committee cochaired by representatives from Citibank, Bank of America, and the Swiss Bank Corporation to coordinate their activities.

The following day, August 20, Silva Herzog spoke to representatives of the 115 banks that held 60 percent of Mexico's private debt. He emphasized Mexico's intention to reach an agreement with the IMF and to introduce austerity measures in the Mexican economy. He stated that Mexico hoped to maintain good relations with its creditor banks and would continue making interest payments on its outstanding debt. What Mexico required from its creditors, however, was a ninety-day suspension of principal payments, as well as $1 billion in new money during 1982 and 1983.

While the banks reluctantly accepted the ninety-day moratorium on principal payments, the bankers' advisory committee focused its attention on Mexico's request for a long-term rescheduling of its debt, and particularly on the request for $1 billion in new money. The advisory committee was uncomfortable with the issue of new loans since each of the major banks was reluctant to make any new loan commitments to Mexico. The problem was finally taken up personally by de Larosiere of the IMF on November 16.

By the time Mexico formally agreed to the IMF's terms on November 10, every major participant in the Mexican financial crisis—with the significant exception of the commercial banks—had undertaken considerable risks. The Mexican government had agreed to terms that would lower the standards of living of most Mexicans. The IMF was about to commit just under $4 billion at a time when its funds were severely limited. The U.S. government had already advanced Mexico $2 billion during the Washington weekend, its Federal Reserve system had loaned $925 million to match the loan made by the BIS, and it was in the process of arranging for another $2 billion loan through the Export-Import Bank. All that the commercial banks had done thus far was to postpone payments of the principal on their loans—they were still being paid interest. To many people involved in the Mexican financial rescue, it appeared that the banks were getting a free ride.

On November 16, de Larosiere met with the heads of the major banks and dropped a bombshell. Now that Mexico had agreed to swallow the bitter medicine of IMF conditionality, he wanted the banks to lend $5 billion in new money *before* he could recommend authorization of the Mexican agreement by the directors of the IMF, scheduled to meet on December 23, 1982. De Larosiere gave the banks one month, until December 15, to provide the additional funding. The leading bankers were dumbfounded by de Larosiere's action, as such "forced" or "involuntary" lending by commercial banks had no historical precedent. However, because the agreement between the IMF and Mexico was the linchpin to the overall solution of the debt crisis, the banks had few alternatives to cooperating with his demands.

The bankers' advisory committee created a formula for distributing the $5 billion commitment by requesting additional funding equivalent to 7 percent of every bank's exposure in Mexico. The real challenge would be convincing smaller banks to participate in the "7 percent solution," since many of these banks had already signaled their preference to cut their losses and withdraw from Mexico altogether. Moreover, the larger money center banks worried about the regulatory implications of expanding their lending beyond prescribed limits. Federal Reserve chairman Volcker issued a statement assuring bankers that new loans to Mexico would not be subject to supervisory criticism. For its part, the Mexican government also encouraged hesitant bankers with an announcement that banks participating in the "involuntary lending" would receive priority repayment, whereas nonparticipating banks would be paid only if funds continued to be available. Under this pressure, most of Mexico's private creditors ultimately fell in line. Although only $4.3 billion was subscribed by the December 15 deadline, de Larosiere declared that the sum constituted an acceptable amount, and he took the agreement to the IMF board for approval.

The only issue remaining to be resolved, rescheduling the principal on Mexico's privately held debt, was completed on December 8. After the tough negotiations to implement involuntary lending, it was much easier convince the banks to stretch the maturities on about a quarter (or approximately $20 billion) of Mexico's outstanding debt. The rescheduling extended principal payments due in the next two years over an eight-year period, but the interest rate on these rescheduled loans was extremely high: 2.5 percent above the London Inter-Bank Offered Rate (LIBOR).[22] In addition, the banks charged Mexico an additional 1 percent fee for the rescheduling, which amounted to about $200 million in front-end fees. The rescheduling thus added $700 million to Mexico's already heavy debt-servicing burden. Many in Mexico found the terms of rescheduling as outrageous as the oil deal, but the cash-strapped nation had few alternatives. Silva Herzog, however, paid a price for his central role in negotiating the agreement, and his meteoric rise in Mexican politics slowed considerably. Many in the United States also thought that the price of the loan deal did not contribute to a solution of Mexico's debt crisis, but the extra costs may have been necessary to entice the private banks to participate. With the completion of the rescheduling agreement and the IMF's December 23 approval of Mexico's economic program, the 1982 Mexican rescue was complete—at a total cost of $14.07 billion (Table 5.4).

APPENDIX: THE MEXICAN POLITICAL SCENE

Mexico won its independence from Spain in 1821, eleven years after its initial declaration of independence. This delay reflected sharp differences of opinion within the Mexican polity on how the region should be governed. After independence, these political battles raged on. Independent Mexico could not find the political formula to resolve these disputes peacefully, nor could it ensure economic stability and growth. The resulting endemic political instability, civil strife, and very limited economic advancement persisted for almost half a century. The termination of this destructive cycle came only after two foreign interventions and at the price of dictatorship.

In its 1846–1848 war with Mexico, the United States took advantage of its neighbor's political instability and captured over one-half of Mexican national territory. Less than a decade later, civil war in Mexico provided the opportunity for the French to invade and occupy Mexico from 1862 until 1867. Political instability had made Mexico highly vulnerable to the expansionist and imperialist objectives of foreign powers.

Mexico's political uncertainty and economic stagnation ended only in the last two decades of the nineteenth century under the leadership of Porfirio Diaz. Under the theme of "Peace, Order, and Progress," the nation elected Diaz president in 1876. Diaz kept his promise of bringing political peace and economic development to Mexico. In the process, however, he instituted a dictatorship that lasted thirty-five years, oversaw the extreme and expanding concentration of wealth and political power in the hands of a very few privileged Mexicans, and permitted a dramatic increase in the economic and political power of foreigners, particularly Americans, in Mexico. Not only were the majority of Mexicans left landless and impoverished, but members of the upper class not favored by the regime were increasingly closed off from economic and political opportunity. By 1910, rising discontent created an explosive situation.

The spark igniting the Mexican revolution was the clearly fraudulent 1910 reelection of President Diaz. Middle- and upper-class supporters of the losing presidential candidate, Francisco Madero, took up arms to oust the discredited dictator, reestablish democracy, and reduce foreign involvement in Mexican life. At the same time, disdain for the Porfirian regime and desire for profound social and economic changes led to spontaneous uprisings in support of Madero among Mexican workers and peasants across the nation. With their support, Madero's revolt successfully forced Porfirio Diaz to flee Mexico in May 1911. Following arguably the fairest elections in Mexican history, Madero was inaugurated president in November 1911.

Mexico's new government faced the daunting task of satisfying the demands of its supporters while reaching an accommodation with the former dictator's military, the economic elite, and foreign investors. This difficult task was made virtually impossible by expectations for rapid resolution of peasant and worker grievances generated by the successful revolt against Diaz and the rise of the legendary revolutionary leaders of the Mexican masses: Emiliano Zapata and Pancho Villa. When Madero did not act immediately to institute land and labor reform, Zapata and Villa led their followers in revolt against his government. This action awoke a fear of chaos among former Diaz supporters, particularly within the military and among foreign investors, which culminated in the overthrow and assassination of President Madero, along with the reestablishment of the Porfirian system under army tutelage.

Madero's death and the reemergence of dictatorship unified the old allies just long enough to oust the Porfirian regime once again. With the elimination of their mutual enemy, however, the revolution degenerated into an extremely violent and destructive civil war between the supporters of the murdered president under the leadership of Venustiano Carranza and the supporters of Villa and Zapata. After three years of warfare, the destruction of the Mexican economy, the death of one in ten Mexicans, and the seven-month-long U.S. occupation of Mexico's main port at Veracruz, Carranza's army emerged victorious. Their challenge now was to consolidate this victory in a political system able to avoid future civil conflict and ensure economic advancement for the entire nation.

The first step in this process was the 1917 drafting of a new constitution. Still in effect today, this document reflects the goals for which the revolution was fought: a presidential system protected by a no-reelection provision; use of Mexican patrimony for national advancement rather than personal or foreign benefit, to be guaranteed by state control over land and natural resources; an improved distribution of national wealth and opportunities through agrarian and labor reform; and a reduction of the influence of the religious elite through a strict church-state separation.

Constitutional provisions alone, however, could not ensure cooperation among revolutionary leaders. Although agreement existed on the national goals reflected in the new constitution, the victorious leaders of the revolution did not agree fully on how to implement the constitutional provisions, nor on who should lead the nation in the process. The 1917–1940 period was crucial to Mexico's postrevolutionary development. During these years, Mexican leaders gradually consolidated the nation's postrevolutionary political system based on two key institutions: the party and the presidency.

Originally formed in 1929, the central purpose of the Party of the Mexican Revolution was to control latent conflicts in Mexican society and within its leadership and thereby provide the basis for effective government in revolutionary Mexico. The party thus integrated the politically relevant sectors of Mexican society into an institution headed by the leaders of the revolution. In its post-1940 structure, the Institutional Revolutionary Party (PRI) incorporated the three popular sectors of Mexican society: peasants, workers, and bureaucrats. Notably absent from party membership were the military and the business sector. The military's exclusion reflected its dramatic decline in political influence during the twentieth century. Although every Mexican President from 1917 to 1946 was a military figure, since 1946 every president has been a civilian. The absence of the business sector from party membership reflected the desire of the revolutionary leaders to prevent a repetition of the economic elite's Porfirian-era political hegemony, which enabled them to manage the national economy for their personal benefit at the expense of the nation.

A key element of the party's leadership and integrative role is the choice of who will occupy the presidency for a constitutionally limited single six-year term. The institution of the presidency in Mexico is extremely powerful (Mexicans often refer to their president as "king for six years.") Serving as leader of the party and of the nation, the president's actions seem to be limited only by the necessity of maintaining the consensus on which his power is based. The nature of this ruling consensus defined Mexican politics prior to the 1982 debt crisis, and thus is critical to an understanding of Mexican economic policy.

According to two analysts of Mexican politics, this consensus long consisted of "industrialization with social justice."[23] The revolutionary leaders agreed that Mexico had to industrialize, but because of the weakness of the Mexican private sector, industrialization would require a prominent role for the state as well as foreign investment. Mexico's leaders also agreed that the demands of the workers and peasants for increased social justice should be met in an effort to prevent renewed unrest from the two groups that had demonstrated a capacity to express demands violently during the revolution. The general political consensus on the goals of industrialization and social justice did not, however, extend to the means by which these goals would be achieved, nor to the priority given to either one of them.

The PRI leadership has historically been of two minds regarding the consensus: Cardenista and Alemanista. Cardenista policy prescriptions emphasize social justice and reflect the policies of former president Lazaro Cardenas. During his presidency (1936–1940), Cardenas nationalized the foreign-owned oil companies, actively enforced constitutional provisions protecting workers' rights, redistributed more land to peasants than all his revolutionary predecessors, and rapidly expanded the state's role in promoting economic growth. The Alemanistas favor an emphasis on industrialization, as occurred during the presidency of Miguel Aleman (1946–1952). Aleman dramatically reduced land reform, oversaw a real reduction in worker purchasing power, invited foreign investors to participate in the Mexican economy, worked closely with the private sector, and employed state investment and credit policies to strengthen the role of the private sector in the Mexican economy. After a dozen years of sharp internal debate (1940–1952), this difference of opinion coalesced into a general agreement that social justice would be achieved through economic growth and industrialization. The result was what came to be known as the "Mexican miracle": thirty years of political stability in a nation that had suffered endemic instability for most of its independent existence, and an annual economic growth rate averaging 6 percent for three decades. This "miracle," however, did not come without consequences for the future.

By the late 1960s, Mexico's development strategy had generated an extreme maldistribution of wealth and continuing economic dependency on the United States, despite revolutionary rhetoric to the contrary. These economic consequences began to take a toll on the consensus undergirding the PRI's development strategy. Concurrently, new societal actors, born of Mexico's economic development, emerged on the national scene. These groups, a growing and educated urban middle class and a marginalized urban underclass, expressed concerns outside of the revolutionary consensus and operated outside of the control of the party structure. The resulting tension in the Mexican political system burst into the open after the government violently repressed student demonstrations in 1968. The cost was 300 lives and a serious rupture in the PRI-led political structure. The disintegrating PRI consensus was recast in the form of two distinct, opposing camps within the ruling party and within Mexican society as well: national populists and liberal rationalists. The national populists argued that continued economic advancement depended on a more equal distribution of the benefits of industrialization, whereas the liberal rationalists contended that only through further industrialization could social justice be ensured.

This sharp division within the ruling party, combined with the political imperative of the Mexican presidency to maintain the revolutionary consensus, severely constrained economic policy choices. To favor one party faction over another would risk the dissolution of the postrevolutionary system that had so successfully brought about political stability and economic advancement in a nation whose history taught that neither could be taken for granted. Yet holding the party together without an internal consensus implied that the demands of both camps would have to be met simultaneously. This option would entail a sharp increase in government spending.

President Luis Echeverria (1970–1976) chose the latter option. His strategy was to ensure social justice through job provision based on state-led industrialization. Since the private sector was unwilling or unable to invest at the necessary levels and further foreign investment was distasteful to the nationalist sentiments of a significant part of the ruling coalition, the state would expand its role in the economy and thereby create jobs for the urban unemployed. The Echeverria government also increased social spending to help reduce the cost of living in urban areas. Echeverria coupled this economic strategy with a highly nationalistic foreign policy designed to appeal to influential intellectuals and student groups operating outside of the PRI.

Echeverria's policies did not, however, succeed in their objective of pleasing both sectors in Mexican politics simultaneously. The president did shore up support for the regime among its most vocal opponents (labor, students, and intellectuals), but his policies also undermined the confidence of the increasingly powerful business community. The Mexican private sector had long accepted state involvement in the economy as part of an implicit understanding between the two. The state would limit its economic involvement to those sectors where it did not directly compete with the private sector, and to infrastructure investments, credit provision, and other mechanisms supporting private-sector development. The dramatic growth in the state's involvement in the economy under Echeverria suggested to the business community that its agreement with the regime was no longer valid, and some members of the community believed their investments were now at risk. In this context, Echeverria's nationalist foreign policy raised business concerns about the president's commitment to the post-revolutionary capitalist development program.

The president's attempt to raise taxes on Mexican businesses (to pay for social policies and state investments they opposed) did little to restore business confidence in the regime. The business community successfully defeated the tax proposal but apparently at the cost of presidential responsiveness to private-sector concerns, which only further intensified worry in business circles. Additionally, the defeat of Echeverria's tax measure forced the government to finance its economic program through foreign borrowing and deficit financing on an unsustainable scale. The economic outcome was rising inflation rates, a growing undervaluation of the peso, and, not surprisingly, rapidly expanding capital flight. As foreign exchange reserves shrank, Mexico was forced to turn to the IMF for assistance in August 1976.

When Lopez Portillo took over the presidency in December 1976, he faced many of the same political problems confronted by his predecessor but now compounded by an economic crisis and a crisis of confidence within the Mexican business community. These circumstances prohibited adoption of the politically low-cost strategy of concurrently pursuing the development goals of the two factions within the ruling party. Yet it was still the President's task to seek out the elusive consensus on which he could govern. By incorporating representatives of each of the party's two factions into his administration, Lopez Portillo successfully forged a consensus to implement the IMF stabilization plan. He also reached out to the private sector to shore up their confidence in the regime and initiated limited political reforms to meet middle-class demands for more participation in the political system. He could offer little to the workers and peasants, however, other than the promise of a better future.

Lopez Portillo's consensus-based support of stabilization was very fragile, and it (in somewhat of an ironic turn) began to unravel in 1978 because of the program's positive performance during the preceding year. The national populists asserted that stabilization had been so successful that it could be abandoned ahead of schedule, whereas the liberal rationalists contended that the very success of the stabilization program argued for its continuation. Lopez Portillo bridged this gap in the short term by using in his economic program elements from each of these opposing viewpoints. Bridging this gap permanently, however, would have been extremely difficult. It was in this context that Mexico began to produce significant quantities of petroleum from its newly discovered oil fields.

Oil influenced the political-economic situation in Mexico in several ways. First, it provided a vast store of wealth with which Mexico would be able to finance economic growth well into the future. Second, it provided a source of collateral for foreign loans that could immediately finance economic development and replace the politically higher-cost options of foreign investments or increased tax collection. Equally important, it created a belief (both in Mexico and abroad) that Mexico's financial problems were virtually solved. It thus seemed to the Mexican government that it could return to Echeverria's politically low-cost economic strategy of state-led industrialization, combined with expanded social welfare spending, a nationalist foreign policy, and significant limitations on foreign investment.

This perception persisted until 1981, when oil prices fell further, and interest rates rose higher, than imagined possible. Meanwhile, the underlying polarization

within the Mexican political system remained unresolved. As the economy declined, divisions within the ruling party increasingly constrained Lopez Portillo's
policy options and seemingly led to governmental paralysis throughout late 1981.
In this political-economic context, the Mexican government faced the 1982 financial crisis.

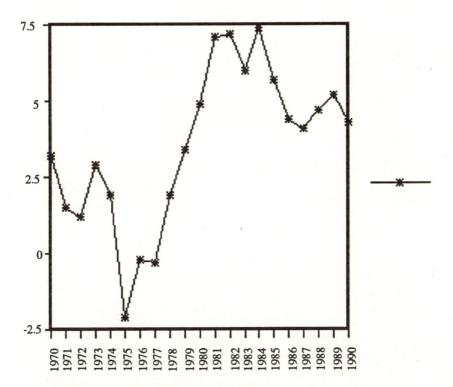

FIGURE 5.1 Real Interest Rates, 1970–1990
Note: The real interest rate is calculated as the LIBOR minus the U.S. GDP deflator.
Sources: IMF, *International Financial Statistics Yearbook* (Washington, D.C.: International Monetary Fund, 1985 for 1970–1972, 1988 for 1973–1975, and 1991 for 1976–1990).

TABLE 5.1   Mexican Economic Indicators

	1977	1978	1979	1980	1981	1982
Total exports (billions of US $)	4.5	6.0	9.0	15.6	19.6	21.2
Petroleum exports (billions of US $)	1.0	1.8	3.9	9.8	13.8	16.7
Price of Mexican isthmus crude (US $/barrel)	--	--	17.1	32.0	38.5	32.5
Debt service /exports	--	11.0	6.9	4.9	11.7	22.3

Sources: IMF, *International Financial Statistics Supplement on Economic Indicators*, 1985, and *International Financial Statistics* (Washington, D.C.: International Monetary Fund), various years.

TABLE 5.2   Mexican Trade and Financial Indicators

	1977	1978	1979	1980	1981	1982
Central government deficit (% GDP)	3.3	2.7	3.3	3.1	6.7	15.4
Total imports (billions of US $)	5.9	7.6	12.1	19.5	24.1	15.1
Current account deficit (billions of US $)	1.9	3.1	5.5	8.2	13.9	2.9
Total long-term debt (billions of US $)	20.6	25.5	29.0	33.7	42.7	51.4

Sources: IMF, *International Financial Statistics Supplement on Economic Indicators*, 1985, and *International Financial Statistics* (Washington, D.C.: International Monetary Fund), various years.

TABLE 5.3   Mexican Growth and Inflation Rates

	1977	1978	1979	1980	1981	1982
Consumer prices (% change over previous year)	29.0	17.5	18.2	26.4	27.9	58.9
GDP at 1980 prices (% change over previous year)	3.4	8.3	9.2	8.3	7.9	-0.6

Sources: IMF, *International Financial Statistics Supplement on Economic Indicators*, 1985, and *International Financial Statistics* (Washington, D.C.: International Monetary Fund), various years.

TABLE 5.4   Emergency Lending to Mexico, 1982

IMF	$3.92 billion
BIS	$0.925 billion
U.S. Federal Reserve	$0.925 billion
U.S. government	$2.0 billion
Private banks	$4.3 billion
U.S. Export-Import Bank	$2.0 billion
Total	$14.07 billion

Source: Table XI in Adhip Chaudhuri, *The Mexican Debt Crisis, 1982,* Case study no. 204, The Pew Diplomatic Initiative (Washington, D.C.: Georgetown University School of Foreign Service, 1988).

NOTES

1. "The Crash of 1982?" *Economist*, October 16, 1982, p. 24.

2. As a result of the large infusion of petrodollar deposits from members of the Organization of Petroleum Exporting Countries (OPEC), the international commercial banks had an excess of funds available for loans during the 1970s. In fact, competition among banks to extend loans was fierce, as too many lenders chased too few borrowers. In this environment, developing countries like Mexico obtained loans easily.

3. Norman Gall, "The World Gasps for Liquidity," *Forbes*, October 11, 1981, p. 152.

4. Although capital flight is impossible to measure precisely, it is significant that the "errors and omissions" column of the Mexican balance of payments went from a positive $756 million in 1979 to a negative $8.3 billion by the end of 1981.

5. These currency swaps are arrangements between central banks by which currencies are exchanged without entering the foreign exchange markets. Thus, Mexico was able temporarily to swap pesos for dollars at the official rate of exchange without disrupting foreign exchange markets.

6. Joseph Kraft, *The Mexican Rescue* (New York: Group of Thirty, 1984), p. 13.

7. When this occurs, foreign exchange conversions are permitted only through the central bank; all private foreign exchange market transactions are prohibited.

8. "It's the Neighbors Again," *Economist*, October 9, 1982, p. 23.

9. "The Markets See a Grain of Hope for East-West Trade," *Economist*, January 16, 1982, p. 60.

10. "How Long Can Bankers Pull Rabbits out of a Sombrero?" *Economist*, August 28, 1982, p. 59.

11. U.S. Congress, Senate, Subcommittee on International Finance and Monetary Policy of the Committee on Banking, Housing, and Urban Affairs, *International Debt*, 98th Cong., 1st sess., 1983, pp. 5–6.

12. U.S. Congress, House of Representatives, Subcommittee on International Trade, Investment, and Monetary Policy of the Committee on Banking, Finance, and Urban Affairs, *The Mexican Economic Crisis: Policy Implications for the United States,* 98th Cong., 2nd sess., 1984.

13. U.S. Congress, Senate, Subcommittee on International Finance and Monetary Policy, *International Debt*.

14. Harvard Business School, "Mexico's Adjustment Program" (Cambridge: Harvard Business School, 1983), p. 5.

15. Kraft, *The Mexican Rescue*, p. 5.

16. Ibid., p. 13.

17. One such occasion was in 1976.

18. Roger S. Leeds and Gale Thompson, *The 1982 Mexican Debt Negotiations*, (Baltimore: Foreign Policy Institute, School of Advanced International Studies, Johns Hopkins University, 1988), p. 26.

19. Ibid., p. 21.

20. The SPR was established in the wake of the 1973–1974 oil crisis to create a buffer stock of petroleum reserves that would be available to the U.S. market in the event of another oil shortage.

21. Kraft, *The Mexican Rescue*, p. 14.

22. Mexico was accustomed to a rate of approximately 1 percent above LIBOR.

23. Roberto Newell and Luis Rubio, *Mexico's Dilemma: The Political Origins of Economic* Crisis (Boulder, Colo.: Westview Press, 1984).

6

Restructuring Zaire's Debt, 1979–1982

Thomas M. Callaghy

On April 15, 1979, Erwin Blumenthal, a retired German central banker, wrote a confidential letter to Jacques de Larosiere, then managing director of the IMF.[1] In the letter, Blumenthal described his experiences over the previous eight months as principal director and head of an IMF-sponsored team of experts working in the Central Bank of Zaire, in the central African country ruled by the autocratic but "pro-Western" Mobutu Sese Seko. Under enormous external pressure from the United States, other major Western governments, the IMF, and the World Bank, the government of Zaire had granted this and other IMF-sponsored teams working in the Finance Ministry, the Customs Office, and the Planning Ministry unprecedented formal decisionmaking powers. In a move reminiscent of the gunboat diplomacy of the nineteenth-century customs house takeovers, these teams of expatriates were in Zaire to ensure the payment of debt service by a recalcitrant but "friendly" and strategically important debtor.

"I deeply regret," Blumenthal wrote to de Larosiere, "to add to your problems as you already have more than enough, but Zaire remains a child that is causing much trouble!" Blumenthal noted a series of problems involving threats to the Bank of Zaire's autonomy, relations with the new governor of the bank, and impediments to the effective functioning of his team. "What worries me about the economy here," he wrote, "is the low level of production of GECAMINES,[2] embezzlement of export receipts, the growth of smuggling in all parts of the

---

The original version of this case was prepared for The Pew Diplomatic Initiative at Columbia University and previously distributed as case no. 206. The case has been shortened considerably and edited especially for this volume.

country, [and] illegal barter deals." In a later, secret report, Blumenthal identified the source of his problems: "There was and there is only one obstacle in the way, but destroying everything: the CORRUPTION of the ruling clique." Yet he also indicated why he and the IMF willingly undertook this seemingly impossible mission in Zaire: They believed Mobutu, head of state, when he signed the letter of intent committing himself and his country to the IMF's terms. As Blumenthal learned, however, "Mobutu and his government [did] not care about the repayment, about the servicing of the external public debt; they rather count[ed] on the generosity of the creditors to reschedule the service on the debt again (and again)!"[3]

When Blumenthal left the country in June 1979, Zaire had not had a viable agreement with the IMF for over a year. The economy was in chaos, the productive capacity and infrastructure of the country were deteriorating rapidly, standards of living were falling dramatically, debt service arrears were enormous and growing quickly, and the mineral-rich region of Shaba (Katanga) in the southeast had been invaded by dissidents twice in the two previous years (stopped each time only by direct Western military intervention). How, given these problems, could the United States and other creditors induce Zaire to service its international debt?

THE POLITICAL ECONOMY OF ZAIRE'S DEBT CRISIS

Zaire was born, and exists, in the international arena.[4] External assistance, influence, and intervention, especially American, have been continuous and pervasive factors supporting the emergence, consolidation, and survival of the Mobutu regime in Zaire. U.S. support was crucial to Mobutu's control of the armed forces in the early days, crucial to his first "coup" in September 1960, and crucial to his seizure of full power in 1965 as an African caudillo. It was also central to the emergence and consolidation of a heavily personalized authoritarian state and to its ability to survive a severe debt crisis and external invasions in 1977 and 1978.

Nevertheless, external influence has clearly had its limits in Zaire. Since his earliest days in the turbulent crucible of Zairian politics, Mobutu has shown a Machiavellian flair for establishing and manipulating shifting coalitions of support, both internally and externally. In the specific case of Zaire's international debt negotiations, Mobutu often exploited the interstices created by the competing interests of the actors (the United States, other Western governments, the IMF, commercial banks, etc.) involved. In this way, the Mobutu regime managed throughout the period under consideration here to maintain some room for autonomous action.

Organized around a presidential monarch (Mobutu), the Zairian state is a personalized version of the old Belgian colonial structure. It incorporates weak bureaucratic elements with strong forms of personalized power and administration. Over time, Mobutu has appropriated the administrative, coercive, and financial means to sustain and increase his power. Specifically, he has used police, military forces, and a cadre of territorial administrators to control all key societal groups via the corporatist elements of a single party, the Popular Movement of the Revolution (MPR). In addition, he has encouraged the growth of an unproductive, nontechnocratic "political aristocracy" that is financially dependent on the state and thus owes its privileged position and livelihood to Mobutu. Finally, he has used state finances to sustain these domestic power networks and (ultimately) perpetuate his ruling position.

Given his regime's financial dependence, it is ironic that domestic finances have been Mobutu's chief weakness. Although the Zairian state has had a sizable income, its financial structure has been weak, inefficient, and massively corrupt, especially in its revenue collection and distribution activities. Consequently, the regime came to rely on extraordinary financial measures such as questionable loans, extortion, confiscation, currency debasement, and the operations of foreign businesses and financiers. When such measures proved insufficient, the regime turned to massive external borrowing for its survival.

Mobutu borrowed extensively, often rashly, and was able to do so because of Zaire's vast potential wealth. Between 1967 and 1973, Zaire's external public debt quintupled; in 1972 alone it doubled to $1.5 billion. At first the government tried to hide the actual amount of debt service payments, but in the first half of 1973, actual payments exceeded 80 percent of the budget estimates for such payments for the entire year.[5] By 1977, the total debt was estimated at over $3 billion, and debt service payments were the equivalent of 43.4 percent of export earnings and 49.5 percent of total state revenue.[6] As the 1980s approached, Zaire was nearly $5 billion in debt and on the verge of economic collapse.

Although the Mobutu regime's rampant corruption and rash borrowing laid the groundwork for this crisis, other immediate factors were also important. The dramatic fall in copper (which accounted for two-thirds of Zaire's foreign exchange) and other commodity prices in the mid-1970s, the closure of the Benguela Railroad across Angola since the civil war there in 1975–1976, the Zairianization moves of 1973–1975, rising oil costs, and a world recession contributed to Zaire's economic problems as well. This situation was aggravated by the 1977 and 1978 invasions of Shaba province by dissidents based in Angola and by additional mistakes on the part of Mobutu's government: grandiose and unproductive development schemes (the Inga-Shaba power line, the Maluku steel mill), the almost total neglect of agriculture and infrastructure, and a lack of understanding and concern about the rapidly deteriorating situation. As one observer put it, "the top government leadership has traditionally known nothing of or cared little for economics, and this shows."[7]

The IMF, the United States, and other Western governments pressured Zaire to sort out this situation and helped Mobutu and his government to devise two stabilization plans (the "Mobutu Plans"), the first in March 1976 and the second in November 1977. In both cases, Zaire entered into a standby agreement with the IMF, which pledged substantial credit. The plans reflected the IMF's conditions and aimed to cut corruption, rationalize expenditures, increase tax revenues, limit imports, boost production in all sectors, improve the transportation infrastructure, eliminate arrears on interest payments, make principal payments on time, and generally improve financial management and economic planning. In 1976 and 1977, Zaire's public and publicly insured debt was also rescheduled by the United States and other Western countries via the Paris Club mechanism. Finally, three World Bank and Western country aid donor, or consultative group, meetings were held (one in 1977 and two in 1978) to generate additional official assistance. Without this support, the regime might well have collapsed, but for both economic and politico-strategic reasons, the Western countries feared such an outcome.

Mobutu and his political aristocracy could not politically afford, however, to comply fully with the international financial community's reform demands. Implementing the bureaucratic changes called for by the United States and other actors would have undermined the very basis of the regime's power and political survival—access to and free use of the state's resources, especially foreign exchange. The Mobutu government therefore went to great lengths to avoid reforms and repayment of its debts (except with new debts) and schemed constantly to gain access to new internal and external resources. Borrowing, nonpayment of debts, and rescheduling became routine activities of the Zairian state.

Foreign officials undertook elaborate measures to ensure proper financial administration in Zaire, but they were simply unable to maintain constant monitoring, even of reforms they had helped to initiate. Reforms ostensibly in progress were, in fact, easily manipulated.[8] The Zairians knew that only partial and temporary changes were necessary, that they could outflank, circumvent, or wear down the reform efforts. They understood that the United States and other external actors were unable to watch all areas and arenas simultaneously and consistently over time. One U.S. official described the situation as a video game in which the reformers had only one ship and sequential shots, and the Zairians had wave after wave of invaders coming at and around the reformers; not all the invaders could get through, but a good number of them would.[9] In fact, by the time of Blumenthal's departure in mid-1979, the Mobutu regime had blocked all efforts by international lenders to control its financial practices.

KEY ACTORS

The Government of Zaire

The government of Zaire had no clear understanding of what it had agreed to do when it signed the first two standby agreements with the IMF in 1976 and 1977 and evidently no intention of living up to the agreements. Because of the gravity of Zaire's situation, the degree to which the government could have lived up to the agreements is not clear. Since no real effort was made, however, this ability is impossible to gauge. The Mobutu regime viewed international organizations and aid agencies not as sources of development assistance but as channels for access to additional resources. In assessing this early period, the World Bank identified corruption as a primary factor inhibiting a satisfactory governmental response to the nation's economic crisis. The Bank noted that corruption spread "despite condemnation by the highest political authorities," that government employees were "neglecting their official duties in order to pursue other work to supplement their income," and that "the incentive to smuggle outweighed the ability to control such practices." Consequently, the socioeconomic conditions of the Zairian population were "seriously aggravated."[10]

In addition to the issue of political will, there remained the question of the regime's administrative capability. It had been plagued by intragovernmental disorganization, lack of coordination, political and personality conflicts, massive corruption, and a lack of sizable numbers of technically qualified personnel. The government took many policy decisions, but they were rarely implemented coherently or for any length of time, if at all. There had been major jurisdictional and policy squabbles among the presidency, the Bank of Zaire, Finance, and the debt administration office created in 1976. According to the World Bank, "through 1978, the Government's response to the crisis was for the most part ad hoc." It pointed to "the inherent weaknesses of Zairian institutions," which "interfered with investment selection, debt management, allocation of foreign exchange, implementation of projects, distribution of commodity assistance, and monitoring of the economy."[11]

As a consequence of its limited political will and administrative capacity, Zaire lacked a rational debt service policy. Even very basic debt data often did not exist, was inconsistent, or was uncoordinated. Principal and interest figures, for example, were often confused, or one administrative unit's figures would not match those of another. The regime had no idea what the total of the debt was or to whom money was owed. Furthermore, debt servicing was largely based on the ad hoc exercise of personal discretion by key regime officials rather than on any coordinated, preplanned payment policy. Thus payments were rarely made on time or in the complete amount. The efforts of external actors (such the UN and World Bank) to improve the government's "managerial" capabilities, including such basic skills as determining how much was owed, to whom, and when it was due, had only a marginal positive impact. Zaire did have a number of competent and dedicated people who, with proper political will and protection, could work to ameliorate Zaire's situation. However, there were clear indications that these people, for good political and personal reasons, were not willing to take "sensitive" actions.[12]

Beyond the short-term financial and debt-servicing difficulties of the regime lay even more severe problems. Foremost among these was the regime's preoccupation with foreign exchange: how to get it quickly and in large amounts. Additionally, there was a lack of understanding of the real, long-term underpinnings of the economy and, above all, of the necessity of patterned, sustained, and substantial medium- and long-term investment in key sectors of the economy to maintain current production levels, much less to increase and diversify them. The regime was fixated with money as a source of wealth and failed to see savings, investment, and production as the true sources of wealth and growth.

IMF and World Bank Expatriate Teams

Owing to the meager results of the first two stabilization plans, the IMF and the World Bank, after close consultation with the United States and other major Western creditor countries, decided to send their own teams of experts into Zaire in 1978 to take over key financial positions in the Bank of Zaire, the Finance Ministry, the debt administration office, the Customs Office, and Planning Ministry. In large measure, the teams were an effort to create a technocratic core of competent Zairian officials, to buffer them from political pressure, and thus to bring some rational order to the chaos of Zairian mismanagement. Many Zairians, however, viewed the expatriate teams as a crude form of neocolonialism.

In December 1978, several months after his arrival at the Bank of Zaire team, Blumenthal took dramatic measures that struck at the heart of the political aristocracy's power. He cut off credit and exchange facilities to firms of key members of the dominant group, including several of Mobutu's closest collaborators, and imposed very strict foreign exchange quotas. Since President Mobutu needed the foreign exchange to keep warring elements of the political aristocracy in line, these actions appeared to threaten his regime. It is not surprising that he and his political aristocracy employed creative, persistent, and largely successful maneuvers to detour such measures.

Efforts to impose budgetary control over the presidency and the military were for the most part delayed or circumvented, and ways were usually found around the foreign exchange controls. As Blumenthal noted, "There just is no effective control over the financial transactions of the Presidency; one does not differentiate between official and personal expenses in this office . . . . All endeavors to improve budgetary control in Zaire had to stop short before the operations of the central governing authority: *la Presidence!*"[13] In addition, Nguza Karl-i-Bond, appointed prime minister in 1979 largely at the behest of the United States and other Western creditor countries and banks, quickly discovered that "any effort to implement the IMF program of reforms would inevitably lead to confrontation with the personal interests of the President."[14] Finally, in response to Blumenthal's attempt to impose exchange controls, Mobutu and his supporters exerted substantial pressure on a variety of foreign and domestic actors to provide foreign exchange, legally or illegally.

The political aristocracy systematically harassed and wore down the teams over time. Blumenthal recounted a striking example of one means by which this was achieved: "At the end of January 1979 one evening (around 7 p.m.), when I was still in the bank, soldiers of General Tukuzu (father-in-law of [Bank of Zaire governor] Bofossa), threatened me with submachine guns when they could not get their hands anymore on the head of the foreign department where they wanted to demand foreign exchange for their general."[15] Toward the end of his year-long stay in Zaire, Blumenthal reportedly slept with a shotgun under his bed and had a radio that kept him in contact with the West German and U.S. embassies, and the U.S. Marines in particular. Such machinations on the part of Mobutu's government meant, in the words of one British banker, that "the leakages of foreign exchange [were] simply pushed further upstream."[16] The various internationally sponsored teams could not substitute for domestic political will and administrative capability.

The Western Governments

The United States and other Western governments only began to realize the seriousness and structural nature of Zaire's economic and fiscal crises after the first invasion of Zaire's Shaba province in 1977. Their early preoccupation had been with politicostrategic concerns, mainly in southern Africa. Western policymakers also tended to downplay the seriousness of the economic situation, in particular by seeing it as merely another periodic downswing that would be ameliorated by a rise in commodity prices or other factors. This perspective characterized the thinking of the Zairian government and the international commercial banks as well.

"Western" governments had insured 75.8 percent of Zaire's private bank loans and thus had a direct economic interest in Zaire's ability to meet its debt payments. Fourteen governments were directly involved in the 1979 Paris Club rescheduling: the United States, France, Belgium, Britain, Italy, Germany, Japan, Canada, the Netherlands, Norway, Sweden, Switzerland, and Abu Dhabi. The most heavily involved countries, however, were the nations providing the largest amount of loan guarantees: the United States, France, Belgium, and Italy. In late 1979, Zaire's outstanding debt to these four countries was nearly $2.4 billion, almost one-half of Zaire's total debt. It was distributed as follows: United States, $894 million; France, $593 million; Belgium, $487 million; and Italy, $392 million.[17]

French, Belgian, and Italian interests in Zaire were fairly straightforward: at minimum, to preserve their economic and political interests in the region and, if possible, to expand them—at one another's expense if necessary. U.S. relations with Mobutu's Zaire, by contrast, were characterized by a striking ambivalence. The United States has long tried to reconcile complaints about the regime's recalcitrance, authoritarianism, and corruption with attempts to protect larger political, strategic, and economic interests. This dilemma was heightened for the administration of Jimmy Carter (in power during most of the period covered by this case) because of its well-publicized views on human rights.

Four considerations were in fact central to U.S. relations with Mobutu's Zaire. First, Mobutu was seen as the only person who could hold this strategic and important country together. Second, Zaire played a major role in U.S. intelligence-gathering activities and covert operations, especially in southern Africa. Third, the country was a prime supplier of key minerals, especially cobalt (filling 60 percent of the West's demand). Finally, and most importantly, Mobutu was perceived to be very pro-Western. Although most external actors would have been pleased to see Mobutu replaced with someone less corrupt and unproductive, no one really knew how to effect such an exchange without precipitating a dangerous power vacuum (i.e., one that could be filled by a Marxist) and/or a civil war in this central African giant. Zaire borders nine other countries, and the fear of contagion was real.

After 1975, these considerations were heightened by renewed East-West tensions in the region. In the midst of a bitter civil war in which the United States was indirectly involved, a new Marxist government in Angola turned to the Soviets, Cubans, and East Germans for help. Over 15,000 Cuban troops were sent to the region, and thus the Soviets and their clients were seen to be "moving into Africa" at the expense of U.S. global and regional interests. This fact greatly affected the Carter administration's decision to support the two "rescue" operations during the invasions in 1977 and 1978 of Shaba province by dissidents from Angola, and to participate in the externally mandated political, human rights, military, and economic "reform" efforts that followed them. It was clearly easier, cheaper, and less risky to keep Mobutu's leaky but important regime afloat.

The interests of the other Western governments did not always coincide with those of the United States or with one another. Thus, it is not surprising that these actors only partially and fitfully coordinated their efforts to get Zaire to service its debt, control its expenditures, diminish corruption, take hard economic decisions and implement them, and undertake badly needed "managerial" reforms. Nevertheless, they did reschedule its public and publicly insured debt five times via the Paris Club mechanism and helped to generate additional assistance for Zaire from a variety of sources. Given their influence on the IMF and the World Bank, their constant diplomatic presence in Kinshasa, and the substantial amount of Zairian debt guaranteed by or owed to them, the Western governments were dominant actors in the external efforts to cope with Zaire's debt crisis.

The Commercial Banks

There was general agreement by 1979, even among bankers themselves, that the banks had loaned excessive amounts of money to Zaire without any clear indication of what they were getting into. General agreement also existed that a 1976 memorandum of understanding with Zaire, which was essentially a Citibank-led rollover effort that eventually failed, was a mistake. Although it preserved Zaire's creditworthiness, at least temporarily, it also helped delay recognition of the seriousness of the country's situation both by the bankers and by Zaire's government. The banks strongly resisted a rescheduling, in part because they wanted to let the Western governments and international organizations reschedule Zaire's public debt (including the publicly insured private bank debt) and provide much-needed "adjustment" assistance, thereby leaving more foreign exchange available to service the uninsured private debt. In fact, the banks' repayment ratio had been ten times that of the public creditors. This tendency was reinforced by the banks' holding out the enticement of further lending, even though much of it was offered to individual members of the political aristocracy rather than to the state.

THE DEBT GAME

In early summer 1979, about the time Blumenthal was deciding to abandon his post in protest, the United States, Britain, Belgium, and France informed the Mobutu government that there would not be another comprehensive Paris Club rescheduling until Zaire reached new agreements with the IMF and the London Club. However, Zaire was in a catch-22 situation. The London Club banks did not want to reschedule until there was a new IMF agreement and a Paris Club rescheduling. The IMF, for its part, did not want to put together a new stabilization effort and in fact would have difficulty doing so unless there were commitments of substantial new donor country assistance and precise rescheduling agreements. Fund staff were also quite leery of Zaire, given the dismal results of the 1976 and 1977 standby agreements and their recent experience inside the Zairian policy establishment. With the IMF's reputation at stake, another stabilization attempt would be highly problematic.

Under enormous U.S. and Western country pressure, however, both the Fund and the government of Zaire agreed in early summer to start negotiations for a new standby arrangement. Basic agreement was reached by mid-August, and the new standby became effective on August 27. Zaire was to receive SDR 118 million over eighteen months if it adhered to quarterly performance targets. The bargaining had been tough because of Zaire's track record and the consensus that now existed within the Fund about the need for major reforms. Indeed, corruption was by now a major preoccupation of all the external actors. The IMF also made it very clear that successful implementation of this standby agreement depended on the provision of a substantial amount of aid, in the form of debt reschedulings, from Zaire's creditors and donors. Given the size of its external debt and payment arrears, Zaire could institute the structural changes needed to ensure sustained and broadened stabilization efforts only if it received outside assistance.

Realizing the damage done by Blumenthal's early departure (in June 1979) and the need to reestablish his legitimacy with his Western friends, President Mobutu in August hired three foreign investment banking firms—Lazard Freres, Lehman Brothers Kuhn Loeb, and S. G. Warburg. For very high fees, these firms assessed the actual size and structure of Zaire's debt (they found substantially more than the World Bank had earlier); compiled a series of information memoranda; assisted Zaire in Paris and London Club reschedulings and in several consultative group meetings; and dealt with the IMF, the World Bank, Western governments, and private banks in an ongoing, albeit informal, way. The importance of these "advisers" to Zaire's bargaining strength cannot be overestimated. These firms came from some of the creditor countries (the United States, Britain, and France) and had close ties to their governments, the IMF, the World Bank, and the international banking community.

After hiring these advisers, Mobutu toured Western capitals in September and October 1979 with a message of commitment to major reforms and reliable debt service. In the process, he met with President Carter, Robert McNamara (then president of the World Bank), Jacques de Larosiere (IMF director), and senior private banking officials in New York.

LONDON CLUB: ROUND ONE

The next major arena of activity was the London Club.[18] The commercial bank rescheduling proved to be a very long and difficult process, lasting nearly seven months. The 134 banks involved in the Zaire case were represented by a negotiating committee of ten agent or syndicate banks. Their views were influenced by recent bank experiences in Peru, Turkey, and Iran, as well as by their unfortunate experience with Zaire over the 1976 memorandum of understanding and the failed Citibank-led attempt at a new $250 million syndicated loan. In addition, they, too, were increasingly preoccupied with the magnitude of corruption in Zaire. In earlier dealings with Zaire, the banks had found the government's economic and fiscal analyses to be a major bone of contention. Because of the predominant role in these negotiations of Zaire's investment bank advisers, however, economic and fiscal analyses were not a central issue this time.

Preliminary negotiations with the banks began in October, with the main issues being the amounts and terms of repayment, the mechanics of implementing an agreement, and the legal safeguards in case of its collapse. Zaire and its investment bank advisers felt they could achieve a favorable London Club agreement and then use it to get better treatment from the Paris Club than Zaire had obtained in 1976 or 1977. They argued that Zaire needed generous treatment so it could stimulate strong international support for its recovery and reform efforts, thereby ensuring more reliable debt service. (Zaire had not made any substantial principal payments since 1976, and only semiregular interest payments.)

The banks, however, were not uniform in their interests. Although they all shared a concern for Zaire's debt-servicing ability and reliability (and thus wanted a large payment up front), the U.S. and Japanese banks were more stringent in their demands than their European counterparts. The U.S. banks were under particular pressure from federal bank examiners over the quality of their Zairian loans. They therefore wanted an agreement that would at minimum keep Zaire's loans on a performance basis and thus avoid write-downs and official losses. Yet they also wanted the most that Zaire could pay. In fact, the major U.S. creditor, Citibank, wanted both a short repayment period and a large payment up front. Belgium, France, and Italy, however, were under no such pressure from their governments and had good political and economic reasons to favor more generous terms.

These October discussions were followed by a two-month period in which the ten agent banks consulted with the other 124 banks in their various syndicates and at the same time kept in touch with Zaire's investment bank advisers. Then, at a one-day meeting in New York on November 11, 1979, the Zairian government (through its investment bank advisers) presented its formal proposal to the agent banks. The terms of the proposal were unusually lenient (for example, a ten-year maturity and five-year grace period), which concerned the banks a great deal. They feared such an agreement's likely precedent-setting effects and, particularly, its impact on countries struggling to make payments without a rescheduling. Its effect on the Paris Club creditors was also a concern. Nevertheless, after considerable discussion, the banks accepted Zaire's proposals on interest rates and payment and grace periods. They insisted, however, that all arrears on interest payments be paid when the agreement was signed, and they demanded $20 million more than Zaire had originally proposed in payments up front on principal arrears.

The agent banks now had to "sell" this proposal to the other 124 banks—not an easy task. This effort entailed a special trip by Zaire's negotiators to Tokyo in late November to meet with the Japanese banks, which held over one-third of the debt and had to get Japanese Finance Ministry approval for any rescheduling. The Japanese were extremely skeptical about Zaire's ability and willingness to meet even the generous terms proposed. A number of other banks wanted the agreement tied to certain levels of government aid, but this proposal was dropped after the "Brussels Club"—most of Zaire's main donor countries—met on November 29–30 and agreed to supply $334 million over the next year to help cover an expected balance-of-payments deficit for 1980 of $422 million. Considerable agreement existed, however, that there was still not enough in up-front payments of principal arrears.

At a meeting with Zaire's investment bank advisers in London on December 11, the agent banks therefore proposed increased payments in years two through five of the grace period. This proposal was passed on to the Zairians, who accepted it the next day, primarily because it meant that no more money had to be paid out right away. They also did not want the agreement to come apart, since the Paris Club was meeting that very day in the French Finance Ministry on the rue de Rivoli. Round one of the London Club was thus concluded. The next step for Zaire was to turn this basic agreement into a legal document and obtain its formal approval.

THE PARIS CLUB

The Paris Club rescheduling of December 10–11, 1979 was Zaire's third in four years.[19] As usual, prior agreement with the IMF was a precondition, but this time the United States and the thirteen other Western countries also insisted on prior agreement with the London Club banks, at least in principle. Any Paris Club rescheduling thus had to be comparable to a London Club agreement. This was particularly important to the Carter administration, since Congress insisted that the government not look as if it were bailing out the banks. Finally, this being Zaire's third Paris Club rescheduling, the issue of previously rescheduled debt became central and contentious.

Zaire and its investment bank advisers went to Paris optimistic about the outcome, especially since the Brussels Club meeting had gone so well. In Brussels the same basic set of countries that constituted the Paris Club had accepted Zaire's analysis of its economic and financial situation and had been quite forthcoming with assistance. In addition, Zaire had taken the unprecedented step of making its own formal rescheduling proposal on November 26, just prior to the Brussels meeting. However, the Zairian delegation, headed by Finance Minister Bofossa W'amb'ea Nkoso (who had moved from the Bank of Zaire in March), was visibly shaken after an informal meeting with the U.S. delegation just prior to the Paris Club's first plenary session on Monday morning, December 10, 1979. The United States expressed concern about reports that Zaire was not in compliance with the terms of its August standby agreement with the IMF and pointed out that if this were so, the United States might not have the authority to sign any Paris Club agreement.

The position of the United States is nearly always central to a Paris Club rescheduling because of its status as the largest creditor, a major world power, and the state with the greatest economic reporting and analytic capabilities. These strengths did not, however, make the U.S. negotiators' job easy. Since Congress had to be kept informed, the reaction of legislators to any rescheduling agreement had to be considered. The case of Zaire was particularly sensitive because of the venal and brutal reputation of the Mobutu regime. Zaire's reputation for corruption had also become widespread in the U.S. press, and Zaire was becoming an important concern on Capitol Hill. Congressman Stephen Solarz of Brooklyn, chairman of the Africa Subcommittee of the House Foreign Affairs Committee, focused much attention on Zaire and, in particular, held a series of hearings on U.S. policy toward the Mobutu regime. Finally, in late summer 1979, the House Foreign Affairs Committee voted to discontinue all military aid to Zaire.

How, then, could a U.S. administration protect long-run U.S. interests in dealings with this difficult friend? The primary tactic employed by the State Department was to create an appearance of serious reform efforts under way in Zaire. The deputy assistant secretary of state for African affairs, Lannon Walker, used this tactic in his May 1979 testimony before a Senate committee: "In summary, progress to date has been mixed, but the outlook [is] nonetheless encouraging. More has been accomplished over the past year than most would have thought possible. What is needed now is continued effective implementation of the full range of reform processes now under way. Sustained forward movement will restore the badly eroded confidence of the international community in Zaire's ability to meet its full potential."[20] The administration's public position was hardly a fully accurate picture of Zaire in late spring 1979.

The view inside the administration was distinctly less sanguine and unified. Even within the State Department, there were strongly etched differences of opinion about Zaire between Walker and his boss, Richard Moose, the assistant secretary of state for African affairs. Intragovernmental tensions over debt reschedulings also frequently existed between the "politicos" at State and the "green eyeshade" types at Treasury. An interagency task force on the Zaire Paris Club rescheduling was formed in October 1979 to reconcile these differences of opinion. Chaired by the Treasury Department and incorporating officials from the State Department, the U.S. Agency for International Development, and the Export-Import Bank, the task force met for two months to iron out the U.S. position. Discussion covered the usual issues of what debt is eligible to be rescheduled, the repayment period, and the grace period, as well as some unusual proposals such as the creation of an escrow account into which Zaire's future mineral export receipts might go to service the debt.

On one key point, however, there was no disagreement: All concurred that the normal prohibition against rescheduling previously rescheduled debt was not to be broken or even bent for Zaire, even though previously rescheduled debt was a major issue for Zaire by this time. In spite of the Carter administration's public support for the Mobutu regime, a key Treasury official noted that if the United States were to break precedent on the issue of previously rescheduled debt, "it has to be the 'right' country on grounds either of foreign policy or the fact that the debtor is making extraordinary efforts to improve its economic management. Neither is true of Zaire."[21] On foreign policy grounds the administration had Congress, the press, and its own human rights record to worry about; in terms of economic management, Zaire was on very shaky ground, Walker's testimony notwithstanding.

At the first formal session of the two-day, December 1979 Paris Club meeting, the IMF representative, Evangelos Calamitsis, made the opening presentation, describing Zaire's overall financial and economic condition. Although he made no comment about the level of Zairian compliance with the August stand.by arrangement, he did indicate Zaire's need for additional resources for imports crucial for rehabilitating the country's productive capacity. The World Bank representative, Benison Varon, then followed with an assessment of the underlying structure of the economy, stressing that "a significant and sustained improvement in Zaire's debt service capacity cannot be achieved without first restoring and then expanding the productive capacity of Zaire."[22]

In his opening statement, Finance Minister Bofossa asserted Zaire's desire to honor the Paris Club agreement this time and thus its need for generous terms, such as those requested from the London Club and already agreed to in principle. The Zairians believed they could afford $108 million in debt service to the Paris Club during 1980 without jeopardizing the country's ongoing economic recovery. This figure allowed for a 10 percent increase in imports over 1979. Zaire was also requesting the rescheduling of $60 million in previously rescheduled debt (the large bulk of which was already in arrears), extended over ten years. This called for a major change in Paris Club behavior. These terms were also based on the Zairians' assumption that another Paris Club meeting would take place at the end of 1980. Other departures included in the proposal were the inclusion of arrears on short-term commercial debt and a cap on interest rates.

In the question period following Bofossa's presentation, the U.S. delegate, Charles Meissner, immediately asked the IMF representative whether Zaire was currently in compliance with its IMF standby. Calamitsis replied that Zaire had exceeded performance targets in a number of important areas and would not be able to make the second drawing in December.

After the luncheon, the creditors met by themselves, with Calamitsis and Varon present, and argued until 6 p.m. with only one short break. The two central issues were Zaire's lack of positive performance under the IMF agreement and the Mobutu regime's level of corruption. Corruption in Zaire increasingly prevented many of its creditors from taking its macroeconomic and financial situation seriously, despite the presence of Zaire's internationally respected investment bank advisers.

At the conclusion of this creditor session, the French chairman of the Paris Club, Michel Camdessus (who became the managing director of the IMF in 1988), visited the Zairian delegation at its hotel and "informally" presented the creditors' first offer. He asked for a response by 8 p.m. Shocked by the proposal, the Zairians and their foreign advisers worked feverishly until 9 p.m. to put together a counterproposal. At the evening session, Camdessus said that the creditors would not concern themselves with Zaire's balance of payments and that trade issues should properly be dealt with in other fora (implicitly, the Brussels Club or a World Bank consultative group). As a result, the creditors insisted on a payment of $477 million in 1980. The fourteen creditor countries also categorically refused to reschedule any previously rescheduled debt or consider a cap on interest rates. On several other key issues, the creditors were still divided among themselves.

Bofossa immediately pointed out that a payment of $477 million in 1980 would entail a reduction of planned 1980 import levels to roughly 40 percent below what the IMF, much less the World Bank, deemed minimally necessary. He insisted that "the import levels necessitated by your proposals are totally incompatible with the stabilization of the economy and will result in a further deterioration of the country's economic and social situation."[23] The finance minister then presented Zaire's counterproposal, which backed away from the interest cap proposal and incorporated a $166 million payment in 1980.

After this session ended at 10 p.m., the creditor countries caucused again until 1 a.m., Tuesday, December 11, at which time they made another offer to Bofossa and asked for his response by 9 a.m. The new offer included payments in 1980 amounting to $300 million. The Zairians and their investment bank advisers worked the rest of the night putting together a second counterproposal. At 9 a.m. the same morning, both sides met again, all clearly in a state of considerable fatigue. Finance Minister Bofossa again stressed his concern about the impact of the creditor's proposal on Zaire's import capacity. Their second proposal still would entail a 30 percent reduction in Zaire's 1980 imports from the 1979 level.

Although the Zairian delegation's use of import level considerations and their implications for productive activity and recovery was a very useful negotiating technique, it was not necessarily the prime worry of President Mobutu and key members of his ruling group. They were more concerned with the available levels of foreign exchange, which could be used for a whole host of purposes other than the rehabilitation of the Zairian economy. Their perception of this debt-rescheduling process was rather different from that of the creditors, Finance Minister Bofossa, or his investment bank advisers.

Previously rescheduled debt was still a major bone of contention, with the creditors refusing to budge. This meant that Zaire would owe $142 million more in 1980 than the $300 million of the creditors' second proposal—a serious blow to the Zairian delegation's hopes for the rescheduling. Bofossa did not want to take such an agreement back to Kinshasa and President Mobutu as the result of "his" delegation's labor and the very expensive investment bank advisers' effort. He thus made a second counterproposal, which included payments of $40 million of previously rescheduled debt, with the rest to be rescheduled under a new formula. The remaining $102 million immediately became the major focus of the negotiations.

In an interesting ploy, Bofossa put both the IMF and the World Bank representatives on the spot by asking their opinions about the impact the import levels resulting from the creditors' latest proposal might have on Zaire's economic stabilization and recovery efforts. In so doing, he effectively forced them to violate the unwritten norm of IMF and World Bank neutrality in Paris Club operations. Both

Calamitsis and Varon stated that the latest creditor proposal was far too tough, although Varon was more adamant than his colleague from the Fund. The World Bank had a reputation for taking a broader, developmental perspective than the IMF, but Varon's answer also reflected recent Bank thinking on Zaire's economic situation. An October 1979 confidential report, *The Zairian Economy: Current Situation and Constraints*, had assessed the impact of various rescheduling levels on Zaire's recovery and criticized the short-term perspective of Paris Club reschedulings and commercial bank behavior alike. Thus, although the World Bank was far from an advocate of Mobutu's Zaire,[24] Bofossa had ensured that the Bank's representative would interject these sympathetic views directly into a Paris Club negotiation, a fact deeply resented by several creditor countries.

Breaking with their reluctance to discuss aid issues in the Paris Club arena, these countries suggested to Varon that if the situation in Zaire were really as bad as he said and Zaire did indeed need generous treatment, surely the World Bank would offer Zaire a large balance-of-payments support loan. Now in an embarrassing position largely because of the Bank's own ambivalence toward Mobutu's Zaire, Varon had to reply that the Bank did not have any such plans. He did offer to bring the issue to the attention of his superiors when he returned to Washington.

After Bofossa argued that the Paris Club's latest terms were much too harsh and might jeopardize the London Club agreement, the creditors' irritation shifted to the London Club banks, who insisted on Paris Club comparability for their rescheduling agreement of December 11 to take effect. Who were they to judge any Paris Club agreement? The banks were owed only about $400 million, whereas they, the Paris Club creditors, were owed over $3 billion. In addition, the Paris Club had already rescheduled twice previously, whereas the banks resisted it for years, trying one maneuver after another, all of which ended in failure. Besides, the London Club agreement was really not that generous; the banks were getting full interest and not taking any real losses. With considerable tension in the air, the session ended at 10:30 a.m. The Zairians and their advisers were told to stand by for the creditors' last offer within the hour. Bofossa, drained and aggravated, felt the battle over the $102 million gap had been lost completely. This clearly was not an agreement he could take back to Mobutu. Bofossa ruled out not signing any agreement and returning to Kinshasa empty-handed, although his foreign advisers suggested just such a response; Mobutu had expressly told him to come back with an agreement—and a good one. His staff and advisers thus prepared a statement that he would read into the minutes indicating that Zaire would sign the agreement, but with severe reservations: "Zaire sincerely believes that the creditors' proposal is unrealistic. It will make its best efforts to honor it, but doubts it can be successful in this effort."[25]

As Bofossa was reviewing this statement, Camdessus requested to see him. The Paris Club chairman offered a final compromise on the total $142 million in previously rescheduled debt. It would still not be rescheduled, but it could be spread out, with half paid on June 30, 1980 and the rest on January 31, 1981. In fact, this only added another month to the payment period, but it made it appear as if the previously rescheduled debt were being paid over two years; 1980 would at least look better for the Zairians. Bofossa made one last effort to make it look even a little better, as this would ease his return to Kinshasa. He proposed that one-third be paid in June 1980 and two-thirds in January 1981. Camdessus took this offer back to the creditors who accepted it at 1 p.m.—right on schedule for a normal Paris Club meeting.

The final agreement, drawn up and signed that afternoon, had Zaire paying $211 million in 1980, plus one-third of the previously rescheduled debt, more than twice its original proposal of $108 million. The creditors settled for less than half of their original proposal of $477 million and only one-third of the previously rescheduled debt in 1980, but the other two-thirds would come in January 1981. This agreement underscored the creditors' ambivalence and mistrust of their central African "ally." It included stipulations that the bilateral accords, which now had to be negotiated individually with each of the fourteen creditor countries, would take effect only if Zaire came to terms with the IMF on policies and performance criteria for 1980, and if final agreement were reached with the London Club banks. The Paris Club did agree in principle to consider another rescheduling to cover 1981 maturities but only if Zaire were still in compliance with the IMF and with all previous Paris Clubs and the bilateral agreements attached to them.

After two exhausting days, Bofossa and his advisers returned to Kinshasa to face Mobutu and to solve two major problems: putting the IMF program back on track and concluding the London Club rescheduling.

THE IMF AGREEMENT: GETTING BACK ON TRACK

Fully one month before the Paris Club agreement, by early November 1979, it was very clear that the IMF standby signed in August was in serious difficulty. Zaire's budget deficit was $50 million over the target deficit ceiling of $170 million. Major problems also developed in foreign exchange management, statistical reporting, interest rates, and taxes, as well as with an upsurge in smuggling, mainly of coffee by individuals operating out of the presidency and other high government circles. Zaire had thus only been allowed to draw SDR 20 million of the SDR 118 million authorized for the eighteen-month agreement.

In late December 1979, the Zairian government also implemented a forced exchange of old currency notes for a smaller number of new notes to reduce money supply in the economy. Not only was this program undertaken without any discussion with or advance notice to the IMF, but the corruption and abuse involved in the process was staggering. New five-zaire notes were introduced with a low ceiling on the amount of cash people were allowed to convert. Many people without political connections thus lost vast sums of money. Corruption aside, the program was badly administered, leading to further losses for the Zairian population. Two IMF officials were sent to Kinshasa to assess the situation. To control the damage, in early Janfuary 1980 the regime replaced Finance Minister Bofossa with an individual held in high repute by most external observers, Namwisi Ma Koyi. Although Zaire was allowed to make its December drawing on the standby, a larger IMF team was due to visit soon to evaluate the overall damage.

The virtual collapse of the August 1979 standby posed considerable problems for the IMF, Zaire, its investment bank advisers (especially since the London Club process was entering a very sensitive stage), and the U.S. and other Western governments that wanted to give Mobutu assistance. The United States in particular was torn between the need, on the one hand, to defend its interests in and actions toward the Mobutu regime, and the secret fear, on the other, that Mobutu's regime was beyond repair. At the March 5, 1980, House Foreign Affairs Subcommittee on Africa hearings on military and development aid to Zaire, Deputy Secretary of State Walker used the strategy of emphasizing U.S. strategic interests in Zaire and exaggerating Mobutu's progress with reforms. He freely admitted the existence of problems with Zaire's economic reforms, but Walker contended that these efforts were "finally beginning to show progress, although it has been a slow and painful process for all concerned and it is far from being over." He further noted that although "Zaire's performance under the first four months of the [1979 IMF standby agreement] was less than satisfactory," Zaire was in the process of renegotiating this agreement, and Walker implied that a successful outcome was the best way to ensure continuing reform efforts by the Mobutu government.[26]

Privately, however, the U.S. administration's view was less optimistic. In a secret 1980 interagency intelligence memorandum (IIM) entitled "Zaire: Is It Reformable?" the U.S. government's intelligence and policy community decided that the Zairian reforms amounted to no more than "tinkering" with the country's thinly rooted institutions in response to foreign pressure. The IIM concluded that Mobutu neither intended nor perceived the possibility of fundamental structural reform.

Nevertheless, two weeks after Walker's testimony and following difficult, acrimonious, and protracted negotiations, Mobutu signed another letter of intent for the same August 1979 eighteen-month standby, in effect restarting it by establishing new performance criteria. The Fund's executive board approved the new letter of intent on May 16, 1980, and Zaire was allowed to make more drawings, the first since September 1979, when the previous agreement took effect. On June 12, 1980, Zaire drew SDR 39.2 million, and on both August 20 and September 22, it drew SDR 19.6 million.

LONDON CLUB: ROUND TWO

On December 12, 1979, the day after the conclusion of the Paris Club rescheduling, the government of Zaire accepted in principle the modified terms of the London Club agreement put to its advisers the previous day in London. Despite their earlier warnings about comparability with the Paris Club, the agent banks did not seriously examine the results of the rescheduling by the Western countries. By Christmas, a bank agreement in principle was fully in place with the agent banks. The next difficult step was to turn this agreement into a legally binding document. From Christmas until late February 1980, a battery of creditor lawyers, and Zaire's investment bank advisers, and their lawyers fought intensely over a number of important issues.

This process required a four-day meeting in Paris in mid-February. A central issue was the definition of default and the actions that could be taken by the creditor banks if Zaire did default on the complex terms of the agreement. Because of Zaire's reputation and debt service track record, the banks took these provisions very seriously. They especially wanted to be able to seize any of Zaire's mineral assets that were outside the country. Given the recent efforts of U.S. banks to tie up Iran's assets, the creditor banks also wanted assurance that none of the 134 banks would get preferential treatment or be able to attach liens on Zairian assets outside the context of the London Club agreement. In this regard, a bank version of the most-favored-nation principle was adopted.

A related issue involved bank monitoring of Zaire's economic and financial condition. Zaire was to submit detailed reports on its condition every six months, as well as all IMF and World Bank reports on Zaire. Unlike the Paris Club, the banks did not require that Zaire remain in compliance with its IMF agreements in order for the London Club rescheduling to remain valid. Given the difficulty of keeping an IMF agreement on track (just described), they were afraid Zaire would miss IMF targets and did not want to jeopardize their own agreement with Zaire. The agent banks merely stipulated that Zaire must remain a member of the IMF and be entitled to draw on its resources. The last major issue, the mechanism for implementing the agreement, was resolved by designating a nonagent bank, the Bank of Tokyo Trust Company, as the servicing bank.

Thus, after nearly seven months of effort, a rescheduling agreement was finally ready to be signed, and that date was fixed for April 21, 1980. Then, out of the blue, Citibank dropped a bombshell by insisting that Zaire pay it roughly $3 million owed (but not guaranteed) as part of an Export-Import Bank loan. This move was consistent with Citibank's reputation as a hardball player. It threatened to allow the entire London Club agreement to collapse if this demand were not met. Zaire and its advisers were afraid that other banks would challenge the agreement on grounds of preferential treatment if Citibank were paid. Just three days before the deadline, Citibank relented, and the 185-page London Club agreement was signed, as scheduled, much to the relief of Zaire's investment bank advisers.

THE IMF AND "THE GOOD 1980"

The second half of 1980 proved to be a surprise to most people; things actually went relatively well by Zairian standards. A new air of optimism set in, affecting most major actors. An IMF mission visited Kinshasa from August 18 to 31, 1980, to conduct an overall review of the 1979 standby program. During the mission, Mobutu made several key personnel changes, including replacing Blumenthal's old nemesis at the Bank of Zaire, Governor Emony Mondanga, with a much-respected former governor, Sambwa Pida Nbagui. The United States and other external actors were most pleased by these encouraging moves. On September 5, Mobutu signed yet a third letter of intent for the 1979 standby, which included modified performance targets for the remainder of the year. The executive board of the Fund approved these changes on October 15.

In its October 30 report on the August mission, the IMF concluded that "provided the strong corrective measures are sustained throughout the year, the staff considers that the ceilings of the revised program can be observed."[27] Zaire was allowed to make its last drawing on the 1979 standby in December. In assessing the last half of 1980, the Fund observed that "after some initial difficulties, in 1980 performance under the program was satisfactory. Although recovery in world copper prices, coupled with highly favorable prices for cobalt, contributed significantly to this outcome, the improvement was also due to a relatively effective implementation of the program."[28] Having garnered these favorable assessments, Zaire looked toward a larger and longer program with the IMF—a three-year extended fund facility. On September 24, 1980, Finance Minister Namwisi met with U.S. businesspeople, bankers, and government officials at a luncheon in New York organized by the U.S. Chamber of Commerce. The finance minister highlighted Zaire's advances in recent months, including its strict adherence to the performance criteria contained in the 1979 standby agreement, as compared with past failures in the 1976 and 1977 IMF stabilization programs. On the basis of this success, he noted, "the Government of Zaire plans to seek from the International Monetary Fund an extended fund facility and supplemental facility obtaining, thereby, direct support of its balance of payments and thus the expected level of imports. At this time we are in the process of designing the framework for such an agreement which we hope would be put in place in the near future."[29] Namwisi concluded his speech by emphasizing that a strong Zaire was important for the West.

Discussions with the IMF for an EFF began in Kinshasa in November 1980 and finished seven months later after two Zairian trips to Washington and three

IMF missions to Zaire. On June 5, 1981 Mobutu signed a letter of intent for an EFF worth SDR 912 million, or about $1 billion over three years. This longer program "aimed at alleviating the structural distortions in the economy and achieving a viable external payments position over the medium term."[30] The Fund's executive board approved it on June 22, 1981. Because of this agreement, the Paris Club met in July for the fourth time in six years and rescheduled $3.34 billion in external debt.

The Mobutu regime and its external advisers and friends were flush with success, but this euphoria was to be short-lived. By September 1981, the EFF was already in serious trouble. The first two drawings, or "purchases," under the EFF were made, totaling SDR 175 million, but Zaire was not allowed "to make the third scheduled purchase of SDR 100 million because of failure to observe three of the four performance criteria established for end-September 1981."[31] The Fund sent two missions to Kinshasa to find out what was going wrong, one from October 15 to 25 and the other from November 30 to December 13, and in early 1982 it issued confidential reports of its findings. The Fund pointed to "a further weakening of Zaire's overall situation, not only on account of major shortfalls in export earnings [due to a sharp decline in copper prices] and capital inflows but also because of slippages in policy implementation."[32] It appeared that Mobutu and those around him had not changed their ways:

> There were slippages in budgetary expenditure controls, notably in the areas of the Presidency and Political Institutions, education, and subsidies. On the basis of developments through the end of the third quarter of 1981, it is estimated that outlays of the Presidency and Political Institutions for the year as a whole amounted to about Z 500 million, or roughly double the programmed figure.

> There have also been certain unbudgeted outlays, including a large subsidy to the state oil importing company, cost overruns for a number of capital projects, and apparent slippages in the effectiveness of revenue collection.

> Thus, the 1981 overall government deficit (on a cash basis) was in the neighborhood of Z 1.3 billion, as against a target of Z 550 million; this was equivalent to 5.2 per cent of the estimated GDP, or more than double the ratio envisaged in the program.[33]

In June 1982, the EFF was canceled for noncompliance. Zaire was never allowed to make the third drawing under the EFF; it thus only received SDR 175 million out of the original SDR 912 million offered. The reform efforts had apparently ground to a complete halt.

EPILOGUE

Spring 1982 had been a rough one for Mobutu in other ways as well. His private visit to the United States in May received some quite unfavorable treatment from the press. One newspaper, among others, criticized his visit "with 93 of his wives, friends and children in a lavish vacation trip to Florida and New York." It reported that "the Mobutu party may have spent as much as $2 million in expensive hotels and restaurants, trips to Disney World and other activities at a time when Zaire is in arrears in official loan payments to the United States."[34]

Despite strong willingness on the part of the Reagan administration to support Mobutu, Congress was not inclined to be very helpful. Shortly after Mobutu's visit, the House Foreign Affairs Committee voted to reduce military sales credits for Zaire from $20 million to $4 million and rejected the administration's request for $15 million in budgetary support. The committee members wanted "to distance the United States from a regime lawmakers described as repressive, unstable and corrupt."[35]

The Mobutu regime reacted very strongly, declaring that it was renouncing all U.S. aid because of the congressional action. It further denounced "insulting remarks" and the "intolerable attitude" of some members of Congress and asserted that there was an "anti-Zaire lobby in Congress." Zaire also complained bitterly that its January 15, 1982, decision to abstain on an Arab-backed resolution in the UN Security Council to impose sanctions on Israel for annexing the Golan Heights "has not brought us any good fortune."[36] Finally, the Zairians resented, according to one press report, "the hearing last September when the House committee heard former prime minister Nguza Karl-i-Bond, who resigned his post and went into exile last spring [1981], charging corruption and mismanagement by Mobutu. According to Karl-i-Bond's testimony, Mobutu and close members of his family withdrew more than $150 million in foreign exchange from the Bank of Zaire in 1977-1979 alone."[37]

A final springtime blow to the Mobutu regime was the surprise victory of the Socialists in France. Mobutu had enjoyed close ties with the defeated government of Valery Giscard d'Estaing, as well as a close personal relationship with the outgoing president. The Giscard government had solidly backed Zaire during the two Shaba invasions, sending Foreign Legion troops during the second incident. Giscard's France had also counseled favorable treatment for Zaire in the 1979 Paris Club rescheduling. The Socialists, by contrast, had criticized Giscard for his close ties to Mobutu and other corrupt African leaders. These developments on both sides of the Atlantic, coupled with the humiliating cancellation of the EFF, created a gloomy outlook for Mobutu in the second half of 1982.

By late 1982, Zaire's situation was particularly grave and uncertain. Not only had the EFF agreement collapsed, but Zaire also was substantially behind in its payments to the private international banks based on the 1980 London Club agreement, and efforts to refinance the arrears had been unsuccessful. Many of the banks began quietly writing down Zaire's debt. Only two bilateral agreements (the French and the American) had been signed for the 1981 Paris Club rescheduling and only very modest sums paid. In addition, with the collapse of the EFF, payments due in 1982 that had been rescheduled by that agreement technically now came due. The amount of medium- and long-term debt service payments due in 1982 was about $946 million ($771 million contractual debt plus $175 million in arrears). This did not include commercial arrears or the SDR 52 million owed to the IMF. Since the best forecast of Zaire's foreign exchange earnings for 1982 was between $1.2 and $1.3 billion, these repayment figures translated into a debt service burden for late 1982 equal to 75.7 percent of Zaire's export earnings. It was thus apparent that, barring substantial external assistance, Zaire would be unable to meet its 1982 and 1983 debt service payments. By the end of June 1982, Zaire was about $863 million in arrears.

Zaire felt it had played the reform game for well over a year in late 1981 and early 1982 and thus had earned the 1981 EFF agreement. For this reason, the government relaxed its performance, and the situation deteriorated rapidly. Other factors may also have contributed to Zaire's reform failures. U.S. officials in 1982 admitted that the Western governments had not sufficiently coordinated and sustained their Zairian policies.[38] Certainly their interests and outlook were not uniform. The Europeans, for instance, took a more realpolitik view of Zaire's situation than did the United States. Belgian banking and business interests had a good deal to lose, especially in minerals marketing and prefinancing arrangements, if reforms went too far. Furthermore, many foreign businesses, banks, and European officials believed Mobutu would outlast the IMF, World Bank, and Western government reforms, so that the issue for them was maintaining access to the regime (and their interests) even if this meant sacrificing the reforms. Overly optimistic estimations of foreign capital inflow and mineral export earnings, on the part of IMF staff, may also have contributed to Zaire's perceived economic failures.

In the final analysis, there are two ways of viewing the reform efforts. First, there were those who believed that the reforms had some chance of success. Second, there were others who believed from the beginning that the reform efforts had no or very little chance of success but realized that they were a convenient way of continuing to support the Mobutu regime for other reasons. The first group clearly misperceived the nature of the regime and thus the chances for success; the second used the misperceptions of the first for their own ends.

NOTES

1. The source for this entire section is Erwin Blumenthal's "Zaire Report on Her International Financial Credibility," typed manuscript, April 7, 1982. After this secret report was leaked to the European press in September 1982, several versions of it circulated, some of them in French, The body of the text was written in English, although most of the appendices are in French, I am certain of the authenticity of my copy, as Blumenthal handed it to me personally in 1984.

2. GECAMINES is the copper and cobalt parastatal that supplies about two-thirds of Zaire's foreign exchange revenue every year.

3. Blumenthal, "Zaire," pp. 8, 18, 9, and 6.

4. For more detailed information of Zaire's political economy, see Thomas M. Callaghy, *The State-Society Struggle: Zaire in Comparative Perspective* (New York: Columbia University Press, 1984), chapters 1 and 4; and Crawford Young and Thomas Turner, *The Rise and Decline of the Zairian State* (Madison: University of Wisconsin Press, 1985). On early U.S. ties to Mobutu, see Madeleine G. Kalb, *The Congo Cables: The Cold War in Africa from Eisenhower to Kennedy* (New York: Macmillan, 1982); Richard D. Mahoney, *JFK: Ordeal in Africa* (Oxford: Oxford Unversity Press, 1983); and John Stockwell, *In Search of Enemies: A CIA Story* (New York: W. W. Norton, 1978), which covers the period up to the Angolan civil war.

5. P. A. Wellons, *Borrowing by Developing Countries on the Euro-Currency Market* (Paris: OECD, 1977), pp. 119-120.

6. Crawford Young, "Zaire: The Unending Crisis," *Foreign Affairs*, 57, 1 (1978), p. 177.

7. Kenneth Adelman, "Zaire's Year of Crisis," *African Affairs*, 77 (1978), p. 37.

8. Confidential interviews, Kinshasa, July 29 and August 6, 1982; Washington, D.C., July 9, 1982.

9. Confidential interviews, Kinshasa, August 5,6, and 9, 1982; Brussels, July 22, 1982, and January 13 and 14, 1982; and Washington, D.C., March 2 and 3, 1981; December 16, 1981; August 9, 1982.

10. World Bank, "From Economic Stabilization to Recovery: An Appraisal of the Mobutu Plan," Washington, D.C., unpublished report, May 15, 1980, pp. 3, 4, 14, and 27.

11. Ibid.

12. Confidential interviews, Kinshasa, July 29 and August 5,6, and 10, 1982; Brussels, January 14, 1982; Paris, January 21, 1982; and Washington, D.C., December 16, 1981, and July 9, 1982.

13. Blumenthal, "Zaire," p. 19.

14. Nguza Karl-i-Bond, "Current Political and Economic Situation in Zaire," testimony before the U.S. House of Representatives, Foreign Affairs Committee, Subcommittee on Africa, September 15, 1981, pp. 13, 15. For his participant-observer view of the external reform efforts, see *Mobutu ou l'incarnation du mal Zairois* (London: Rex Collings, 1982), pp. 143–146, 165.

15. Blumenthal, "Zaire," p. 13.

16. Confidential interview, London, January 7, 1982.

17. Calculated from data in World Bank, "Zaire: Economic Memorandum, Recent Economic Developments and the Path to Recovery," Washington, D.C., unpublished report, May 20, 1981; and Bank of Zaire, "The Republic of Zaire: Recent Economic and Financial Developments," June 1982. The latter report is one of a series of information memoranda produced by Zaire's investment bank adviser triumvirate of Lazard Freres, Lehman Brothers Kuhn Loeb, and S.G. Warburg.

18. This section is based on the author's confidential interviews on the London Club and on Jeffrey E. Garten, "Rescheduling Third World Debt: The Case of Zaire," Ph.D. dissertation, School of Advanced International Studies, Johns Hopkins University, 1981.

19. This section is based on the author's confidential interviews on the Paris Club and on Garten, "Rescheduling Third World Debt."

20. Quoted in Crawford Young, "The New Optimism on Zairian Recovery: Illusion or Reality?" unpublished manuscript, p. 28.

21. Quoted in Garten, "Rescheduling Third World Debt," p. 158.

22. Quoted in ibid., p. 118.

23. Quoted in ibid., p. 129.

24. In September 1979, ten of the World Bank's fifteen projects were in serious trouble, and senior Bank management decided not to increase its exposure in Zaire. President McNamara was particularly skeptical and informed Mobutu that there would be no consultative group meeting for Zaire until he demonstrated a more serious effort and reached agreement with the IMF and creditor clubs.

25. Quoted in Garten, "Rescheduling Third World Debt," p. 136.

26. Lannon Walker, "Opening Statement," testimony before the U.S. House of Representatives, Foreign Affairs Committee, Subcommittee on Africa, Hearings on Military and Development Aid to Zaire for FY-81, March 5, 1980, typed text, pp. 5, 13–14.

27. IMF, "Zaire—Review and Consultation Under Stand-By Arrangement and Request for Modification for Performance Criteria," Washington, D.C., unpublished report, October 3, 1980.

28. IMF, "Zaire—Staff Report for the 1983 Article IV Consultation and Request for Stand-by Arrangement," Washington, D.C., unpublished report, November 30, 1983, p. 5.

29. Namwisi Ma Koyi, "Text of Speech by Minister of Finance for the Republic of Zaire, to the Chamber of Commerce of the United States in New York on September 24, 1980," typed text, pp. 2, 3–4, 7–8.

30. IMF, "Zaire—Staff Report for the 1983 Article IV Consultation," p. 5.

31. IMF, "Zaire—Use of Fund Resources—Compensatory Financing Facility," Washington, D.C., unpublished report, February 11, 1982, p. 4.

32. IMF, "Zaire—Staff Report for the 1981 Article IV Consultation," Washington D.C., unpublished report, January 19, 1982, p. 1.

33. IMF, "Zaire—Staff Report for the 1981 Article IV Consultation," pp. 2, 5; IMF, "Zaire—Use of Fund Resources," p. 4; IMF, "Zaire—Staff Report for the 1981 Article IV Consultation," p. 5.

34. *Washington Post,* May 14, 1982.

35. Ibid.

36. Ibid.

37. Ibid.

38. Confidential interview, Kinshasa, July 29, 1982.

7

■ ════════════════════════════════ ■

Nigeria, 1983–1986:
Reaching Agreement with the Fund

Thomas J. Biersteker

In the wake of its large-scale borrowing, the accumulation of its debt, and the global economic recession at the beginning of the 1980s, Nigeria found itself unable to meet its debt obligations and entered into negotiations for a standby agreement with the IMF. The stakes were very high, and many of the disputed issues had significant implications for the direction of national development and the determination of winners and losers in the domestic economy. Accordingly, reaching agreement on the policy changes expected by the Fund has proven exceedingly difficult. This case examines the course of the IMF's three and a half years of negotiation with Nigeria, a country that resisted the Fund's policy conditions under three successive governments before signing an agreement in November 1986.

ROUND ONE: NIGERIA APPROACHES THE FUND

Ever since OPEC first succeeded in raising the price of crude petroleum dramatically in 1973-1974, Nigeria has been a monoculture economy dependent on the export of petroleum. Petroleum proceeds accounted for nearly 95 percent of

This case was originally prepared under the auspices of The Pew Diplomatic Initiative at the University of Southern California. This is a revised and edited version of the case, prepared especially for this volume.

government revenue during the late 1970s and continued at this level throughout Nigeria's negotiations with the Fund. The petroleum income came at a time when Nigeria was already experiencing a decline in agricultural production. Hence, though it created new opportunities, Nigeria's newfound oil income exacerbated a number of other structural problems in its economy: lagging agricultural performance, inflation, and inequality. The Nigerian economy has long been characterized by high levels of import demand, and the oil income fueled an explosion of consumer-goods imports during the 1970s. It also reinforced the development of a heavily import-intensive manufacturing sector in the country.

When it assumed power from a military administration in October 1979, the civilian regime of President Shehu Shagari faced relatively few external economic constraints. The price for Nigerian crude petroleum was at an all-time high; national oil income had reached unprecedented levels; and prices for Nigeria's major agricultural export (cocoa) were at higher levels than they had been for a decade. The debt service ratio was an easily manageable 1.5 percent, and foreign exchange reserves increased by a factor of two (to more than $10 billion) during its first year in office.

The Shagari administration was the first elected regime in Nigeria's second republic (civilians had previously ruled the country under a parliamentary system from the time of its independence from Britain in 1960 until a military coup in January 1966). The new constitution that gave birth to Nigeria's second republic was based on a U.S.-style presidential system of governance, with separate legislative, executive, and judicial branches of federal government. Although it was challenged by opposition parties from their bases in state governments, the Shagari administration used Nigeria's new federal system to concentrate political power at the federal level, a concentration that had originally begun under the military during the Nigerian civil war (1967-1970).

The Shagari government was regionally based in northern Nigeria, but it had received strong support in the 1979 elections from the middle-belt and central regions of the country. The ruling National Party of Nigeria (NPN) was widely viewed as a conservative political party that represented the interests of the traditional oligarchy in northern Nigeria, the emerging political and economic class in the north (an influential segment of which was sometimes referred to as "the Kaduna mafia"), and elements of Nigeria's influential commercial and industrial elite throughout the country. The NPN was the best-funded of the five political parties that competed in the early days of the second republic, and during the 1979 elections it was popularly referred to as the "Naira Party of Nigeria" (a reference to Nigeria's currency, the naira).

During the Shagari government's first two full years in office (in 1980 and 1981), the level of imports into the country more than doubled. The naira was highly overvalued at the time, hence the cost of imported goods was relatively low. To control the volume of imports into the country, the government maintained an elaborate import licensing scheme in which individual importers received governmental approval (in the form of licenses) to import set quantities of goods. However, the arrangement was fraught with corruption, and the volume of imports was only partially controlled. The new civilian government granted import licenses principally to its political supporters, giving them quasi monopolies to import goods and control the market in specific sectors. In return, state and party officials regularly received kickbacks for the granting or, in some instances, the direct auctioning of import licenses (in the name of "federal character").

For a time, the oil income fueled the increased volume of imports (Table 7.1). However, existing levels of public expenditure were maintained; the exchange rate appreciated in real terms; and oil production decreased to 69.7 percent of 1980 levels. Petroleum export earnings fell from $25 billion in 1980 to $17.5 billion in 1981. As a result, foreign exchange reserves were drawn down at a rather rapid rate during 1981 to make up for the difference from lost oil revenues. Foreign exchange reserves plummeted from more than $10 billion in 1980 to $3.9 billion in 1981 (Table 7.2). After a slump in oil exports in the first half of 1981, new external borrowing increased to more than $2 billion (Table 7.2).

In September 1981, the Shagari government introduced its first austerity package, designed to cut public expenditure by about $1.6 billion. When the 1982 budget was announced at the end of the year, further cuts (in excess of $3 billion) were announced, along with plans to increase foreign borrowing to make up the balance-of-payments shortfall. In April 1982, Nigeria drew down its remaining reserves with the IMF, and throughout the year it continued to increase the level of total external borrowing (Table 7.2). The volume of crude petroleum exports continued to drop, and by November, Nigeria was three months in arrears in settling its routine trade debts in foreign exchange. By the end of the year, the fiscal crisis had deepened, and Nigeria's debt service ratio had shot up to 11.3 percent (Table 7.3).

In February 1983, as the backlog of short-term import debt continued to increase, the Shagari government approached foreign commercial bankers on a $1 billion Eurocredit to help settle its trade arrears. Two months later, Nigeria initiated negotiations with the IMF. At the outset, Nigeria sought to borrow $2 billion from the Fund, largely to help refinance its trade debt (then estimated to be somewhere between $3 billion and $5 billion). Since Nigeria had already drawn down its reserve with the Fund, the IMF indicated a number of conditions that would have to be satisfied before it agreed to commit any new funds. The stabilization package the Fund proposed included a devaluation, a tightening of the money supply, an increase in interest rates, a cutback in recurrent government expenditure, the abolition of a number of consumer subsidies (particularly on petroleum), a wage freeze, and the relaxation of exchange and import controls.

Nigeria's trade debts continued to pile up, and a number of foreign banks began to stop confirming Nigerian letters of credit. With an election scheduled for August 1983, the Shagari government accelerated its efforts to increase the level of external borrowing and during the month of June an agreement was announced between Nigeria and twenty-four international banks. The banks agreed to refinance $1.6 billion of the country's trade arrears into a three-year medium-term loan, with repayment to start after the elections, in January 1984. Nigeria's decision to go to the Fund was described as "helpful" in persuading the banks to negotiate. On the eve of the elections, a World Bank loan of $120 million was announced, with prospects of an increase to $500 million.

President Shagari and the NPN were reelected by a wide margin in August 1983 elections that were widely viewed as severely rigged.[1] Corruption was nothing new in the history of Nigerian politics, but the NPN had apparently taken it to unprecedented levels. Shortly after the elections, a second refinancing agreement was reached, this time with a total of sixty five international banks.

Negotiations with the IMF had been continuing throughout this period, and agreement had been reached on a number of conditions. The Nigerians had agreed to reduce government expenditures; increase budgetary discipline; review the feasibility of ongoing projects; reduce the level of subsidies for parastatal firms; end grants to state governments; rationalize customs duties; increase interest rates; reduce money supply; gradually remove fertilizer subsidies; review industrial incentives and policies; promote exports; increase producer prices for agricultural commodities; better-manage the external debt; and improve the efficiency of government revenue collection. Despite the progress, however, three major issues blocked an agreement: devaluation, trade liberalization, and an end to petroleum subsidies.

The IMF was primarily concerned with the overvaluation of the naira and the price distortions it produced throughout the economy. The Fund wanted at least a 33 percent devaluation of the currency. The Nigerians countered that a devaluation would have little immediate effect. Since the price of their major export (petroleum) was already denominated in dollars, the Nigerian negotiators contended that a major devaluation would do little to promote exports. Further, they argued that the prices of their other commodity exports were also externally determined and undergoing a decline to postwar lows at the time. The Shagari government feared especially the consequences a devaluation would have on import prices and the level of domestic inflation.

Trade liberalization was less pressing for the IMF at the outset of the negotiations, since the Fund staff thought that the overvalued exchange rate by itself created the principal source of trade protection. The Nigerians argued that the elimination of the trade licensing scheme could lead to the dumping of goods on the Nigerian market, which could destroy the capacity of the country's infant industries and lead to the potential importation of hazardous substances. The Fund opposed petroleum subsidies, as it does nearly all government price subsidies of any kind. Nigerian authorities resisted the cut in petroleum subsidies on the grounds that it would produce unacceptable levels of domestic inflation.

From September 1983 to the end of the year, the negotiations between the IMF and Nigeria were stalemated on these three issues. In a sense, Nigeria and the

Fund were engaged more in discussions for policy reform than formal negotiations. As one IMF official put it, the Fund missions were "essentially pedagogical. . . .We were just trying to talk economic sense to them."[2] Another Fund negotiator observed, "There is some question whether these were negotiations at all. We seldom knew when decisions were made. We seldom knew, or had access to, the people who decide. The people we saw didn't always deliver."[3] Hence, there was apparently not much give-and-take in the discussions during successive IMF missions to Nigeria. The two principal protagonists appear to have talked at each other as much as they talked with each other.

In his annual budget speech on December 29, President Shagari announced new austerity measures. Among them were plans for a reduction in the level of imports; a further cut in the federal budget; a further revision downward of the fourth development plan targets; and the privatization of a number of state-owned companies. There was no mention of any devaluation. Shagari announced his intention to continue to approach the Bank and the Fund for structural adjustment and balance-of-payments assistance. Two days later, his government was overthrown by a military coup.

ROUND TWO: STABILIZATION WITHOUT THE FUND (JANUARY 1984–AUGUST 1985)

When the military returned to power at the beginning of 1984, it faced a number of significant economic problems. Price levels within OPEC had weakened, and as Nigeria's oil production share continued to decline (Table 7.4), its market was increasingly threatened by other producers. Oil income was down, from $25 billion in 1980 to less than $10 billion in 1983 (Table 7.4). Nigeria's debt service ratio had climbed to 18.7 percent, and its foreign exchange reserves were virtually drained (Table 7.2). Domestic inflation was running at a level of 23.2 percent, and industrial production was sharply off.

In his first speech after assuming power, the new head of state, Major General Muhammadu Buhari, emphasized discipline, austerity, self-reliance, and fiscal conservativism—ideas that were to become the basis of his government's policy and its subsequent approach to the Fund. At first, the new regime was greeted with a good deal of popular enthusiasm, coming as it did after what was increasingly perceived as the widespread civilian waste and corruption of the preceding four years. At the outset, the new government appeared to be a continuation of the last military government of generals Murtala Muhammed and Olusegun Obasanjo, the regime that had handed power back to the civilians in 1979. Several members of its governing council had served under Muhammed and/or Obasanjo (Buhari himself had been petroleum minister), and some of the language of the new government—of state management of the economy—was familiar.

However, there was also some continuity with the ousted civilian regime. Although it legitimated itself as a corrective regime, intent on cleaning up the economic and political mismanagement of the civilians, the new military government was conservative politically and, like the Shagari government, it, too, was dominated by northerners. Significantly, a northerner again controlled the distribution of import licenses at the Ministry of Trade. The new regime differed primarily in two major respects: the degree of its distrust of the private sector (which had so effectively penetrated the ousted civilian regime) and the degree of its overt authoritarianism. Nigeria previously had experienced three successive military governments in its post-independence history up to this point (military officers ruled between 1966 and 1979), but the Buhari regime was to prove the most authoritarian.

Shortly after assuming power, the regime launched its "War Against Indiscipline," a national campaign that invoked patriotic appeals in an attempt to increase order and discipline within the country. It also enacted highly controversial decrees (Decree No. 2 and Decree No. 4) that centralized state power to levels unprecedented since the Nigerian civil war, giving it the power to arrest and detain without trial and effectively censoring Nigeria's lively press.[4] These measures provided the new regime with far greater direction and decisiveness in policymaking. However, they were also indicative of a tendency within the new leadership to rely on authoritarian measures to bolster its political position rather than use ideology to mobilize popular support for its programs.[5]

At the outset, observers at the IMF viewed the new regime with a certain amount of optimism, especially when General Buhari described his approach to Nigeria's accumulated debt: "given prudent management of the existing financial resources, determined substantially to reduce waste...it will be possible to clear the accumulated domestic payments arrears, reduce the rising budgetary deficit, and the weak balance of payments deficit.[6] The Fund's hopes for an early resolution to the stalemated talks were short-lived, however. Shortly after his initial speech to the public, Buhari appealed to the IMF for greater understanding of Nigeria's predicament, especially on the question of devaluation. Moreover, he ruled out any reduction of petroleum subsidies (and hence any increase in domestic fuel prices).

Less than a month after it assumed power, the new military government resumed negotiations (originally begun under Shagari) with a number of OECD country export credit agencies under Paris Club auspices. They were negotiating a rescheduling of Nigeria's backlog of short-term trade debt, estimated by some observers to have reached $6.7 billion by the time the military resumed power. There were also disagreements on the amount of interest that Nigeria should pay on the considerable trade debt not covered under the insurance schemes of official OECD government export credit agencies (in excess of $4 billion), but progress was being made. Nigeria had originally wanted to complete this refinancing agreement by the end of February, but the talks had been interrupted by the coup. Given the degree of corruption associated with the preceding regime, major questions were being raised about whether some of the goods claimed to have been exported to Nigeria had ever arrived in the country. Hence, the precise size of the uninsured trade debt became a major issue. The Nigerian government appointed Chase Manhattan Bank of New York to reconcile claims for trade payments outstanding.

At about the same time, Barclay's Bank of London took the lead in a syndicated loan to Nigeria of approximately $1 billion to repay exporters insured by Britain's Export Credits Guarantee Department (ECGD). Barclay's had acted as agent during the July and September 1983 refinancing negotiations and had now been designated to manage a new loan to repay insured exporters. Nigeria's punctual repayment of the first installment on those agreements only a few days after the coup facilitated the reopening of lines of credit.

Despite the progress in refinancing its $6 billion to $7 billion officially insured short-term trade debt, agreement on the balance of Nigeria's $20 billion debt was dependent upon the state of its negotiations with the IMF. A Nigerian team left for Washington on February 15, 1984, to resume discussions with the Fund. The IMF continued to insist on a major devaluation for the naira. Fund staff and their counterparts in the World Bank agreed that the overvaluation of the naira was the single most important source of economic distortion in Nigeria. In their view, Nigeria had become one of the most extreme cases of overvalued exchange rates and economic distortion in the developing world. In addition, the IMF called for a number of additional demand management measures, including further cuts in government expenditures; further reductions in subsidies; the stoppage of federal government loans to state governments; and the division of parastatal firms into economic and social categories. It also asked for a further review of domestic interest rates and a number of trade policy reforms, including a relaxation of import restrictions, vigorous export promotion, and a simplification and rationalization of Nigeria's tariff structure.

Most of these terms were initially deemed acceptable by Nigerian finance minister Onaolapo Soleye. But the same three issues that had prevented an agreement under the civilians prevented an agreement under the military: devaluation, relaxing import controls, and cutting petroleum subsidies.

The Buhari government did not rule out a devaluation altogether. In fact, it oversaw a gradual reduction in the value of the naira from $1.38 in 1983 to $1.12 in 1985 (Table 7.5). However, it disagreed strongly on the pace and magnitude of the devaluation requested by the Fund. Nigeria wanted a gradual reduction of approximately 30 percent to bring the naira to parity with the U.S. dollar. The IMF was holding out for a single, more significant cut in Nigeria's exchange rate. Many of the arguments against devaluation that had been employed by the civilian negotiators were used again by the military ones. They argued that since Nigeria's major export, oil, was denominated in dollars, a major devaluation would have no appreciable impact on exports. Furthermore, since Nigerian manufacturers could scarcely provide 50 percent of Nigeria's consumption needs, high levels of imports would have to be maintained. Nigeria's existing industries also relied heavily on imported raw materials and intermediate goods for their production. Finally, the negotiators expressed fear that inflation would rise dramatically in the wake of a major devaluation. Thus, as General Buhari stated in a widely quoted interview, "devaluation could be considered only as a last resort."[7]

The Nigerians resisted trade liberalization because they argued that without import controls and other restrictions, the Nigerian propensity to import everything would flood the domestic market with goods. The objected to reducing the level of petroleum subsidies for two reasons. First, there were fears that a major rise in petroleum prices would have an unacceptable inflationary impact. Second, ever since the emergence of OPEC and the identification of petroleum income with the wealth of the country, domestic petroleum prices had become an important symbolic issue in Nigeria. (When higher prices and spot shortages developed within the country in 1974, they helped create a political crisis that undermined a previous military government.)

Talks with the Fund continued intermittently throughout spring 1984, as Nigeria's foreign exchange reserves dipped to below the $1 billion level. In early April, a consortium of foreign suppliers concerned about whether they might ever be repaid decided to drop their insistence that Nigeria reach an agreement with the Fund and agreed to a rescheduling of its uninsured trade arrears, along the lines of a Nigerian proposal that provided for a two-and-a-half-year grace period and an interest rate of 1 percent above LIBOR. About $2.5 billion of debts were settled with this agreement.

Talks with the Fund resumed in May 1984, but fueled by fears of inflation, public opposition to a devaluation began to grow. As the dollar appreciated in its relationship to other major currencies throughout the spring, the naira-dollar relationship remained basically unchanged. Thus, the naira was being revalued upward in relationship to the currencies of its major European trading partners. In June, another Nigerian delegation flew to Washington to explain the country's adjustment package. However, the talks were soon broken off over Nigeria's refusal to agree to a one-time devaluation of 30 percent to 35 percent, a reduction of its petroleum subsidies, and a further relaxation of its curbs on imports. In July, the Fund declared that Nigeria's latest proposals for stabilization and adjustment were insufficient for it to qualify for a loan under the Fund's extended fund facility. The Nigerians had hoped that their austerity program and policy changes would serve as an alternative to a major devaluation, but the Fund rejected their position.

It was at this time that the Buhari government devised a strategy for stabilization without the Fund. Several elements of its approach had been introduced under the guise of austerity shortly after it came to power (e.g., restricting both imports and demand; placing tight controls on government spending; and increasing the domestic sources of government finance). The Buhari government had also devised a number of schemes to increase foreign exchange earnings, beginning with appeals to OPEC for an increase in its production quota and continuing with experiments in countertrading, oil price cuts, and deliberate overproduction. Yet austerity and increased foreign exchange earnings alone were not enough to cover the interest payments Nigeria had to maintain on its $20 billion debt. After the talks with the IMF broke down in July, Nigeria tried to bypass the Fund and negotiate directly with its principal creditors.

Buoyed by its recent success in refinancing some of its short-term debt into longer-term maturities, the Buhari government offered to convert its official debt denominated in local currency into promissory notes along the lines agreed to in its April 1984 settlement with uninsured creditors. It bypassed the Paris Club and gave OECD trading agencies until the end of September to reply to the proposal. Britain's ECGD assumed a key role for the creditors and advised its policyholders to insist on an agreement with the IMF and reject the Nigerian offer. However, there was a rush of creditors (owed a total of $2.4 billion) anxious to accept the offer, and Nigeria was more than willing to test the authority of the official agencies (like Britain's ECGD) that were attempting to control the negotiations. The conversion of local currency principal proved to be more complicated than originally anticipated, though, and the creditors represented at the Paris Club played down the prospects of an agreement without prior Fund approval.

The OECD agencies eventually reasserted their authority to negotiate for officially insured creditors, and in October, the Paris Club formally rejected Nigeria's proposal. It claimed that 1 percent over LIBOR was inadequate and insisted that any settlement had to await an agreement with the Fund. Nigeria tried to leave the door open for a Paris Club settlement without a Fund agreement and proposed to pay holders of insured debts around $220 million in interest due on obligations from 1983 and 1984. For the moment, however, its attempt to bypass the Fund and the Paris Club had failed.

Informal talks with the IMF resumed briefly at the annual IMF-World Bank meetings in September 1984, but little progress was made. After the Paris Club rejection in October, the U.S. government stepped up pressure on Nigeria to settle with the Fund, and there were reports of disagreement within the Buhari administration about how to proceed. In November, the IMF staff hinted that it might relax its demands on petroleum subsidies and trade liberalization, if Nigeria agreed to a major devaluation. However, the talks bogged down in December over the nature of the devaluation necessary for an agreement.

In January 1985, General Buhari set his priorities for the coming year in his annual budget speech. He stressed the need for continued austerity and a nationwide freeze on wages. He indicated that 44 percent of the anticipated foreign exchange earnings of the country were going to be set aside for debt servicing during 1985, giving the country one of the highest debt service ratios in the world. An IMF team arrived in Lagos for routine discussions later in January and argued for an immediate devaluation of at least 25 percent, followed by a further downward float of another 25 percent. However, in an interview after the negotiations in February, Buhari once again rejected such a large devaluation and contended that the devaluation of the naira "is the most sensitive issue as far as we are concerned."[8] He also rejected any reduction in the level of subsidies on domestic fuel.

After only a year in office, Buhari had imposed a severe deflationary stabilization program on the country, without receiving any of the benefits of IMF financial assistance. Public expenditures had been reduced (with severe implications for employment and local business), and strict import licensing had been utilized to cut import levels back to their lowest levels (in current terms) in ten years. At the same time, oil production levels had recovered; the country's negative trade balance had been reversed; foreign exchange reserves were slowly being built up; and new external borrowing had virtually ceased (Tables 7.1 and 7.2).

Many difficult policy reforms had also been initiated: reducing the state's role in production, increasing interest rates, and initiating a reform in the tax structure. As a result of these policy reforms and the deflationary measures associated with them, thousands of civil servants were laid off; urban unemployment skyrocketed; new taxes were introduced; industrial-sector activity was drastically curtailed; and the cost of many social services was passed on to consumers for the first time. Throughout the period, Nigeria continued to pay interest on the portion of its debts that had been rescheduled. In 1984 alone, it paid out $3.5 billion in debt servicing, or 33.6 percent of its total export earnings for the year (Table 7.3). In February 1985, Buhari publicly declared his opposition to a 50 percent to 60 percent devaluation of the naira, and the talks with the IMF were effectively stalled. On August 27, his government was overthrown by a military coup.

ROUND THREE: FROM STABILIZATION TO ADJUSTMENT (AUGUST 1985–DECEMBER 1986)

When Major General Ibrahim Babangida assumed power in August 1985, he inherited a stabilized but drastically deflated economy. The external economic conditions confronting the new military government were the worst any regime had faced since independence. Less than four months after Babangida took over, the international price for oil fell precipitously (Table 7.6). Nigeria's oil income was cut nearly in half, as the spot price for Nigerian Bonny Light crude petroleum dropped from $27.88 per barrel in August 1985 to a low of $9.94 in July 1986. The country's debt service ratio climbed to nearly 40 percent. The foreign exchange reserves that had been built up under Buhari (Table 7.2) were sufficient to cover import needs, but there was nothing left to draw down. The country had already gone through two years of austerity and economic stagnation, and with the drop in oil income, the prospects for the short and medium terms were grim.

Like the Buhari government that preceded it, the new regime initially established its legitimacy by deliberately correcting the most evident flaws of its predecessor. The new government repealed the controversial Decree 4, released those detained without being charged or tried, and announced plans for a restructuring of the powerful national security organization. The new leadership was creative, charismatic, and far less insulated and remote than its precursor. Although northerners continued to dominate the military regime, the Babangida government was not controlled by the same group from the far north that had played such a prominent role in the Buhari government. Officers from the middle north occupied many of the key military positions in the new regime and were generally much more comfortable than their predecessors in dealing with southern political and economic elites.

Babangida worked populist themes into his early addresses to the nation and demonstrated his originality and independence by being the first of Nigeria's six military leaders to assume the title of president.[9] He also made a number of bold and highly visible appointments to his cabinet, selecting an unusually large number of professionals who collectively expressed a broad range of views and perspectives (from the populist Olikoye Ransome-Kuti in Health and the outspoken nationalist Akinyemi in Foreign Affairs to the economic conservative Kalu Idikau Kalu in Finance). The appointment of Kalu was significant because he had formerly been an employee of the World Bank and was widely known as a supporter of accommodation with the IMF.

In his first public statement after the coup, Babangida declared his intention to "break the deadlock" and reopen the stalemated talks with the Fund. For the first time, high-ranking government officials appeared willing to support some of the economic arguments of the Fund. Brigadier Sani Sami stated that he thought it was in Nigeria's best interests to obtain an IMF loan quickly. He urged the Nigerian Economic Society to discuss the issues and consider the possibility of a dual exchange rate. The head of Nigeria's largest bank, First Bank of Nigeria, also went on record urging a faster depreciation of the naira. Within a few weeks, two committees were set up to look into the major financial issues facing the country. One focused on the IMF terms, whereas the other concentrated on the costs and benefits of countertrade. It was at this time that the government decided to stimulate informed discussion on the merits of an agreement with the Fund and launched its celebrated national public debate on the issue.

At the outset, it appeared that the government was already predisposed toward some kind of agreement with the Fund and that the public debate was simply a way of generating and possibly mobilizing popular support for the tough conditions that would follow.[10] Some observers outside Nigeria (including the IMF) were concerned about the wisdom of opening public discussions on the technical issues of international finance and worried that the new government might find itself locked into an inflexible position on the issue.

The debate itself consisted of a flurry of speeches, individual pronouncements, street demonstrations, public affairs discussions, and special reports and interviews in newspapers, radio, and television. It provided a unique glimpse into the composition of the coalitions of supporters and opponents of agreement with the IMF. At the start of the debate, the IMF's demands were published, along with the details of past negotiations. The Fund was still holding out for (1) a substantial devaluation; (2) antiinflationary measures (such as a reduction in aggregate public spending; a tightening of the money supply, a mechanism for increasing the efficiency of parastatals and government investments; and the end of nonstatutory financial transfers to state governments); and (3) the restoration of market mechanisms (e.g., trade liberalization, the removal of petroleum subsidies, cuts in subsidies and loans to parastatals, an increase in interest rates and cuts in credit allocations, and a raising of agricultural producer prices). Privatization was not played up as an issue at this point in the negotiations, but it was evident that the Fund wanted some movement in this direction, along with a review of industrial incentives, an export drive, general improvements in the efficiency of revenue collection, and stricter control and management of Nigeria's external debt.

It did not take long for a broad-based opposition to the Fund's program to emerge. Organized labor declared the program (and the Babangida government) "antiworker" and contended that the rich would benefit at the expense of the poor. Labor was concerned about the extent of retrenchment already suffered and likely to continue with the IMF program. The Nigerian Labour Congress (NLC) was especially opposed to privatization and called for greater indigenously based industrialization. Labor was joined by a number of urban-based professionals who expressed concern about the disruptive implications of a major devaluation. Many professionals had already been badly hit by nearly two years of economic stagnation under the Buhari regime and were concerned about the implications of extended austerity under the Fund.

Students, academics, and a number of journalists also joined in the coalition opposed to agreement with the Fund. Many expressed concerns that an authoritarian regime would be required to implement the program, and several argued that the debate itself was a thinly disguised corporatist effort to reconstruct the principal factions of the dominant classes, in disarray since the overt repression of the Buhari government.[11] A few beneficiaries of the import licensing scheme spoke out against trade liberalization, as did a number of prominent northerners who were especially concerned that greater reliance on market mechanisms would disrupt the fragile regional balance in the country.[12] By October, there were reports of disputes within the ruling military council on the wisdom of reaching an agreement with the Fund.

Support for an agreement with the Fund came primarily from prominent indigenous entrepreneurs in the Lagos area, a number of professional economists, the Lagos Chamber of Commerce, and major industrialists (some of whom spoke through the Manufacturer's Association of Nigeria, even though the association held reservations and did not come out strongly for economic reforms until early 1986). The World Bank also began to play a larger role in the process at this point. The Bank had been involved in the background of the two and a half years of discussion with the IMF every IMF mission to Lagos used the Bank's offices and relied on its files of economic data and information about Nigerian officials and policies. However, the Bank began to play a much more visibly active role during the public debate. The resident World Bank representative in Nigeria was a Pakistani by the name of Ishrat Husain. Husain attended every seminar on the Nigerian economy and took every opportunity to make his (and the Bank's) views known. He was a frequent and occasionally outspoken participant during the public debate on the IMF, and he regularly courted and held receptions for the leading economic elite in the country. According to one of his staff members in the Lagos office, "eventually many of his arguments were espoused by [that elite]."[13]

Nevertheless, there were a few reservations about an IMF agreement within the Nigerian business community, especially among the industrialists. Much as they wanted to see a settlement of the debt issue and a resumption of normal trade for their import-intensive facilities, they were concerned that too much trade liberalization would make their investments unviable. Hence, they favored agreement with the Fund, on the condition that it be accompanied by a major tariff reform.

However eloquent or well argued their case, supporters of an agreement were drowned out by the majority opposed to the Fund. Public opinion grew more and more hostile throughout the fall, and once again, the same three issues that had bedeviled previous attempts to reach an agreement emerged as major stumbling blocks: devaluation, trade liberalization, and an end to petroleum subsidies. But the public debate also revealed a new issue. It became apparent that there was a growing reticence on the part of the public about any further government borrowing from *any* source. That is, more than opposition to borrowing from the IMF, there was widespread opposition to the idea of additional government borrowing in general. After years of seeing one corrupt government after another, Nigerians had become fed up and were increasingly suspicious of the ability of its leaders to manage the economy properly. Many argued that if more loans were obtained, the money would disappear just as quickly as it had in the past.

In the wake of growing public discontent, major strikes planned by both the NLC and students' organizations, and further disputes within the ruling military council, Nigeria broke off talks with the IMF on December 13, 1985. If Babangida had ever intended to use the public debate to build a coalition on behalf of an agreement with the Fund, his strategy had clearly failed.

However, a few weeks later, in his annual budget speech delivered on December 31, 1985, President Babangida combined nationalist assertiveness with an acceptance of most of the IMF's original terms—including two of the three issues that had prevented agreement in the past. The nationalist assertiveness was contained in Babangida's call for a reduction in external dependence, for the achievement of food self-sufficiency, for a shift in Nigerian attitudes and tastes, and for a 30 percent cap on debt servicing for the year. But the most significant parts of the speech laid out the plans for major structural adjustments of the economy. According to one IMF official, "The IMF read the budget speech with surprise. The nature of the language was good. We had no idea of what it would mean in policy terms."[14]

Babangida had apparently accepted the public verdict on the IMF but argued that since Nigerians were not willing to borrow additional resources from the Fund, they would have to be prepared to accept tough new economic measures at home. Accordingly, he announced plans for the adoption of a "realistic exchange rate" (one that would allow the naira to find its own level), a substantial (80 percent) reduction of petroleum subsidies, and a large-scale privatization program (an idea traditionally promoted more within the World Bank than the IMF). Explicit reference to trade liberalization was omitted for the time being, but all of the other major components of the Fund's original terms found their way into the speech.

Despite Babangida's rejection of the prevailing public sentiment on the details of the IMF's terms, initial reactions to his speech were generally favorable within Nigeria. The nationalist rhetoric was well received by the Nigerian public. Babangida's references to the most controversial of the Fund's conditions (devaluation and privatization) were vague, especially since the effective consequence of creating a two-tier foreign exchange regime (i.e., a major devaluation) was not evident to the vast majority. Even more significant, he concluded his budget speech with a surprise announcement of his plan to return the country to civilian rule. Two weeks after he delivered his speech, Babangida announced the formation of a seventeen-member Political Bureau with the mandate to design a more viable political and economic structure for the country and lay the groundwork for a return to civilian rule. The Political Bureau was also asked to analyze the contributions made in the national debate on the IMF.

Reaction abroad was guarded. For its part, the IMF expressed doubts about the ability of the Nigerian government (however well intentioned) to implement its austerity program. On an official visit to London in early January, the Nigerian foreign minister received a cool reception, allegedly because of Nigeria's new limit on debt servicing. Nevertheless, there were rumors of an endorsement of Nigeria's new economic recovery program from some significant parties abroad, most notably within the UK's ECGD.

Throughout the first half of 1986, work went forward on the development of the two-tier foreign exchange market mechanism and other details of the new economic recovery program. In April, a ninety-day moratorium on repayments of medium- and long-term commercial bank debt was agreed to in London. Nigeria's principal commercial bank creditors agreed to a moratorium on approximately $7.5 billion of its debts. Nigeria also went to the Paris Club in April but was unable to secure a comparable moratorium on outstanding debt without some kind of settlement with the Fund. Later that month, Ernest Stern, a World Bank senior vice president, visited Nigeria and declared its program essentially "sound." Stern's endorsement was significant because he was one of the most powerful individuals within the Bank at the time and widely considered the Bank's "hands-on man" in charge of operations.

In June 1986, President Babangida announced a new two-year structural adjustment program (SAP) that spelled out the details of the plan first introduced in general terms in his budget speech the previous December. The details of the second-tier foreign exchange market (popularly known as SFEM) that served as the cornerstone for the program had been the subject of extensive negotiations among the Bank, the Fund, and the Nigerian government for some time. The Nigerians had originally preferred a small market, secondary to the official market that would continue to handle all government transactions. The World Bank wanted a SFEM of at least $2 billion (large enough to absorb funds that would otherwise go to the black market). The IMF held out for a market that would be large enough to handle all international transactions (including government imports) and one that could absorb the entire official market within a period of six months. The details of the SFEM announced by Babangida were closest to the proposal put forward by the World Bank, and it was increasingly apparent that the Bank was playing a major role in the design of Nigeria's adjustment program. All transactions were to be handled by the SFEM, with the exception of government debt service payments and contributions to international organizations and institutions. The SFEM was to commence on October 1 and coexist with the official market for a period of twelve to fifteen months before being completely absorbed.

The two-tier foreign exchange market was accompanied by extensive trade liberalization and a major privatization program. Nigeria's system of bureaucratic controls was to be dismantled, along with its controversial import licensing scheme. Six of its major agricultural commodity boards were abolished, and a review of the parastatal sector was initiated. The IMF, however, remained doubtful about the ability of Nigeria to implement its program; declared its dislike of the SFEM program; and continued to hold out for a major devaluation of the naira. The Fund was increasingly "positive" toward Nigeria, but a formal agreement (one that could have provided $1.5 billion from the IMF and up to $1 billion from the Bank) remained elusive. After the announcement of the SAP, however, the World Bank offered to provide $400 million in structural adjustment loans to Nigeria. The commercial bank moratorium originally announced in April 1986 was extended for an additional three months in June.

A week after the announcement of the SAP, the government advanced the SFEM start-up date to August 1, and the central bank issued operational guidelines that significantly relaxed the existing exchange control regulations. A number of interest groups and businesses pressured the central bank to allow them to continue operating at the official exchange rate, but the central bank agreed only to exempt transactions already in process. In effect, the major consequence of this action was to postpone for three months the full impact of the introduction of the SFEM.

In early September, shortly before the first SFEM auction, the World Bank announced agreement on a $450 million trade promotion and export development loan (largely to help start and finance the SFEM) and also promised to increase its project lending to Nigeria to nearly $1 billion a year. The London Club agreed to yet another ninety-day extension of Nigeria's debt service moratorium but was unable to reach a broader agreement because of cross-conditionalities on Nigeria's accumulated debt. Accordingly, on September 19, Nigeria requested IMF endorsement of its SAP in the form of a standard standby agreement that would allow Nigeria to borrow, in principle, funds totaling $785 million for an initial period ending in December 1987.

When the first second-tier foreign exchange auction was held on September 26, 1986, the naira fell 68.6 percent to a level of 4.62 naira to the dollar (Table 7.5). At the second auction a week later, the naira dropped another 9.2 percent and reached the level of 5.08 to the dollar. After some erratic fluctuations throughout the fall (and a fair degree of central bank intervention), the rate stabilized at about 3.5 naira to the dollar, or an effective devaluation of about 57 percent.

In the middle of November 1986, after a month and a half of experience with SFEM, the IMF declared Nigeria eligible for a $540 million standby loan. The Nigerian government refused the funds, but the long-standing deadlock over the rescheduling of Nigeria's $20 to $22 billion of external debts was finally broken. Within weeks of the November agreement with the IMF, the London Club provisionally accepted a rescheduling plan, and the Paris Club followed with an agreement in the middle of December. All that remained was the formidable task of keeping the agreements on track.

TABLE 7.1   Nigeria's Trade Balance (in millions of US dollars)

	Exports (fob)	Imports (fob)	Trade Balance
1976	10,122	7,478	+2,644
1977	12,431	9,723	+2,708
1978	10,508	11,685	-1,177
1979	16,774	12,709	+4,035
1980	25,741	14,636	+11,105
1981	17,961	18,872	-911
1982	12,088	14,801	-2,713
1983	10,309	11,393	-1,084
1984	11,827	8,844	+2,983
1985	13,369	7,634	+5,735
1986	6,599	4,063	+2,536

Source: IMF, *International Financial Statistics* (Washington, D.C.: International Monetary Fund, various years).

TABLE 7.2   Foreign Exchange Reserves (in millions of US dollars)

	Total Reserves (minus gold)	Change in Reserves	External Borrowing (net flows)
1976	5,180	-406	-244.2
1977	4,232	-948	+26.3
1978	1,887	-2,345	+1,252.6
1979	5,548	+3,661	+1,523.4
1980	10,235	+4,687	+1,594.2
1981	3,895	-6,340	+2,176.6
1982	1,613	-2,282	+3,006.0
1983	990	-623	+3,943.2
1984	1,462	+472	-237.0
1985	1,667	+205	-1,202.0
1986	1,081	-586	+105.0

Sources: For information on foreign reserves, the IMF, *International Financial Statistics* (Washington, D.C.: International Monetary Fund, various years). For information on external borrowing, the World Bank, *World Debt Tables* (Washington, D.C.: World Bank, 1980, 1985-1986, 1989-1990).

TABLE 7.3   Total Debt Service and Debt Service Ratios

	Long-Term Debt Service (millions of US $)	Debt Service Ratio (total debt service as % of exports)
1976	374.4	3.4
1977	106.6	0.8
1978	128.2	1.2
1979	264.4	1.5
1980	812.9	2.0
1981	1,337.0	4.7
1982	1,762.0	11.3
1983	2,327.7	18.7
1984	3,462.8	33.6
1985	4,039.0	38.7
1986	1,740.0	29.6

Source: The World Bank, *World Debt Tables* (Washington, D.C.: World Bank, various years).

TABLE 7.4 Nigerian Crude Petroleum Production, Exports, and Earnings

	Production 1980=100	Percent Change	Export Price 1980=100	Export Volume		Export Earnings[b]
				Naira[a]	1980=100	
1976	100.4	—	36.3	6,196	105	9.5
1977	101.4	+1.0	40.9	7,073	109	10.5
1978	92.4	-8.8	39.5	5,671	98	8.5
1979	111.6	+20.7	58.5	9,706	117	16.0
1980	100.0	-10.4	100.0	13,632	100	25.0
1981	69.7	-30.3	108.4	10,681	64	17.5
1982	62.2	-10.7	99.4	8,003	53	11.5
1983	59.7	-4.0	84.6	7,201	49	9.8
1984	67.0	+12.2	83.3	8,841	57	11.0
1985	71.4	+6.5	—	10,891	71	12.0
1986	70.8	-0.6	—	8,369	66	6.5

[a] in millions of Naira.
[b] in billions of US dollars.
Source: All data (except estimates of oil export earnings) from the IMF's *International Financial Statistics* (Washington, D.C.: International Monetary Fund, various years). Oil export earnings, in billions of U.S. dollars, estimated by the *Financial Times* of London, March 2, 1987.

TABLE 7.5 Exchange Rate

	% Variation	US $ per Naira (market rate)
1976	-1.8	1.5959
1977	-2.7	1.5514
1978	+1.5	1.5745
1979	+5.4	1.6591
1980	+10.3	1.8297
1981	-10.6	1.6292
1982	-8.8	1.4854
1983	-6.9	1.3823
1984	-5.3	1.3085
1985	-14.4	1.1206
1986	-73.0	0.3021
January - March		.9997
April - June		.9465
July - September		.7445
October - December		.3021

Source: The IMF, *International Financial Statistics* (Washington, D.C.: International Monetary Fund, various years).

TABLE 7.6   OPEC Spot Crude Oil Prices: Nigerian Bonny Light (US $ per barrel)

Months	1983	1984	1985	1986
January	32.19	29.73	27.53	23.55
February	30.75	30.25	28.55	17.88
March	29.13	30.23	28.44	14.63
April	29.81	30.20	29.28	12.83
May	29.94	30.06	27.02	14.30
June	30.31	29.57	26.53	12.67
July	31.00	28.67	27.21	9.94
August	31.35	28.47	27.88	13.00
September	30.83	28.63	28.55	14.75
October	30.03	28.63	29.07	14.63
November	29.50	28.04	30.33	14.92
December	29.18	27.84	27.78	16.19

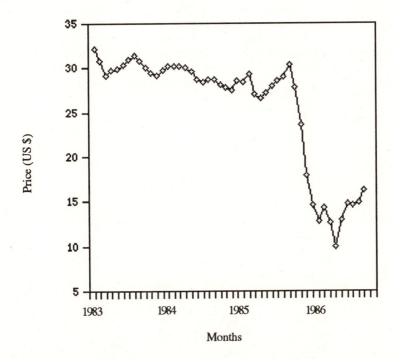

FIGURE 7.1   OPEC Spot Crude Oil Prices: Nigerian Bonny Light (US $ per barrel)
Source: OPEC Bulletin, October 1983 through March 1987.

NOTES

1. For more details, see Larry Diamond, "Nigeria in Search of Democracy," *Foreign Affairs* 62, no. 4 (Spring 1984).

2. Interview with IMF official in Washington, D.C., October 1987.

3. Ibid.

4. For more information, see Larry Diamond, "Nigeria Between Dictatorship and Democracy," *Current History* 86, no. 520 (May 1987).

5. This is a principal argument made by Yusuf Bangura in his article, "Structural Adjustment and the Political Question." *Review of African Political Economy* 37 (December 1986).

6. Interview with IMF official, Washington, D.C., October 1987.

7. Quoted in *West Africa* (February 27, 1984).

8. Quoted in the *Financial Times*'s annual survey on Nigeria (February 1985).

9. Diamond, "Nigeria Between Dictatorship and Democracy."

10. Bangura, "Structural Adjustment."

11. Ibid.

12. The north is the least-developed region of the country and has long feared and opposed southern economic penetration. Historically, northern technocrats and intellecturals have favored a strong state role in the economy to counteract the competitive superiority of the southern bourgeoisie. For an elaboration of this argument with regard to indigenization, see Thomas Biersteker, *Multinationals, the State, and Control of the Nigerian Economy,* (Princeton, N.J.: Princeton University Press, 1987), pp. 160-161.

13. Interview with former World Bank staff member, Lagos, Nigeria, July 1987.

14. Interview with IMF officials, Washington, D.C., October 1987.

8

■ ═══════════════════════════════════════ ■

The Philippines, 1983–1986:
Negotiating Under Uncertainty

Penelope A. Walker

In October 1983, the Philippines became the first Asian country to be caught up in the expanding debt crisis of the 1980s. Although political factors influenced the development of debt crises in other countries, nowhere were they more immediate than in the Philippines. Only in the Philippines did a single political event precipitate a debt crisis. The August 1983 assassination of Benigno Aquino, the most formidable political opponent of President Ferdinand Marcos, sparked the transformation of underlying resentment for Marcos's government into the first mass dissent since 1972. The assassination and its aftermath raised doubts about future Philippine political stability, lowered confidence in the economy, and thus contributed to a massive outflow of capital.

The flight of an estimated $1 billion undermined the Philippine economy. The third-quarter balance-of-payments deficit in 1983 rose unexpectedly to $800 million (on its way to an annual total of $2.5 billion, $1.5 billion over the 1982 level), and foreign exchange reserves declined to the equivalent of less than one month of imports ($430 million), despite the second devaluation of the peso during the year (the total devaluation amounted to 35 percent). Lenders refused to roll over many short-term government credits, reduced loan terms, and even closed trade credit lines. The IMF abandoned the existing standby agreement with the

The original version of this case was written by Penelope A. Walker for The Pew Diplomatic Initiative at the University of Southern California. This is a substantially edited and revised version of the case, prepared especially for this volume.

Philippines and called for expanded economic austerity. With its external accounts in disarray, the Philippine government in October announced its inability to service its debt and declared a ninety-day moratorium (October 17–January 16).

The Philippine crisis was more than economic, however; it extended into the political realm as well. The Marcos regime faced highly vocal and disruptive challenges to its legitimacy from both the articulate urban middle classes and the Catholic church. The Philippine debt-rescheduling negotiations of the next few years would thus occur in a politicized domestic arena, which both prolonged the Philippines' negotiations with its many creditors, the IMF, and the United States and complicated stabilization and structural adjustment of the Philippine economy. Continued political uncertainty was the hallmark of debt negotiations, not only at the end of the Marcos presidency but also during the early months of the subsequent government of Corazon Aquino.

THE MARCOS PERIOD

In order to understand the evolution of the debt negotiations and the behavior of the Marcos government and others in the Philippines, we need to look at the debt crisis in historical terms, both economic and political.

The Economic Record

The economic performance of the Philippines improved in the 1970s as compared to the 1960s. Led by expanding investment (up an average 11 percent per year compared to 8 percent in the 1960s), the national growth rate averaged above 6 percent (versus 5 percent in the 1960s). This improvement, coupled with the order established under martial law, engendered broad support for Marcos during most of the 1970s. However, increased foreign borrowing financed much of the apparent 1970s economic advances. As a result, foreign debt rose from $2 billion in 1970 to $3.8 billion in 1975, $12.7 billion in 1980, and $25 billion in 1983. At the same time, the rise in oil prices in 1973, followed by the collapse of commodity prices in 1976–1977 and the continuing slow pace of industrialization gradually weakened the country's ability to repay. This debt combined with the Philippines' poorer performance compared to its neighbors led to doubts about Marcos's economic management when the 1979 rise in oil prices tipped the debt-laden economy into a sustained downturn.[1] Oil price increases and rising real interest rates on commercial loans further contributed to the total Philippine debt in the late 1970s, and they took their toll on the external accounts.[2]

The IMF authorized seventeen standby agreements with the Philippines between 1961 and 1983 to help alleviate recurring balance-of-payments problems and restore external equilibrium. The IMF has retained an adviser in residence to the central bank director since the early 1970s, and IMF teams visited the

Philippines annually during the 1970s. By 1980, the worsening economic situation induced more frequent visits to monitor progress on current agreements and to negotiate new ones. Each of these IMF agreements was negotiated in secret, which evoked criticism from those who did not participate but were affected by the outcomes. During the negotiations analyzed in this case, the IMF was accused of helping support Marcos and was often blamed for the Philippines' economic problems. Similar charges were leveled against the World Bank for its lending practices.[3]

The Political Record

The nature of the Marcos government was apparent in his governing practices. President Marcos imposed martial law in 1972 with the support of most Filipinos. He suppressed opposition through incarceration, media censorship, and executive decrees; weakened the legislative and judicial branches of government; established a highly centralized governing structure; and increased state intervention in the economy (especially in state regulation, the promotion of business, and expanded public investments). Even after elections in 1978 and the lifting of martial law in 1981, Marcos continued to restrain the opposition. He rigged the elections and still ruled by decree.

Marcos also used his martial law powers and his access to state resources to grant political powers to chosen individuals, including those within his political party, the Kilusan Bagong Lipunan (KBL, or New Society Movement), and to give economic preference to his friends (generally referred to as cronies).[4] He used bureaucratic intervention to help in day-to-day business operations, gave preferences in the awarding of public contracts, and used the expanded state banking sector (particularly the development banks) to channel credit to cronies regardless of their business efficiency. One of Marcos's most notorious actions, particularly during the debt negotiations, was the creation of near monopolies for his friends. Industries were restructured to ensure these individuals controlled key productive and financial institutions, enjoyed access to cheap credit from government banks, and were free from audit or effective accountability.

Spurred by the availability of financial resources from military aid and expanded access to commercial bank loans,[5] this favoritism (or "cronyism") affected governmental and bureaucratic authority at all levels. It shifted the key to business success from competitive performance and ability to political ties and provided a disincentive to reinvestment and expansion among healthy firms because of fears of predatory takeover by a crony. Increasingly, Marcos's political practices interfered with the Philippine economy by diverting limited and expensive resources, by reducing investment efficiency, and by contracting an unserviceable debt. These consequences made Marcos's practices (particularly the creation of crony monopolies) highly contentious. They contributed to growing resentment domestically and became an issue in the multilateral debt negotiations.

The Eroding Base of the Marcos Government

Through graft, apparent economic growth, and martial law, Marcos created a powerful political base that appeared unshakable throughout the 1970s. By the decade's end, however, events had overtaken him. A confluence of economic deterioration, insurgency, and illness (by early 1983, many believed Marcos to be terminally ill)[6] limited Marcos's room to maneuver and constrained his ability to maintain power.

Several traditional bases of Marcos support began to show signs of strain. In the rural areas, both rich and poor became disillusioned as the crony monopolies forced firms into bankruptcy and the military failed to curb a Maoist insurgency led by the New People's Army (NPA). Marcos's political party, the KBL, began to splinter as doubts about Marcos's health grew and succession became an issue. The party no longer automatically granted Marcos his requests, attempted to curb his powers after martial law was lifted, and called for the repeal of his decree powers after the May 1984 elections.[7]

Signs of dissension also appeared by 1983 in Marcos's most important source of support, the military. Under Marcos, the military doubled in size and took more than 20 percent of the national budget and the greatest share of U.S. aid. Its officers enjoyed elite status. Nevertheless, the military was unable to curb either the NPA insurgency or an insurrection by Muslim separatists in the south, partly because of deteriorating morale. Reductions in military aid left troops with poor and inadequate equipment, the army in the field became dispirited and unruly, and many recruits and officers blamed these problems directly on the Marcos government. This unaddressed disillusionment and frustration weakened military support for Marcos and ultimately led to military involvement in his 1986 overthrow.

Thus, throughout the 1983-1985 period, Marcos maintained a functioning but weakening political base. The widening splits among his supporters complicated Marcos's choices, and his ability to heal the breaches was severely constrained by the economic requirements of the prolonged debt negotiations.

Opposition Challenges

By the early 1980s, the long-suppressed opposition forces, which included the NPA, the Catholic church, the vestiges of pre–martial law political parties, the business community, and the urban middle class, became emboldened by Marcos's failures and excesses. He could no longer manage a growing economy, and economic deterioration was visible everywhere: in the budget and balance-of-payments deficits, the huge debt, bankrupted crony firms, capital flight, and financial crises. He was losing against the NPA, could no longer ensure law and order, and his corruption was causing both embarrassment and moral outrage. Although Marcos's government was rapidly losing legitimacy, however, the divided opposition remained unable to oust him. Only the 1986 presidential candidacy of Corazon Aquino would unite these disparate groups.

The business community and the urban middle class, once supporters of Marcos, became particularly vocal in their opposition as the economy weakened and financial scandals broke.[8] After Aquino's October 1983 assassination and the ensuing mass dissent, anti-Marcos businesspeople aligned with middle-class professionals to galvanize public support. Weekly demonstrations by middle-class and wealthy Filipinos called for the overthrow of Marcos, which, after an initial harsh repression and subsequent U.S. reaction, were allowed to continue for over two years. In addition, in November 1983, the annual Philippine Business Conference sent Marcos a list of demands that included a clear designation of presidential succession, an independent judiciary, and restoration of civil liberties. Marcos, in turn, publicly chastised business for its failings, but the opposition's effectiveness was growing, as demonstrated by the 1984 elections.

Despite Marcos's confident predictions and the decisions of several opposition parties to boycott the elections, the opposition won 61 of 184 seats in the national assembly. Diverging from his behavior in previous elections, Marcos had curbed fraud in order to foster an image abroad of flourishing democracy in the Philippines. However, Marcos returned to politics as usual following the elections, and in spite of its electoral advances, the opposition remained too weak and fractured to mount substantial resistance. Nevertheless, protest rallies, business criticism, and a freed press continued to attack Marcos, and as he fought to defend his position, the opposition grew gradually more optimistic.

Ultimately, the most potent curb on Marcos during this period was foreign criticism. The United States, especially the U.S. Congress, became more critical of Marcos as dissent continued and fears mounted that the Communist insurgency might achieve victory. As Jaime Ongpin, one of the most prominent anti-Marcos businessmen, put it: "The involvement of the U.S. government and the foreign banks is of special significance because for the first time in his 18-year reign, Mr. Marcos is confronted with a political crisis in which he cannot ignore, much less manipulate or coerce, the most crucial participants."[9] The IMF also became a more formidable critic. IMF policy reforms cut to the core of Marcos's governing style. These policy correctives did not, however, have the support of the opposition. Businesspeople spoke out against IMF austerity as the downturn worsened in 1984 and 1985. Yet criticism of the IMF was slight when compared to the level of anti-Marcos rhetoric. Marcos and the technocrats who negotiated debt agreements took most of the blame for the economic problems.

Although the growth of Philippine debt and the increased power and presence of the IMF occurred in tandem throughout the 1970s, it was not until 1982, when external financing became more expensive and difficult to obtain, that the IMF came to have a more central position in the economy. This more direct IMF intervention coincided with Marcos's struggle to retain power, and in the joint efforts of the two parties to resolve the debt problems, their interests frequently clashed. Marcos was determined to preserve his power, whereas the IMF was adamant that corrective measures be implemented despite the political cost to Marcos.

The Debt Crisis: 1983

In late 1982, the Philippines was still receiving loans, but their terms were less favorable and conditionality was very tough. In December 1982, the central bank negotiated a syndicated loan for 1983 of $300 million from fifteen banks, but the interest rate was very high (two points over LIBOR), terms were reduced to eight years, and no new money was included. The agreement was merely a rollover of existing loans and debt obligations. The Philippines would also have to roll over $8 billion of short-term debt in 1983. Commercial debt rescheduling, however, had become conditional upon signing an agreement with the IMF.

In February 1983, after nine months of negotiating, the IMF board approved a conditional one-year standby credit of $543 million. Disbursement was contingent on the country's reducing its balance-of-payments deficit (from the $1.4 billion 1982 level to $592 million), limiting the growth of the money supply, curbing government spending, abolishing import and foreign exchange controls, and working to end subsidies. Some in the IMF believed this conditionality to be long overdue, but many in the Philippines were outraged, especially when the IMF was compared to the generally more sympathetic World Bank.[10] The business sector protested. The KBL attacked the technocrats who negotiated the agreement for surrendering Filipino sovereignty, and the government refused to raise oil prices in line with Prime Minister Cesar Virata's promise to the IMF to end oil subsidies. The politicians blamed external creditors and the technocrats for the economic difficulties. Marcos imposed both a 3 percent ad valorem import tax (to reduce imports) and foreign exchange controls, despite his previous promises to the contrary.

In efforts to reduce the growth of the foreign debt and public deficit from 4 to 2.5 percent of gross national product (GNP), Marcos was more cooperative. In June, he cut major public-sector industrial projects in half. After an IMF visit in July, the peso was devalued by 7.5 percent, and oil prices were finally raised. To offset the impact of inflation on purchasing power (plus prepare for the 1984 elections), he increased the minimum wage by 11 percent. Nevertheless, by the end of June, foreign exchange reserves had fallen to $500 million (little more than coverage for one month of imports) with $2.4 billion in loan repayments coming due. The Philippine Monetary Board's attempts to use new import controls to remedy the external accounts' deterioration were futile. The loss of confidence following Aquino's assassination in August and the ensuing mass dissent destabilized the economy.

In response, the technocrats first tried to speed negotiations for new loans along the lines of previous agreements. Prime Minister Virata began discussions with IMF managing director de Larosiere for a 1984 standby agreement and, along with the central bank head, Jaime Laya, went to New York for talks with ten of the Philippines' leading creditors on October 10, 1983.[11] However, such attempts were too late. It is estimated that by August capital flight (which had been at a level of $2 million per day since July 1982) had reached a peak of $5 million per day. At the same time, renewals of $4.5 billion of short-term revolving credits had slowed to a trickle, and some deals concluded before the assassination were withdrawn.[12] Rescheduling appeared inevitable.

On the domestic financial front, there were waves of withdrawals following the Aquino assassination. These subsided when the central bank gave emergency loans but were renewed after a 21.5 percent devaluation of the peso and tightening of monetary policy on October 5. Tighter international credit and the rapid run-up of short-term debt meant debt servicing consumed half of Philippine export earnings, a clearly unsustainable drain. The aftermath of the Aquino assassinatio—the battered capital account, the domestic liquidity crisis, the tottering financial system, the rapid rise in prices, and the widespread shortages caused by hoarding and panic buying—delivered the coup de grace. The national loss of confidence in the Marcos government and fears for future political stability had brought financial crisis.

DEBT NEGOTIATIONS UNDER MARCOS

Stage 1: Deteriorating Relations; Little Progress (November 1983–May 1984)

The Philippines requested a ninety-day debt payment moratorium from its 350 creditors on October 17. The immediate objectives of the moratorium were to use the $600 million savings to prevent the balance-of-payments deficit from rising over $1.6 billion and to reconstitute reserves. The longer-term goal was to replace short-term, high-cost loans with longer-term loans, primarily from multilateral sources. The moratorium was to affect only principal payments, but reserves fell so low that interest payments were withheld as well. Trade credit payments were to be continued in the (unfulfilled) hope that they would be renewed. In any case, the creditors had little choice but to agree, if the Philippines were to avoid default—an event that none of the creditors, particularly the U.S. banks, wanted.[13] This moratorium was only the first step in what would be an excruciatingly long negotiation.[14]

Concurrently, Prime Minister Virata announced a package of supporting domestic economic programs. These included another 21.4 percent devaluation (bringing the total annual devaluation to 52.7 percent), an increase in bank reserve requirements (making the liquidity squeeze even worse), reduction in the availability of foreign exchange to commercial banks, and further measures to reduce government subsidies to business. Later, the government raised oil prices further and granted a general pay raise to workers that was below the anticipated 20 percent inflation rate. Then in December, in an attempt to attract new capital, Marcos liberalized foreign investment laws to allow 100 percent ownership in some sectors.

The Philippines began debt negotiations in early November with the IMF, the World Bank, and the Advisory Bank Committee for the Philippines, drawn from eleven creditor banks and led by Manufacturers Hanover. The needs of the Philippines were immediate and stark: a long-term rescheduling of 40 percent of its $24 billion foreign debt; $1.65 billion in new financing from the banks to relieve the serious financial squeeze and provide acutely needed import financing for 1984; another $1.65 billion from multilateral institutions and trading partners; and an additional $645.7 million seven-tranche standby from the IMF. Talks went well at first, and all sides expected agreement on a package by the end of the ninety-day moratorium (January 19, 1984). A letter of intent signed for the standby in mid-November was expected to receive IMF board approval by mid-January, and the U.S. Congress approved its contribution to the IMF, which unblocked funds.

By December, however, problems began to arise. First, there were coordination problems among the creditors. The banks refused to finalize terms for resumption of trade credits or rescheduling until the IMF credit approval was finalized. The IMF wanted commitment from the banks to precede its own commitment and, in any case, would do nothing before it analyzed economic performance data from the Philippines.[15] Finally, the Paris Club would not begin negotiations for another $1.09 billion loan until agreement was reached with the IMF and the banks. But in December all parties agreed that another ninety-day moratorium would be necessary and that the IMF would lead negotiations on two outstanding issues: a possible peso devaluation and the restructuring of trade credits.

At this point in the negotiations, Virata admitted overstating the size of Philippine reserves in 1983,[16] and the resulting loss of IMF confidence led to new demands. The November letter of intent would have to be completely rewritten after monetary statistics[17] and trade estimates had been revised by the IMF. The IMF team then uncovered another major discrepancy—a huge surge in money supply of 20 percent in October-November, well in excess of the agreed target of 3 percent for the period between September 1983 and January 1984. The IMF now wanted a compensatory devaluation of the peso. Meanwhile, in January, central bank head Laya was replaced by Jose Fernandez (former head of the Far East Bank and Trust Company).

In the background, domestic politics seethed. Marcos refused to make provisions for his succession, angering both the public and his own party. His agreement with the World Bank to end the sugar monopoly in February mollified some critics, but many Filipinos remained skeptical, and his cronies became less supportive (e.g., they failed to repatriate capital at Marcos's request). As economic conditions (production, poverty level) worsened, more businesspeople were openly critical of Marcos's seemingly pointless mortgaging of the economy. They were especially critical of his government's failure to anticipate and correct the situation that had ended in the liquidity crisis and runaway inflation (of 50 percent) now paralyzing the economy.

As a prelude to another round of talks with the IMF, Marcos quite blatantly provoked another surge in money supply to obtain 1984 election funding. Such shenanigans not only reduced the IMF's trust but also complicated Virata's IMF-imposed tasks of rescheduling internal debt and tightening monetary policy. A vicious cycle had developed. Virata would agree to reduce the government deficit and money supply growth, and Marcos would jettison any chances of success in order to maintain political power. Each time Virata went back to the IMF, its demands were more stringent because of past failures to meet agreed targets.

In mid-March, further negotiations and greater austerity were postponed until after the May elections. Instead, the government relied on the foreign exchange and import controls opposed by the IMF to prevent a worsening of the crisis. In response to the liquidity crisis, Citibank and Bank of America froze all assets deposited in their Filipino branches, although they backed down when other banks complained. The banks were not as displeased as they were wary of negotiating during the rising political turmoil and continuing refusal by Marcos to make significant policy modifications and restore democracy. Another ninety-day moratorium was declared in April.

Unfortunately, the elections neither produced the mandate that Marcos had expected nor reduced political turmoil as the Philippines' creditors had hoped. Marcos offered no significant policy changes to either the electorate or the creditors. He ignored the worsening economic crisis and allowed Virata to take the heat. Although Virata was reelected as prime minister, he endured a ferocious attack from the KBL, sparked by the government's inability to continue emergency assistance to weakened banks and to alleviate the liquidity squeeze. The political problems of Marcos and Virata were not an auspicious omen for the new IMF round.

Stage 2: Creditors Get Tough; Some Progress (June 1984–July 1985)

To prepare for the new round, the peso was devalued 22 percent in June. It was not enough. The IMF team in Manila termed the reforms taken since October "purely marginal" and left without an agreement. However, Marcos quickly reopened discussions with the IMF after the United States voted against a World Bank agricultural loan (because of his failure to dismantle sugar and coconut monopolies). The United States refused further assistance unless the Philippines reached agreement with the IMF. This time Virata was successful. He signed a letter of intent that included a free float of the peso by mid-September, unification of exchange rates, rationalization of banking, tight money supply, renewed efforts to curb inflation and control government finances, and reform of the sugar and coconut industries.[18] Virata also promised to eliminate the export and import taxes imposed in June and to remove tax exemptions for state corporations.

This letter of intent allowed the World Bank to approve the stalled agricultural loan over U.S. objections, but it did not guarantee the approval of the IMF board of directors, which was contingent upon securing a minimum of $1.65 billion in new loans from the commercial banks. The smaller regional banks were reluctant to provide new financing and thus forced the Philippines to request an additional $450 million from the Paris Club, beyond their previous $1.65 billion pledge. Recognizing its need to improve relations with the banks and the IMF, the Philippine government abolished the eleven-month-old regulation requiring commercial banks to surrender all foreign exchange to the central bank. By the time the Philippines declared its fifth ninety-day moratorium in October, debt arrears were estimated at $6.4 billion.

Negotiations seemed to be back on track by mid-December, however. The IMF board approved the $607.83 million standby agreement after pledges of new bank credits reached 92 percent of the required $925 million for the eighteen-month period ending in July 1985. The World Bank and the Asian Development Bank agreed to raise an additional $2.1 billion of new development assistance in 1985, and the Paris Club restructured $1.1 billion in official loans. Final figures for 1984 gave the Philippine program much-needed credibility. The balance of payments showed a surplus for the first time since 1977; inflation began to decline from its 1984 peak of 61 percent, reaching a 40 percent rate in March 1985 and 11 percent by year's end; and thus the peso began to strengthen.

There were some delays in disbursement, however, because in February the Saudi National Commercial Bank demanded that priority be given to repayment of trade credits for oil purchases. This demand delayed both approval of an agreement with the banks' advisory committee and the second disbursement under the IMF accord, thus undermining the Philippine commitment to repay the banks $725 million by March 31. This setback was overcome by May (the banks agreed to allow the Saudis to arrange a loan to the Philippines), allowing the $10 billion financial rescue agreement with 483 creditor commercial banks to be signed. This agreement included $925 million in new credits, the reopening of $3 billion trade credit lines, and a $5.8 billion rescheduling of short-term debt. It permitted the release of the second installment of IMF funding (assuming Philippine compliance with performance criteria), which also allowed disbursement of $400 million of new commercial money. At the same time, the Philippine government further reduced subsidies to state companies and was permitted to expand its money supply through gradual interest rate reductions. The creditors' attention began to shift from stabilization to longer-term adjustment and structural reform. All seemed to be on track, but appearances were deceiving.

Stage 3: Policy Reversals;
Elections Called (August 1985–November 1985)

Improved relations with external creditors were not matched by domestic support for the Marcos government. The local economy was still in grave difficulties. The GNP had fallen by 5.5 percent in 1984, over 3 million people had lost their jobs, and even official figures showed a 25 percent unemployment rate in Manila. Interest rates, although dropping, were still too high to induce investment; the need to mop up politically induced excess credit continued to plague efforts to reduce the public deficit; and both foreign exchange and credit were extremely scarce. The poor business climate, pessimism about Marcos's ability to govern or to make the necessary policy changes,[19] and the uncertainty generated by Marcos's refusal to settle the succession issue discouraged the business community. Opposition business leader Ongpin called on the United States to freeze economic aid until Marcos implemented democratic reforms and provided for succession.[20] Even the prime minister, when asked about the economic and political outlook in October, responded: "I think that the best thing the president could do at this point is set up a credible mechanism for succession."[21]

Instead, Marcos continued to use his economic powers to shore up his deteriorating political control and to run afoul of the IMF. Despite pledges to reduce the public deficit, the 1986 budget announced in August made generous provisions for public works in anticipation of the 1986 local elections. Acute and growing problems with tax collections made such spending all the more contentious.[22] In addition, private-sector pressure forced the government to petition the IMF for permission to expand countercyclical spending and to raise budget deficit ceilings. It also vigorously protested IMF calls for further devaluation and tariff reduction. On these issues, government and business were for once in complete accord, but the IMF was unalterably opposed.

Despite successful rescheduling agreements with the banks and the Paris Club, relations with the IMF continued to be strained as trust in the Marcos government declined. The second installment of the December standby accord, scheduled for release in May, was delayed because of failure to meet performance targets. An IMF team in August found that the problems preventing disbursement had not improved: The public deficit was running double the target of 0.9 percent of GNP; money supply was expanding 6 percent over the targeted rate; little progress had been made in restructuring government-owned banks; and the marketing monopolies in coconuts and sugar controlled by Marcos cronies had neither been dismantled nor adequately taxed. The IMF therefore refused to release any funds until November.

Finally, in mid-November, an IMF team reached tentative agreement with the Philippines. They stressed reform of the sugar and coconut monopolies, continued reduction in the public deficit, and improved overall economic management. Once approval from the board of directors was secured, the IMF would release $230 million. However, this long-awaited accord was overshadowed by Marcos's November 15 announcement that presidential and vice-presidential elections would be held in early 1986. When the IMF board approved the agreement in late December, Philippine politics had taken center stage. The electoral contest between Marcos and the compromise opposition candidate, Corazon Aquino, had begun.

Stage 4: Elections;
Regime Change (December 1985–February 1986)

For the 1986 elections, the opposition backed the ticket of Corazon Aquino (widow of Benigno Aquino) for president and Salvador Laurel (head of the largest, best-organized opposition party) for vice-president. Vigorous campaigning, which began as soon as the ticket was announced on December 11, reflected the growing polarization that had taken place in the country since 1983. Marcos's rallies were carefully orchestrated and relied heavily on the draw of celebrity appearances. Aquino's strength was her mass appeal, particularly in the urban areas. Fraud and intimidation were widespread on election day, despite the presence of many poll watchers, mainly from the National Citizens' Movement for Free Elections (NAMFREL)[23] and the U.S. government. Official results were delayed, and quick counts by the government commission and NAMFREL differed.[24] On February 14, the national assembly proclaimed Marcos the winner, but the Catholic church charged Marcos with election fraud. Then Aquino, at a massive rally held February 15, called for civil disobedience, including a general strike on February 26, the day after Marcos's inauguration.

After listening to the reports from congressional observers and his own special envoy, Philip Habib, President Reagan of the United States tried to convince Aquino to accept Marcos's offer to make her a top adviser. She refused. As civil disobedience began and fears for more violent reactions mounted, Reagan made it clear that aid would be withdrawn if civilians were fired on. Marcos was also indirectly urged to withdraw, but the decisive move occurred when Defense Minister Juan Ponce Enrile and Lieutenant General Fidel Ramos sided with Aquino. From Camp Crame in Manila, they appealed for public support, which they received from the Catholic church and thousands of Filipinos who surrounded the camp and faced down the tanks of Marcos loyalists. Although both Aquino and Marcos were sworn in as president on February 25, pressure from the United

States, the church, and divisions within the military convinced Marcos that it was time to flee. Aquino had won.

President Aquino immediately faced several critical issues. Establishing a new government, assuring its legitimacy, and guarding against destabilization by Marcos or his supporters were at the top of the political agenda. Meeting electoral promises of improved income distribution, expanding economic opportunity, and dealing with the continuing debt problem were the most important economic issues. Her government was made up primarily of mmbers of her deceased husband's political party and groups such as NAMFREL and businesspeople who supported her election. No Communists were included, but they initially gave Aquino tacit support. She, in turn, tried to convince the NPA to agree to a truce and negotiate.

By April, Aquino moved to establish longer-term legitimacy by proclaiming a new, temporary constitution, abolishing the national assembly, and governing by decree until a new constitution was approved by national referendum in 1987. She also removed some Marcos appointees at the local level, uncovered corruption, and called on many Filipinos to help. She opened the door to wide-ranging debate and participation, forming various study groups at all levels of society. However, some outsiders saw such open debate as nonproductive and confusing. Bickering among Aquino's advisers led many to question her resolve and, because some of her advisers were left-leaning, to fear the types of policies she might adopt. Nevertheless, the general euphoria, particularly among urban and business groups, combined with the support accorded the government worldwide, served to counter such fears. Aquino's clean government campaign and personal integrity were refreshing departures from Marcos's habits of governing, and they helped to establish her government's legitimacy.

A more immediate political problem throughout the year was the questionable loyalty of the military. Marcos's former vice-president staged a coup attempt with support from part of the military in July. Rumors surfaced of another coup attempt when Aquino went to Japan in November; and her secretary of defense, Juan Ponce Enrile, was believed to be behind it. In early December, Aquino fired him, in part because of the rumor of his involvement in the coup and in part because he was such a harsh critic of her decision to negotiate with the NPA rather than to launch an all-out offensive against it.

Such unsettled conditions and uncertain policies complicated the ensuing debt negotiations. With Marcos, the international financial institutions had to deal with lies. With Aquino, they now feared they were negotiating with a possibly weak and divided government that might not be able, however willing, to deliver.

Changed Economic Agenda

The external negotiators also had to deal with a changed economic environment. Marcos's depredations had continued through the 1986 presidential elections, and his preelection spending binge, combined with reduced tax revenues, meant the 1986 budget deficit was projected to be double that agreed to with the IMF.[25] In addition, the savings rate had fallen from 25 percent of GNP to 15 percent, domestic demand had collapsed, new investment had ceased, many workers were un- or underemployed, and per capita income had fallen by 20 percent since 1981. Still, inflation had dropped significantly, there was relative price and exchange rate stability, the current account and overall balance of payments were in better shape, and capital outflow had ceased. Equally important, oil prices and external interest rates were dropping, and there was considerable accumulation of bilateral foreign aid programs, which had been held back because of Marcos's inability to make policy commitments. Nevertheless, the Aquino administration had inherited an economy weakened by years of resource misallocation and financial drain.

In dealing with the economic situation, Aquino visibly differed from Marcos. In general, she aimed to improve income distribution and equality of opportunity by, first, strengthening democratic institutions and broadening participation and, second, shifting economic policies (toward a tighter monetary policy, for example) to promote recovery. She also emphasized rehabilitation of the agricultural sector[26] and recognized the need to negotiate another rescheduling of the accumulated debt overhang. Without rescheduling, even the moderate growth target of 6.5 percent for the next five years would be unobtainable. Neither sustained development nor stable growth would be possible if 40 percent of Philippine export earnings were needed to meet interest payments.[27]

Aquino selected an economic team, retaining Jose Fernandez as head of the central bank and replacing Virata with Ongpin as minister of finance. She then launched a comprehensive review of the economy, seeking advice from many quarters, including academics and consultative groups from various industrial sectors. Aquino was aided in these choices by the presence of relative financial stability and a growing optimism not only among the Filipino business community but also among foreign observers.[28] Her emphasis on equality of opportunity, market forces, and a nonstatist approach was favored by the World Bank and the Asian Development Bank, which were to be the most important external sources of finance for longer-term adjustment. Other external creditors were more restrained but displayed greater sympathy than at any time since the moratorium in 1983. However, it was recognized that the debt problem had to be addressed quickly and negotiations resumed.

DEBT NEGOTIATIONS UNDER AQUINO

Under previous restructuring agreements, covering debt maturing through the end of 1986, 60 percent of export earnings were earmarked for debt servicing. Negotiations were needed to reduce this burden, as well as make the $350 million worth of undrawn new money from the 1985 rescheduling available. Although the debt profile of the Philippines had improved in March 1986, it was still unfavorable. Total debt stood at $26.4 billion, with 64 percent being medium- and long-term debt, 33 percent short-term, and 3 percent bonds.[29]

Debt rescheduling was the primary occupation of President Aquino's economic managers in 1986. The start was inauspicious, but progress was more rapid and fruitful than under Marcos. In the highly charged political environment after the revolution, particularly with the revelations of the long-suspected corruption and financial malfeasance, there was talk of "selective repudiation" of parts of the external debt.[30] There were discussions of a further moratorium of commercial debt repayments, ceilings on interest paid, and limits on the percentage of export earnings applied to debt repayments. Most of these ideas were floated by Solita Monsod and her staff at the National Economic Development Authority, a cabinet-level organization. But both Finance Minister Ongpin and head of the central bank Fernandez opposed such radical proposals. When these ideas were being debated in early March, Fernandez stated, "Repudiation means letters of credit will not be honored and all transactions will have to be on a cash basis."[31]

The more conservative members of the economic management team won the debate. Economic realities were too constraining in early 1986 to permit an aggressive negotiating stance. Reserves stood at $1.3 billion after a postelection boost, oil prices were down, and tourism earnings were up. Nevertheless, the reviving economy was extremely import dependent for industrial and capital inputs, and earnings from coconut oil, sugar, and copper exports continued to be depressed. Some concessional loans were coming in (e.g., $100 million from the Asian Development Bank, $214 million from the United States, and prospects for more from the Japanese), but there was clear pressure to reschedule old debts and access new money. Most financing, however, was still dependent on obtaining the IMF's seal of approval.

Stage 1: New Agreement;
Expansive Policies (April 1986–October 1986)

In April, Ongpin obtained IMF approval to scrap the previous eighteen-month standby loan that was to have ended in June and keep the remaining draws for the next loan. This move delayed disbursement of the remaining $350 million of new money from the commercial banks, but both Ongpin and the IMF recognized that Marcos's preelection spending had made the budget deficit and reserve money targets impossible to achieve. Ongpin was optimistic that relations with the IMF would be productive and harmonious, and he was correct. Negotiations took only five months (compared to a year under Marcos) and were facilitated by a general willingness to support the Aquino government and Aquino's emphasis on market forces and a stronger role for the private sector.[32] Some observers, including some of the major commercial bank creditors, were also concerned about the longer-term outlook, if the economy did not begin to recover. By June, virtually all the participants in the negotiations agreed that the immediate objective was recovery within a framework of structural reform, without losing financial stability.

The first positive step occurred in May, when the major bilateral aid donors agreed to raise a $600 million financing package if the Aquino government could formulate an appropriate recovery program. The World Bank also wanted to help but was concerned about divisions within the Aquino cabinet.[33] This lack of unity went beyond Manila, however, since the creditors also had differing prescriptions. The IMF was reluctant to allow a wider public deficit, whereas the World Bank recognized the need for the government to take an active role in demand and job creation. The World Bank, in a confidential draft report in August 1986, was critical of the IMF-led austerity drive: "Stabilization was achieved through reduced income and without addressing the medium-term needs of the economy."[34] The banks' concerns continued to focus on factors affecting the Philippines' ability and willingness to repay.

By working closely with the IMF and the World Bank, the Aquino government began a program of economic recovery in the second half of 1986. The process was not without problems. Key elements of the first program adopted by the cabinet were opposed by the more conservative economic managers. The most controversial aspect was the removal of trade restrictions, especially import controls. Manufacturers, supported by the trade minister, Jose Concepcion, protested this policy. They were operating at only 40 percent capacity and feared that a massive flow of imports would put them out of business. They also knew, but were hesitant to admit, that they were not competitive in terms of quality, a fact confirmed by the enormous smuggling of consumer goods into the Philippines. The Philippines Chamber of Commerce and Industry asked that trade liberalization be deferred for two years to permit industry to invest to meet competition. Monsod's more radical group (supported by the majority of the cabinet) argued for free trade to remove distortions in the economy and encourage industrial efficiency. The IMF wholeheartedly supported this plea. Although it did not favor the Monsod group's call for reduction of servicing costs or "selective debt repudiation" (which was not approved by the cabinet), it did seem willing to compromise on expanding money supply to aid recovery. In the end, trade liberalization was postponed, and the money supply was increased to prevent the government from competing with the private sector for funds. As a result, interest rates dropped dramatically (from 30 percent to 15 percent), and the public deficit sharply increased. Inflation, however, remained low because of oil prices and stagnating domestic demand.

In its July review, the IMF supported this program and its macro-objectives, as shown in Table 8.1

A major reason for IMF support was the government's structural reforms, which seemed to address the causes of the deficit. Reforms included rationalization of public financial and nonfinancial corporations (with the goal of privatization in some cases), modification of corporate and income taxation, abolition of export duties, tariff reform, and withdrawal of some tax exemptions and incentives. Another reason for agreeing to the relaxation of austerity policies was an IMF rethinking of its own prescriptions. As Jose Galang put it, "Much of that change in attitude is traced to soul-searching in the IMF about its role in easing the global debt crunch, and it is currently showing more understanding toward countries in financial trouble. Just before the discussions with Manila, the IMF granted Mexico, another huge debtor, fresh credits to pursue a deficit-spending program this year."[35]

Formal agreement with the IMF was reached in October. The IMF endorsed the Aquino recovery plan and the shift of policy from stabilization to longer-term adjustment. The new IMF standby and compensatory eighteen-month financing of $300 million for 1986 and $165 million for 1987 offered adequate financing for 1987, when combined with the delayed $350 million financing from the commercial banks. However, it was contingent on the success of forthcoming negotiations on further rescheduling. There was some new medium and long-term money from multilateral and bilateral creditors, including $240 million in 1986 and $750 million for 1987. In the agreement, no new money was assumed to be on offer from the commercial banks in 1987. The $1 billion financing requirement for 1987 (to maintain reserves equivalent to 3.5 months of projected imports) was expected to come from debt reschedulings with commercial banks and, later, reschedulings with official creditors under the auspices of the Paris Club.

Stage 2: Disagreement; Delays (October–November 1986)

Negotiations with the twelve-bank advisory committee (representing 483 banks) began in late October. The Philippines wanted to restructure $3.6 billion of debt falling due over the next six years, to include the $5.8 billion rescheduled in 1985, and to convert one-third of the $3 billion revolving trade facility into a longer-term loan. Without rescheduling, debt repayments in 1987 would take 90 percent of export revenues. However, talks stalled in early November because of disagreement over the interest rate to be paid. Ongpin rejected an interest spread of 1.375 over LIBOR and instead proposed 0.625 over LIBOR. When the advisory committee rejected Ongpin's rate, he suggested his country might declare a unilateral standstill on some repayments, if compromise were not possible.

Three factors contributed to the Philippines' stance. First, and most important, it paid $80 million for every point above LIBOR. Second, it was willing to wait because reserves (at three months of import requirements) were strong, the last tranche of new money from the 1985 accord was expected by year's end, and positive discussions were under way with the World Bank and the Export-Import Bank of Japan over a $300 million recovery loan approved in December. The third and most important rationale was that the Philippines was only asking for rescheduling terms similar to those granted to Mexico the previous month (which included a twenty-year repayment period and an interest rate of 0.8125 over LIBOR). The banks, led by Citibank, did not want to make the Mexican terms a precedent, however, and therefore refused.

Discussions were resumed in December, with the banks agreeing to a ninety-day moratorium from the first of January. The trade facility also was extended by six months. All other issues were unresolved at year's end, with discussions set to resume in March.

EPILOGUE

The Philippines reached agreement with the banks in March 1987. The terms for the rescheduled debt for 1988 and the $5.9 billion from the 1985 agreement were improved. The 0.875 spread over LIBOR was closer to the Ongpin proposal than the banks' initial offer. However, final approval by all the banks, which had been expected in June, was not accomplished until January 1988. Political controversy, especially calls by some leaders in the national assembly for debt repudiation and Monsod's demands for still easier terms, made several banks nervous.

The domestic economy continued its rapid recovery. GDP, led by domestic demand, was up 5.7 percent; inflation was low; and IMF monetary targets were met. However, continuing import dependence, particularly for intermediate industrial inputs, and IMF-induced import liberalization caused the current account to slip back into deficit. Structural change was also slower than hoped because of low levels of private investment, insufficiency of public funds for investment, inability to develop projects in a timely manner, and political differences over some aspects of structural change, (e.g., land reform, privatization).[36]

By 1988, it was apparent that new money was needed to spur investment and growth if the government target rate of 6.5 percent were to be reached. Once again, the government was asking for easier terms and conditions, including longer-term development money from multilateral agencies such as the World Bank and Asian Development Bank. It did not want to have to use costly short-term money from the commercial banks.

The IMF has eased its terms since 1986 but believes it cannot go much further as the debt of the Philippines continues slowly to mount. In 1988, total debt had risen to $29 billion, and 1989 promised another year of tough debt negotiations. Although there was never a repeat of the 1983 financial crisis, the evidence of recurring problems is not entirely reassuring for future prospects.

TABLE 8.1   Aquino Government Macro-Economic Review and Program for Economic Recovery, July 1986

	1983	1984	1985	1986	1987
GNP (% change)	1.1	-6.8	-3.8	1.5	6-7
Consumer price index (% change)	10	50	23	4	5-6
Exports (% change)	-0.3	7.7	-14.1	-0.6	8.1
Imports (% change)	-2.3	-18.9	-15.8	0.8	12.2
Gross domestic investment (% GNP)	27	19	16	17-18	20-21
Gross national savings (% GNP)	19	15	16	18-19	19-20
Foreign savings (% GNP)	8	4	--	0.9	1.2
Government deficit (% GNP)	-2.0	-1.9	-1.9	4.4	-2.4
External debt (% GNP)	73	81	82	86	81
Debt service ratio (% GNP)	33	35	35	36	35

Source: Penelope A. Walker, "Political Crisis and Debt Negotiations: The Case of the Philippines, 1983–1986," Case no. 133, prepared for The Pew Diplomatic Initiative.

NOTES

1. The Philippines growth, investment, and inflation statistics for the years immediately preceding the debt crisis:

	1979	1980	1981	1982	Peak Year
Real GDP (%)	6.9	5.0	3.8	2.3	1973, 8.7 %
Real investment (%)	21.1	2.9	3.5	11.8	1975, 32.0 %
CPI (%)	18.8	17.8	11.8	12.5	1974, 36.0 %

Source: IMF, *International Financial Statistics* (Washington, D.C.: International Monetary Fund, various years).

2. The Philippines External Accounts

	1979	1980	1981	1982
Trade balance ($ bn)	-1.5	-1.9	-2.2	-2.6
Current account balance ($ bn)	-1.6	-2.1	-2.3	-3.3

Source: IMF, *International Financial Statistics* (Washington, D.C.: International Monetary Fund, various years.)

3. See Walden Bello et al., *Development Debacle* (San Francisco: Institute for Food and Development Policy, 1982).

4. This tendency toward personalization of (and intervention in) the Filipino economy is evident in that from 1972 to 1983, Marcos issued 688 presidential decrees and 283 letters of instruction relating to economic issues. *An Analysis of the Philippine Economic Crisis* (Manila: University of the Philippines, School of Economics, 1984).

5. The commercial banks (because of profit pressures and lack of demand from corporate customers) and multilateral financing agencies alike were under great pressure to recycle petrodollars to the Third World. In retrospect, many of these loans were unwise, but at the time, such recycling took on the aspect of a moral crusade.

6. Benigno Aquino was one of the people who believed the rumors about Marcos's declining health. It was one of the main reasons for his return to the Philippines in August 1983.

7. Richard Kessler, "Politics Philippine Style Circa 1984," *Asian Survey* 24, no. 12, December 1984, 1211.

8. An early example of business opposition was the formation of the Bishop: Businessmen Conference, jointluy sponsored by the Catholic church and business sector. It was not overtly political but did release statements taking issue with goverment policies and the subversion of democratic institutions. Interview with Dante Santos, president of the Philippine Chambers of Commerce and Industry during the Marcos years and leader of several of the anti-Marcos business groups, Manila, April 1988.

9. Quoted in Charles Lindsey, "Economic Crisis in the Philippines," *Asian Survey* 24, no. 12, December 1984, p. 1203.

10. Particular questions were raised about the appropriateness of IMF prescriptions because a World Bank structural adjustment program called for large investments. In April, the World Bank had signed a $302.2 million structural adjustment loan (SAL) that was tied to tariff reform, better promotion of manufactured exports, and tax changes. It was feared that IMF-induced budget restrictions would delay these projects.

11. At the same time, a World Bank team was in Manila to assess the performance of the second SAL in order to be able to disburse the second half of the $302 million loan.

12. Wells Fargo withdrew from the offer of a $100 million facility when it could only raise $35 million.

13. The banks do not make as much money on the longer-term rescheduled loans. However, they do not lose money or come under the jurisdiction of the Federal Reserve for carrying bad loans as they would under a default.

14. The Western financial press at this time had expected speedy negotations, what with the IMF's long familiarity with the country, the relatively small size of the debt, U.S. support, and the reputation of the Filipino technocrats.

15. Even the size of the debt was not known; estimates ran from the IMF's $17.5 billion to $21 billion by the banks. After the moratorium and IMF data verification, the accepted figure was $25 billion, which included some short-term liabilities not previously considered.

16. The drain on reserves began in early 1983. In April, the central bank began to boost reserve figures to meet IMF criteria by borrowing back to back (on behalf of another institution). By the end of September, reserves had been overstated by 43 percent. The numbers were corrected in October, and the fall was blamed on capital flight (which did occur).

17. The necessary statistics included reserve money, net credit from banks to the government, international reserves, external payments arrears, and debt profile.

18. In January 1985, Marcos dissolved the coconut monopoly by decree; in October, the sugar monopoly. However, the other firms in the industries were so weakened they were unable to take advantage of the freeing of the markets. Also, the formal decrees were

not fully implemented because of the importance of their political support to Marcos. A joint IMF-World Bank team in mid-1985 began to formulate reforms for both sectors.

19. Pessimism ran so deep that few businesses utilized the reopened trade credits or new World Bank money make available after the rescheduling.

20. Michael Battye, *Reuters*, September 12, 1985. The U.S. Congress had appropriated $180 million in aid, of which $70 million was military.

21. Jonathan Friedland, "Philippines: The Political Brake on Economic Recovery," *Inter-Press Service*, October 28, 1985.

22. The failure to meet projected revenue targets was a function both of the recession and the shift of taxation sources from external to domestic, which was the heart of the IMF tax reforms.

23. NAMFREL was the most important of the "cause groups" that had been formed since the Aquino killing in 1983. NAMFREL supported the opposition, was associated with the Catholic church, and was dedicated to honest elections.

24. Both showed the race was close, but Aquino was ahead according to NAMFREL and also by CIA estimates. Guy Sacerdoti, "Marcos, Countdown, " *Far Eastern Economic Review*, February 27, 1986.

25. Jose Fernandez, Jr. said in an interview in a special supplement to *Euromoney*, "The Philippines: A New Beginning," September 1986, " I think it was well-known that, in the few weeks prior to the election, a very large amount of spending took place and balances were drawn down very substantially...and we know for a fact that balances held with the rest of the banking system—which were completely outside our control—were also very substantially drawn down."

26. The agricultural sector provided 70 percent of employment on the Philippines but had been stifled by monopolies. The World Bank had begun a SAL for agriculture in 1985 but had problems dismantling the monopolies under Marcos, It was lending money to raise productivity, stimulate both export and import substitution crops, and stabilize farmers' incomes.

27. It should be noted that although Aquino did criticize the IMF stabilization programs' negative effects on the economy and the poor, the IMF and its programs were not an important election issue. The election issues were couched more in terms of abrogation of civil rights and morality should Marcos remain in power versus threats of Communist victory should he be deposed.

28. An example of the foreign enthusiasm is a headline in *Fortune*, March 31, 1986: "Business Turns Bullish on the Philippines." Underneath, the text ran, "President Corazon Aquino has banished the cronyism that stifled enterprises under Marcos, and her economic advisors talk like Reaganites about cutting taxes and fighting inflation. The economy is far from healthy, but daring investors are already placing bets. In the wake of its peaceful revolution, the Philippines is being swept by business euphoria."

29. The creditor composition was 56 percent commercial banks, 12 percent suppliers, 16 percent multilateral, 11 percent bilateral, and 5 percent other.

30. An example of the type of debt suggested for repudiation was the loans for the Westinghouse nuclear plant. There were allegations of payoffs to Marcos and excessive charges.

31. *Financial Times*, March 14, 1986. This is, in fact, what nearly happened to Brazil when it declared a unilateral moratorium in 1987.

32. In April, Aquino told businesspeople that her government would dismantle the "structures of privilege" and and lay down "an enhanced environment for private initiative." *Far Eastern Economic Review*, April 17, 1986.

33. A confidential World Bank memo of May 15, quoted in the *Far Eastern Economic Review*, June 19, 1986, said, "Cabinet members have not yet adopted the discipline of an agreed policy line—on the contrary they frequently make mutually incompatible statements based on their personal views and political constituencies. Perhaps none of this is surprising in the circumstances, but for us it means that the Minister of Finance and the governor of the Central Bank do not have an easy time when they present 'technocratic' arguments and proposals to the Cabinet, and this is bound to complicate our work."

34. *Far Eastern Economic Review*, September 4, 1986.

35. Jose Galang, "More Than Sympathy," *Far Eastern Economic Review*, August 14, 1986.

36. The Asian Development Bank, for example, has been withholding new lending to the Philippines until it improves its financial and project management and clears up its huge backlog of unspent development money.

9

Brazil, 1985–1987:
Pursuing Heterodoxy to a Moratorium

Hugo Presgrave de A. Faria

When the Brazilian military overthrew the civilian government of President Joao Goulart in 1964, it did so with a dual economic and political mission: to be an impartial, honest, and efficient administrator of economic development and to suppress subversion. While the military set out to clean up the political arena, it entrusted economic-policy making to a team of respected technocrats who could approach the economic morass with businesslike, no-nonsense efficiency. The economic team pursued an austerity program designed to balance both the federal budget and the balance of payments, while combating inflation.

Real growth came to a halt between 1963 and 1967, and per capita income fell to 1962 levels. It became increasingly untenable for the military to continue the austerity programs without unprecedented repression, and both the military's image and its unity were affected. The alternative was a rapid change in economic policy that would benefit the industrial elites and allow the fulfillment of some of the ambitions of the middle class. Accordingly, the military changed policy and launched what subsequently became known as the Brazilian "miracle." Between 1967 and 1973, the Brazilian economy grew at a rate of 11.3 percent a year, as

This case is excerpted from Hugo Presgrave de A. Faria's "From the 'New Republic' to the Moratorium" in Inflation: Are We Next?, *edited by Pamela Falk (Boulder, Colo.: Lynne Rienner Publishers, 1989) and is reprinted here with permission of the publisher. It also contains material from Faria's draft case originally prepared in April of 1988 for The Pew Diplomatic Initiative at Columbia University.*

inflation fell to around 16 percent. Internationally, the economy was booming, and recovery in the developed countries increased demand for Brazilian exports. The developed economies were particularly liquid at the time, and Brazil was able to borrow in international capital markets to finance its trade deficit.

The "miracle years" were characterized by a marked trend toward regressive income distribution and increasing levels of foreign debt. Official government policy encouraged foreign borrowing, and the interest rate on foreign loans from commercial banks was up to 11.5 percent below the prevailing rate on loans from domestic sources.[1] By 1974, the military government's economic fortunes had changed again, and General Ernesto Geisel responded by embarking on the path of political liberalization known as abertura, or opening. In the words of former finance minister Luiz Carlos Bresser Pereira: "Abertura was a process controlled by the military, giving in to the process of redemocratization, yet at the same time postponing it as long as possible in order to preserve military power."[2] Since the military regime had employed economic performance to maintain its legitimacy during the "miracle" period, it found it imperative to preserve a growing economy during the *abertura* period, even if at a somewhat lower rate of growth. The Geisel government initiated a large number of ambitious infrastructure projects in transportation, steel works, hydroelectric power, nuclear power, and military technology—financed largely by foreign loans. From 1974 to 1978, gross foreign debt grew 246 percent to a total of $43.5 billion.

Increased difficulty in financing the large state-sponsored projects spilled over into the private sector, as contracts for supplies were canceled or redistributed over longer periods. As private-sector profits began to fall, disaffection with the military grew, as did opposition to further expansion of the state sector. The military split over the choice of General Joao Figueiredo as General Geisel's successor, combined with continued economic deterioration (1981 was the first year since 1966 that per capita income fell in Brazil), helped guarantee that the transition to democracy would continue. The harsh economic reality hit home in the aftermath of the Mexican crisis in August 1982, as Brazil's creditors pressed for a strict IMF stabilization program. International reserves were at their lowest levels since 1972, the rate of new loans decreased by 20 percent, and exports were declining at an annual rate of 15 percent. Secret negotiations with the IMF bought the country some financial relief—in the form of a $5.9 billion facility—but only for a short time.

Brazil's year of reckoning came in 1983. GDP declined by 3.2 percent, leading to an unprecedented fall in per capita income of 5.5 percent. Real wages fell by 16 percent over the already depressed levels of 1982. Inflation reached a record 211 percent, and industrial output fell by 6 percent, while the gross foreign debt grew by 17 percent to $81.3 billion. The only bright spot was Brazil's trade balance, which earned a surplus of $6.4 billion during the year. The country's external obligations became its overriding consideration, particularly after May 1983, when Brazil effectively halted payments on its (by then) nearly $90 billion foreign debt. The de facto moratorium took Brazil out of compliance with its February 1983 letter of intent, and fully one quarter of the country's total external debt was scheduled to fall due by the end of 1984.

In September 1983, Brazil agreed to an orthodox IMF austerity plan in exchange for fresh assistance from the country's creditors. The agreement was discredited within a month, as doubts grew among the creditor community about Brazil's commitment to the program. Brazil had agreed to a reduction in inflation from 170 percent to an annual rate of 55 percent by the end of 1984, along with a reduction in its balance-of-payments deficit from $15 billion to $6-7 billion, and cuts in public spending, subsidies, and the rate of growth of money supply. The plan was widely viewed as a charade,[3] and amended in a new letter of intent filed in November that exchanged sharper cuts in expenditures for a lowering of inflation targets. The revised agreement unlocked $4.2 billion in IMF funds, $6.5 billion in commercial bank loans, $2 billion from a Paris Club rescheduling, and $2 billion from commercial bank lines frozen in May 1983. For its part, Brazil paid $540 million in overdue interest to its principal commercial bank creditors, enabling them to avoid having to declare their Brazilian loans as nonperforming.[4]

The initial results of the austerity plan pleased both Brazilian government officials and their creditors. A positive trade balance of $12 billion and the apparent stabilization of unemployment provided some basis for optimism. At the same time, however, persistent inflation, crumbling domestic demand, and the uncertain political climate brought about by the continued transition to democracy left the prospects for Brazil unclear.

THE BIRTH OF THE "NEW REPUBLIC"

In 1984, impatient with the slow progress of redemocratization and in the midst of a deteriorating economic situation, a popular movement known as the Diretas Ja campaign demanded the direct election of president Joao Batista Figueiredo's successor. While this campaign failed to overturn Brazil's indirect presidential selection process, it strengthened the hand of those opposition figures negotiating the transition to civilian rule with the military. On January 15, 1985, the Brazilian electoral college selected Tancredo Neves, governor of Minas Gerais and member of the opposition party, the PMDB (Brazilian Democratic Movement Party), to succeed General Figueiredo as Brazil's first civilian president in twenty one years; Jose Sarney, former president of the military government–backed party PDS (Partido Democratico Social), was elected vice-president. Then, on April 21, 1985, after the sudden illness and death of Tancredo Neves, Jose Sarney assumed the presidency.

With Tancredo's death, Sarney inherited a number of commitments and alliances that had been personally developed by the president-elect. These were embodied in his ministerial cabinet, which included representatives of the entire political spectrum and illustrated the intricate pattern of compromises behind Tancredo's election. In the economic sphere, for example, Finance Minister Francisco Dornelles, was a technocrat of conservative neoclassical leanings (and Tancredo's nephew). Balancing this perspective was Planning Minister Joao Sayad, an economics professor and a representative of the Sao Paulo PMDB. The central bank president, Antonio Carlos Lemgruber, with his monetarist leanings, completed the economic trio. The rest of the cabinet posts also followed this balancing approach. A number of politicians with strong ties to the recent military past, including Mining and Energy inister Aureliano Chaves and Sarney himself, were placed in highranking posts. Even the previously excluded popular sector was represented.[5]

The cement of this heterogeneous congregation had been Tancredo Neves. Thus, when Sarney was confirmed as president, many questioned his ability to execute the delicate moderating role Tancredo had fashioned for himself. In addition, the two parties whose support had brought Sarney to the presidency, the PMDB and the PFL (Liberal Front Party), ceased cooperating soon after the inauguration. The difficulties were compounded by the increasing strength of various other parties and an extremely fluid electoral panorama. On the other hand, as columnist Newton Rodrigues noted, Sarney had the confidence of the military "with which he had gotten along very well in the previous phases [to the transition]."[6]

Sarney's tenure began with a short-lived honeymoon period. The national mood was one of euphoria tempered by mourning for the deceased president-elect. The Sarney government attempted immediately to give shape to the ideals behind the transition to civilian rule and the drafting of a so-called democratic agenda. A constituent assembly, which would draft a new charter to replace the constitution of 1967, had a prominent place from the outset, symbolizing the return to full democracy.

The political arena was dominated by broad agreement as to the need for changes in the landholding system, the fiscal system, the state bureaucracy, and the management of the foreign debt. The specifics, however, were slow in the making. In agrarian reform, for example, a detailed and moderate plan was proposed in May 1985. By the time it became law six months later, in October, the project fell short even of the timid goals of the military's own land reform program known as the Estatuto da Terra. The crucial difference was that this time the project had been widely discussed, and criticized, both within the government and by Brazilian society at large.

In the early days of the "New Republic," it became clear that the country's economic well-being and the future of democracy required some immediate changes. The tremendous concentration of income (the world's highest)[7], the foreign debt (the developing world's largest), and the threat of hyperinflation presented pressing and potentially explosive problems. However, the expectation of most Brazilians that the new government would swiftly return the country to a growth path and concomitantly address the grave social issues facing the country was crucial. By the end of May, the new government came under conflicting pressures and demands for action. Tancredo had left no clear-cut economic strategy. He had envisioned the first six months of his government as a period when the key economic ministries would evaluate the country's situation before moving ahead with reforms.[8]

Saddled with a cabinet picked by the late president-elect and faced with rapidly mounting expectations, Sarney cast aside this nonpolicy without substituting any clear guidance of his own.[9] The transitional nature of the period, emerging cabinet rifts, mounting—but still not unbearable—pressures from business groups, union leaders, and politicians, and the prospect of nationwide mayoral elections in November 1985 all contributed toward a period of indecision. As Sarney emerged from his brief honeymoon period, searching for the support to build his own cabinet and policies, his calls for a socially responsive, growth-oriented policy became the only guideline for the "New Republic's" economic policy. The economic decisionmaking process of the Sarney government evolved largely in response to this amorphous embodiment of popular aspirations, subject to the constraints of Brazil's political and economic heritage from the military years, as well as to the new dynamics of incipient civilian rule.

THE ROAD TO THE CRUZADO PLAN

The three major international economic issues facing Brazil in 1985 were direct consequences of the policies of the previous decade. Brazil's relationship with the international financial community was dominated by the crushing weight of its $105 billion debt. The need to service this debt led to the country's policy of running very large surpluses (approximately $12 billion) in its trade accounts. This, in turn, set the tone for most of Brazil's commercial relations: importing ever-smaller quantities of goods while pushing for greater export markets in a recessionary world economic environment. Third, government-to-government relations between Brazil and its major creditor and trading partner (the United States) were perilously strained by the enactment in Brazil of a computer market reserve statute—known as the "informatics law"—which sharply restricted U.S. exports to the growing personal computer market in Brazil. It was within this climate that the new civilian government set out to tackle the mounting domestic and international troubles of the Brazilian economy.

In its first month, while Tancredo Neves was still alive in the hospital, the new administration took only a few steps in the field of economic policy, with no fundamental change in orientation from the last years of military rule. These measures reflected to a significant extent the views of Finance Minister Francisco Neves Dornelles. Tancredo had intended significant changes in social policy during his administration, but economic policy was to be run essentially on orthodox lines under the Finance Ministry's guidance. In the words of the Planning Minister, Joao Sayad, "Tancredo envisioned the Planning Ministry as something ornamental,...[Dornelles] arrived with a menu ready, and went ahead despite proposals for alterations, complaints, and arguments against that path."[10] Meanwhile, Sarney refrained from playing an active role in any aspect of policymaking until a few weeks after the death of the president-elect.

The Sarney administration's first economic package consisted of (1) a cut in the government's fiscal budget, (2) a slowdown of operations at federal credit institutions, (3) alterations of the indexation methods and greater reliance on government bonds to increase the public debt, and (4) strengthening of the Interministerial Price Council (CIP) guidelines, amounting to a short-term price freeze. These measures did not constitute any shift in terms of economic policy design; in fact, they were fundamentally the same measures that had been unsuccessfully implemented many times before. Public reaction to the package was generally unenthusiastic. Scholars and business people cited the well-known limitations, in terms of conception and implementation, of the austerity measures and the price freeze. The most criticism was directed at the change in the process of calculating the exchange rate and the *correcao monetaria*—the key index that periodically readjusts most financial prices.[11] Nevertheless, the prevailing public attitude was to give the government the benefit of the doubt and to allow it time to enact more energetic reforms.

Sarney, meanwhile, remained uncomfortable with his cabinet, which acted as if it controlled him, and not the reverse: "In the beginning of the government, [Sarney's] office was often invaded by his unannounced collaborators. [His ministers] addressed him in the familiar *voce* and presented papers for his signature as if he was a clerk."[12] Sarney voiced misgivings about the presidency: "I prepared to be a discreet and circumspect vice-president, without ambition."[13] By early June 1985, however, he had clearly decided to stay and attempt to take control of the presidency. Economic policy remained far from the president's mind as he focused attention on convoking the constituent assembly—which would determine the duration of his mandate as it formulated a new national charter—and on enacting cabinet reform.

Differences among President Sarney's economic staff became increasingly public by the end of May 1985. The rift between Dornelles and Sayad widened as the government came under greater pressure to act. The Sao Paulo private sector, represented by the presidents of the Sao Paulo Federation of Industry (FIESP), the Commerce Federation, the State Commerce Association, the Agricultural Federation, and the Brazilian Rural Society, promised support for the continuation of Dornelles's economic program.[14] Meanwhile, Sayad voiced his disagreements publicly, and his popular support soared, mainly because of his PMDB affiliation and his appealing proposals for adjustment with growth.

Sarney was caught between his two economic ministers. Because of the mildly expansive economic climate and his temporarily successful attempts to associate himself closely with the heritage of Tancredo, Sarney gained popularity. He needed the continued support of both the public and the senior partner in the governing Alianca Democratica (the PMDB) in order to govern and to carry out cabinet reform. For these ends, Dornelles's recessionary policies held little political utility. In addition, Dornelles accused Sarney of "simply start[ing] to spend without any list without any description" after Tancredo's death.[15] While Sayad did not offer Sarney a free-spending economic policy, he did propose an attractive controlled growth and adjustment strategy. Dornelles resigned at the end of August along with the Central Bank president, Carlos Lemgruber.

The new finance minister, Dilson Funaro, and the new central bank president, Fernao Bracher, were more closely aligned with Sayad's adjustment-with-growth strategies than with the monetarist orientation of their predecessors. The choice of Funaro, a Sao Paulo businessman—neither an economist nor a traditional technocrat—and Bracher, a well-connected banker, brought a much-needed boost of confidence to the government's economic team from businesspeople and bankers, both domestic and foreign, who had become uneasy over the confrontations between Sayad and Dornelles.

In the aftermath of the the New Republic's first cabinet changes, it was widely rumored that Sayad might also be removed to allow Sarney to control economic policy through "his" ministers, as opposed to the cabinet inherited from Tancredo. These rumors, combined with the natural transition period from one minister to another in the Ministry of Finance, yielded a two-month policy void. This interlude, however, gave Funaro and Sayad the opportunity to get acquainted and to forge a good working relationship.

Sayad and Funaro recognized the need for major economic reforms that would (1) bring inflation under control, (2) provide for continued economic recovery, and (3) promote gradual income redistribution. Funaro also advocated deindexation to help solve Brazil's chronic inflation. Deindexation would amount to the elimination of the well-established mechanisms (instituted since 1964) of periodic adjustment of nearly all prices (financial rates and wages among them) based on the official inflation index. This economic outlook left external debt policy, considered by many foreign critics to be a necessary key element in addressing the country's economic morass, as a residual, deriving from domestic priorities. To Brazil's foreign creditors, the insistence of the new economic team on not sacrificing growth for the sake of the country's external obligations, signaled imminent changes in debt-servicing arrangements. Beyond these broad points of agreement, the specifics on both the domestic and the foreign front were slow in developing.

By mid-1985, the economy had finally emerged from its deepest recession in recent history and was quickly gaining momentum. In the nine months from January through September 1985, consumer purchases skyrocketed in relation to the same period in the previous year: Car sales increased 27.4 percent, supermarket sales were up 25.6 percent, and building material purchases went up 7.6 percent.[16] This demand boom rapidly returned industrial output to near capacity level, boded well for employment, and fed into a virtuous growth cycle. However, it also fed into an inflationary cycle. The monthly inflation rate in September reached 9.1 percent, with a slight decline to 9 percent in October. Still, the inflationary pressures indicated that the 10 percent threshold would be easily surpassed in November.[17]

The government responded to the mounting inflationary pressures with a consumer credit reform during the last week of October. Reiterating the government's top priority of economic growth, Finance Minister Funaro stated that "we continue to desire economic growth, but we want it to be orderly and lasting." In effect the new measures shortened the maximum maturity for consumer credit for durable consumer goods from twenty-four to twelve months. The credit reform met with the general approval of the entrepreneurial classes as voiced by Abilio Diniz, head of Pao de Acucar, the country's largest retailing group: "It was only a signal from the government to avoid an explosion of demand." The president of the Sao Paulo Federation of Industry, Luis Eulalio de Bueno Vidigal, was more explicit when he stated that "the industrial sector supports this measure, because supply is indeed not adjusted in relation to consumption."[18]

On November 15, 1985, nationwide elections for mayors of former "national security areas"—including all state capitals—were held. The results were mixed. The governing Alianca Democratica parties (PMDB and PFL) split in various states, yielding victories to other parties, but fared well in some areas. After the elections, national attention quickly shifted back to the economic arena as the November monthly inflation rate reached 15 percent and rumors of major economic reforms permeated the media. Then, on Monday, November 25, President Sarney announced that a cabinet shake-up was next on the political agenda. Later that month, the national weekly *Veja* wrote off Sayad's cabinet seat as a result of the mayoral elections and Sarney's announced cabinet shuffle: "Minister Joao Sayad, who was already weak before the municipal elections, became even more exposed after them. Sarney feels obligated to give the Minas Gerais governor, Helio Garcia, a share in the federal government, earned by his capacity to pacify the party and lead it to a spectacular electoral show in the state capital. This share would be exactly the chair today occupied by Sayad."[19]

Still, Sayad remained and shortly thereafter emerged as one of the principal articulators of an economic strategy designed to lead the country to the desired path of adjustment without recession. Developing the reforms that became known as the Plano Cruzado sidetracked all other issues. The foreign debt, cabinet reform, the constituent assembly, and eventually the elections of 1986 all became a function of this economic formula. Before the plan was announced, however, Funaro and Sayad—and their teams of economists—still needed to fine-tune their ideas.

On November 27, Minister Funaro announced a new package of reforms, which consisted of the same tired and unconvincing measures: higher taxes and government austerity.[20] This package was received with the usual public cynicism and criticism by tax specialists, small-business leaders, and labor leaders. One part of the package, however, attracted even more attention than the naturally controversial issue of tax reform. Funaro announced a change in the calculation of the official inflation index and the establishment of a sole index for all price adjustments—wages, monetary correction, and the exchange rate.[21] Public outrage then arose because the new index set the November inflation rate at 11.1 percent, whereas the old index set the monthly rate at 15 percent. This difference opened the government to charges of manipulation. The issue of indices has been a traditionally sensitive one in Brazil. Throughout the dictatorship years, the government was accused of manipulating indices, ranging from inflation to budget figures. In the first nine months of the "New Republic," there were three changes of indices (including this one). Minister Sayad had championed a change from the Fundacao Getulio Vargas's (FGV) index—which had been used for forty years — to the more broadly based, and therefore arguably more representative, index of the Instituto Brasileiro de Geografia e Estatistica (IBGE). The two indices differed widely in their bases, but neither was consistently lower than the other. In fact, in January 1985, the IBGE's inflation figure was 14.6 percent, whereas the FGV's was a *mere* 12.6 percent. Sayad had been advocating such a shift for months, and Funaro also supported a single index for all prices as part of his aim to deindex the Brazilian economy.[22]

In the midst of the public outcry, the former planning minister, Mario Henrique Simonsen, clearly outlined the essence of the indices problem: "The substitution of the IGP [general price index], of the Fundacao Getulio Vargas, by the IPCA [broad consumer price index], of the IBGE, as the parameter for the calculations of monetary and exchange rate corrections is a defensible measure, but it was taken at the wrong time."[23] The issue of timing was crucial. However, the fact that Funaro personally ordered the change of index illustrated a hitherto unnoticed side of the minister's character: his almost dictatorial behavior once he had made up his mind and a sense of "mission," which he held above all other considerations.

On Wednesday, December 18, 1985, a *Folha de Sao Paulo* headline made public the debate that had been raging among the government's economists: "Planning Ministry does not reject the use of heterodox shock." Heterodox shock referred to the then recent economic reforms in Argentina and Israel (June and July 1985, respectively). These policies were based on the belief that high inflation is the result of "inertial inflation," and they usually included orthodox internal and external adjustment measures (currency devaluations, restrictive fiscal and monetary policies, as well as deindexation), combined with unorthodox elements such as monetary reform (the creation of a new currency), wage and price freezes, and pegged exchange rates.[24]

The possibility of deindexation was first raised outside closed meeting rooms by the interim planning secretary, Andrea Calabi, while Joao Sayad was on a trip to Washington. The reactions to Calabi's remarks were immediate. The black market dollar exchange rate shot up 8.9 percent over the previous week's level, the stock market went on a downward slump, and nervous attention was focused on the projected monthly inflation of 18 percent for January 1986. Sayad immediately called from Washington, demanding explanations from Calabi and sending him on a damage control mission. In retrospect, Minister Sayad was characteristically candid: "Calabi made a mistake. He needed to have taken the same position that we all did at the time and lie," that is, deny any knowledge of the impending reforms.[25] The government's economic team had monitored developments in Israel and Argentina; both the nature of their original troubles and the success of the policies made "heterodoxy" attractive. The press thus attributed to Calabi what had been on nearly everybody's mind: that Brazil was ready to opt for radical changes in economic policy.

Meanwhile, developments on the international front further complicated economic plans in Brazil. On October 1, 1985, just prior to the annual IMF-World Bank meeting, the new U.S. secretary of the treasury, James Baker, met with leading commercial bankers in Washington to discuss developments in the management of international debt. Rumors immediately began to circulate that the U.S. administration was about to change its position on developing country debt. The Brazilian delegation to the IMF-World Bank meeting, held that year in South Korea, pursued its own offensive strategy at the meeting. Minister Funaro presented the Brazilian consensus position that moderate economic growth must be maintained at all costs to then IMF managing director Jacques de Larosiere. Funaro clearly distanced himself from the accommodating approach of his best-known predecessor, Delfim Neto. In addition, Funaro presented Brazil's position before the IMF's interim committee and in a closed-door meeting with U.S. Federal Reserve Bank chair Paul Volcker and Treasury Secretary Baker. Funaro insinuated that Brazil might demand new approaches to the debt issue and might proceed with its plans regardless of international pressures for austerity. Brazil's commercial bank creditors, headed by Citibank's William Rhodes (chair of the bankers' steering committee), were unhappy with the new combative tone being set by Funaro.

Toward the end of the IMF-World Bank meeting, Secretary Baker announced a new U.S. approach to managing developing country debt: the Baker Plan. The plan promised new commercial bank funds (equivalent to 2.5 percent of private bank exposure to the fifteen largest debtors—or about $20 billion) over three years to indebted countries willing to undergo medium- to long-term economic adjustment programs administered by the international financial institutions—particularly the World Bank. Baker also issued a stern warning against protectionist, "market reserve" legislation, such as Brazil's informatics law.

While Baker's proposal was a departure from previous U.S. efforts, it would certainly not solve Brazil's—or any other major debtor's—long-term financing difficulties. At best, it afforded both the Brazilian government and its creditors more time to negotiate. More importantly, Baker's decision *not* to require an IMF agreement as a condition for access to new financing signaled to Brazil that there was no hurry in embarking on a new austerity program—a factor that complicated Brazil's impending negotiations with its commercial bank creditors. In late November 1985, Funaro announced in Washington that Brazil would seek a new renegotiation of its foreign debt without the IMF.[26] He argued that since Brazil was one of the few debtors up-to-date on its interest payments, it expected easier debt-servicing terms in the future. To press the point home, the Brazilian government broke with its long-standing tradition of honoring the nonguaranteed debts of private Brazilian banks and liquidated three commercial banks owing a total of $455 million in nonguaranteed commercial bank loans abroad.[27]

On December 17, declarations by Finance Minister Funaro further exacerbated the debate. While in Uruguay, Funaro stated that economic policy for 1986 would not be recessionary and that the possibility of price and wage freezes had been discarded. He also commented that Israel's heterodox shock recipe, based on a consensus among the government, unions, and industrialists, was preferable to Argentina's reform-by-decree formula.[28] The nature of Funaro's trip to Montevideo to discuss foreign debt with other Latin American finance ministers also complicated matters. Upon his return, Funaro attempted to cool discussions of imminent reform: "At no time did I defend freezing prices and wages."[29] On the crucial issue of foreign debt, he was less cautious: "Economic growth will not be interrupted in 1986, even if it requires postponing payment of the foreign debt."[30] From this point on, both economic ministers consistently placed the servicing of Brazil's foreign debt in the context of domestic economic recovery. The year 1985, and the first nine months of the "New Republic," ended with December inflation running at a record annual rate of 235.1 percent, while economic growth had recovered to an 8.6 percent yearly level—the highest in ten years.

In February 1986, under the shadow of rumors about economic reform, President Sarney finally felt he had the opportunity to alter his cabinet. Positions were redistributed between the two Alianca Democratica parties, the PFL and the PMDB. While the PMDB—to which Sarney officially belonged—obtained fifteen cabinet positions, the PFL—in which observers believed Sarney felt ideologically more comfortable—picked up five. Still, the numerical division of positions did not reflect actual power; the five PFL ministries' budgets surpassed the fifteen PMDB cabinet members' spending power 2.5 to 1.[31] However, the crucial reforms were yet to come; the PMDB would rebound in the political battle against the PFL with the initial smashing success of the Cruzado Plan engineered by its economic ministers.

THE CRUZADO ERA

The conservative shift in Sarney's cabinet did not eliminate growing speculation over the heterodox path of impending economic reform. Indeed, the innovative Cruzado Plan, announced on February 28, 1986, at 9:30 a.m. by President Jose Sarney on nationwide radio and TV, was far from conservative. The plan's essential features were the following: (1) deindexing of the economy, beginning with the elimination of correcao monetaria—used for indexing wages, savings accounts, and other financial instruments; (2) immediate and indefinite price freeze of over 80 percent on goods and services; (3) redenomination of the currency from cruzeiro to cruzado, at a rate of 1,000 to 1; and (4) a 33 percent increase in the minimum wage and an 8 percent bonus to wage earners. The government estimated that the inflation rate, which had reached 255 percent annually in February, would fall to zero in March.[32]

Initially, the Cruzado Plan surpassed all expectations in promoting growth and boosting government popularity. In the polls immediately following the announcement of the monetary reform, Sarney's approval rate reached 95 percent,[33] and Minister Funaro was congratulated and applauded in the streets. Economically, the measures engineered an unprecedented consumption explosion. The real wage hike, which resulted from the concomitant 33 percent minimum wage increase (plus the across-the-board 8 percent pay bonus), and the price freeze amounted to the largest real buying power gain in decades. The April sales index, relative to the same month in the previous year, increased 36.2 percent in Rio de Janeiro and a similarly impressive 29.5 percent in Sao Paulo.

As the consumption rise that began in mid-1985 developed into an unquestionable consumption boom by April 1986, the need to safeguard long-term prospects for recovery and to ward off inflationary pressures became acute. Shortages of consumer goods (particularly food items such as potatoes, eggs, milk, meat, and poultry), consumer durables (new cars, most noticeably), intermediate goods (steel), and raw materials (electricity) all became commonplace by June. Demand pressure created a black market for most of the scarce consumer items, taking the form of the payment of agio, or surcharge. On the positive side, employment levels and production rose steadily. In its editorial "The Giant Goes Back to Shopping," dated July 15, 1986, the widely respected Conjuntrua magazine warned of the dangers ahead:

> In this new phase of the Cruzado Plan, the Government will have to face many challenges. The moderation of consumption and the incentive to save are certainly two of them. The economic surgery carried out by the deindexation program was successful. The important point, now, is to care for the economy's post-surgery health. The clearest symptom that the patient still requires attention is the exacerbation of consumption. This, however, has its roots in the recently adopted expansionary policies, and in some of the measures enacted by

the Monetary Reform. Without appropriate correction, the excess of consumption will inhibit investment due to the shortage of financing, will reduce the exportable surplus and increase the already existent price distortions. In the end, there would be left inflation and the need to apply even more restrictive economic measures. Thus, there still remains much to be done.[34]

Meanwhile, the external context had shifted significantly, reflecting both the effects of the Cruzado Plan and exogenous developments in international trade and finance. The trade balance soon became the most pressing concern. The enviable trade surplus that Brazil had maintained since 1983 quickly collapsed due to the simultaneous export decrease and import increase brought about by excessive consumption.

After the unexpected smashing success of the Cruzado Plan, the Funaro-Sayad team stumbled onto the plan's shortcomings without producing the needed solutions. Minister Sayad stated that from May 1985 onward the principal problem was the supply of goods. The pressure on prices could not be ignored. On July 23, the so-called Cruzadinho Plan was announced, ostensibly as a set of measures for controlling consumption, promoting continued growth, and, ultimately, in Sarney's words, "eliminating misery by the year 2000."[35] Critics viewed the plan as a mere stopgap decree to raise revenue to finance the increasing public deficit the government had failed to curb.

The package consisted of (1) a 28 percent compulsory deposit on gasoline and alcohol (for motor vehicles), which would be returned to consumers, with market interest, three years later based on average consumption; (2) compulsory deposits on car purchases: 30 percent for new cars, 20 percent for cars up to two years old, 10 percent for cars up to four years old (shares of the newly formed National Development Fund [FND] were to be issued for the value of the deposit and could be traded within three years); (3) a 25 percent tax on international airline tickets and dollar purchases for foreign travel, with the proceeds also going to the FND (this tax, however, would not be returned to consumers); (4) an end to government-set interest rates for savings accounts and the introduction of floating rates; (5) the creation of the FND to administer both the new revenues, estimated at Cz$35 billion for 1986 ($2.5 billion at the official rate, $1.4 billion at the black market rate), and 33 percent of government pension funds, valued at Cz$38.8 billion in 1986 ($2.8 billion at the official rate, $1.55 billion at the black market rate)—the FND was created to invest in state-owned enterprises and long-term infrastructure projects; (6) income-tax-free government bonds; and (7) increased taxation of short-term financial investments (open-market, overnight, and thirty- to sixty-day certificates of deposit), gradually increasing in inverse proportion to the length of the investment.[36]

The Cruzadinho package clearly demonstrated the limits of the Sarney government's power, particularly in an election year. The measures were by no means a radical alteration of economic policy, but wage compression was ruled out and the measures implemented aimed at the top layer of consumers rather than the masses. While this approach was consistent with Sarney's espoused socially responsible economic policy, it also reflected the needs of the PMDB in view of the November elections for the entire lower chamber of congress, two-thirds of the senate, and all governorships.

Despite the clear political constraints, pressures still existed within the government for alterations to the Brazilian "heterodox" model. Political considerations prevailed, however, and proposals to switch from a blanket price freeze toward a system of administered prices—such as that in place in Argentina at the time—were swept aside. Sayad explained that:

> as far as the price freeze was concerned, which was the most criticized aspect of the plan, there was a perception within the government that it was a barrier, a wall, a dam that could not have any gaps or otherwise everything would collapse. So the government took a position, on the President's orientation, of inflexibility. My position which maintained that [the price freeze] was not working, lost force in face of the two arguments which stated that the problem was about to be solved [presented by Funaro], and the other which said that we cannot open or otherwise everything will come crashing in.[37]

This tension within the government was initially confined to closed-door cabinet discussions while outwardly the PMDB presented a united face, basking in the positive aspects of the program. Then at the end of July, Planning Secretary Sayad and the president of the Brazilian Institute of Geography and Statistics, Edmar Bacha, publicly clashed over the issue of inflation indices. Sayad, with the support of President Sarney and Funaro, requested that the official inflation index exclude the effects of the taxes and compulsory deposits enacted by the Cruzadinho. Bacha, trying to preserve the respectability of his institute's index—which had been the official index for only eight months—insisted on including the effects of the government's measure in the official index. In the spirit of an election year, a compromise was reached whereby two indices were published by the IBGE, one containing the effect of the July 23 reforms, the other purging that effect.

In the only other major attempt to address the building inflationary pressures, the government attempted to suppress the symptoms rather than address the causes of the problem. In the first three weeks of August, the federal police cracked down on the dollar black market as the surcharge reached 90 percent. The dollar black market, as well as the black markets rapidly developing for other items in short supply, revealed the true state of inflationary trends. Rumors of imminent major exchange reforms abounded. In anticipation of future price increases, inflation climbed to its highest level since the beginning of the Cruzado Plan. The reversal of the downward price trend of foodstuffs was the main cause of the inflation surge, leading to a 2.24 percent monthly rate in the Sao Paulo area (1.1 percent was the purged index).[38]

Prior to the November election, beef and milk supplies reached crisis levels for the average consumer. The government therefore took a few token moves against cattle raisers hoarding produce. But the prospect of possible armed confrontation with influential growers caused the government to step down. Once again plainly demonstrating its lack of enforcement infrastructure and to some degree its lack of political will, the government opted for the nonconfrontational, costly, and inefficient option of importing thousands of tons of European beef.

The government justified opening the door to imports—not only beef, but a wide range of foodstuffs and scarce consumer goods and a number of luxury items—as necessary to preserve the reforms' integrity from sabotage by cattle raisers and others who were hoarding goods. Critics condemned the liberalization of imports as catering to the preelection interests of the PMDB and the PFL. Regardless of motivation, however, the importing spree led to an increase of about $1.3 billion in the country's import bill, or roughly 25 percent of international reserves at the time.[39] The confrontation over the beef supply discredited Sarney's economic team more than any other episode since the reforms' inception. Still, the government, and the PMDB in particular, succeeded in focusing national attention on the tremendous increase in real purchasing power—even with goods in short supply and with black market surcharges.

To counter the calls—both domestic and foreign—for austerity in the country's external accounts, the government cited supposedly exogenous factors as restricting its range of options. Foremost on the government's list was the unwillingness of the financial markets to offer new money. The success of the country's adjustment with growth necessitated consistent, if diminishing, injections of new foreign loans, which in the uncertain environment of mid-1986 were not forthcoming. Another crucial, and related, issue raised by government economists was the shift in foreign investment trends in Brazil. In 1985, for the first time in decades, net foreign investment was negative, and projected figures for 1986 were even more worrisome. Both the lack of new loans and the net foreign investment flows dampened prospects for sustained recovery.

The PMDB swept the November 15 nationwide congressional and gubernatorial election, gaining nearly a two-thirds majority in both houses of congress as well as twenty-two of twenty-three governorships. The major defeat of left- and right-wing parties was seen by many analysts as an endorsement of the Cruzado Plan. However, the consumption boom continued, with shortages ranging from imported industrial inputs to eggs, and from electricity to cars. Most goods that were available sold at a surcharge in the neighborhood of 100 percent over the official government prices.

On Friday, November 21, a mere six days after the elections, Ministers Funaro, Sayad, and Pazzianotto announced what quickly became known as the Cruzado II Plan. The new measures included a rash of major price increases that, according to many, dealt the final blow to the price freeze of February 28, 1986. Whereas the subsidies and prices of steel, meat, and milk remained unchanged, the prices of many consumer goods went up: beer and cigarettes by 100 percent; new cars by 80 percent (80 percent of which was to go to the government); gasoline and alcohol fuel by 60 percent; different varieties of sugar by over 20 percent; and, finally, government services such as electricity, telephone, and mail by 35 percent on average.

The second and perhaps most controversial element of the Cruzado II package was a further alteration in the inflation index. The official inflation index would be based on a typical basket of goods, that is, one that might be purchased by a consumer earning up to five times the minimum wage per month (about $280), thus purging the effect of most of the recent price hikes. This latest index alteration contributed to the resignation of IBGE president Edmar Bacha, one of the original architects of the Cruzado Plan.[40] Third, the new package spelled out the mechanism by which an automatic wage adjustment scheme, instituted by the original Cruzado Plan, would function. When the inflation rate reached 20 percent, wage increases of at least 50 percent of the official inflation rate would take effect, after discounting any voluntary pay raises granted over the previous nine months. Fourth, a new policy of minidevaluations (the first one was of 0.26 percent, on November 21) set by the central bank on an almost daily basis would control the exchange rate. Noticeably, this measure was the only reform that directly impacted Brazil's pressing foreign account situation.

Fifth, the Cruzado II Plan also included a number of measures aimed at promoting savings (for example, the introduction of a new tax-free retirement fund) and at recapturing some of the money floating in the parallel economy through a fiscal amnesty. Finally, as a further step along the road of deindexation, treasury bills became free of inflation indexing and started to float with interest rates.[41]

In sum, the package was aimed at containing consumption through sales taxes, rather than income taxes, in order to increase revenue without major government spending cuts. The new measures had a projected revenue of $11.3 billion—nearly 4 percent of GNP. According to Finance Minister Funaro, the government's share of the adjustment in the form of cuts and privatization would account for slightly more than 20 percent of the total new revenue. In the words of Funaro, after a month of negotiations within the PMDB and the administration, "We did not have a choice."[42] Minister Sayad, however, later argued the government did have a choice: "The President had two options before him, one which I presented and another presented by the Finance Minister."[43] However, Sayad's reforms, which favored more sustained structural reforms and less tributary emphasis, lacked the immediate impact of Funaro's recipe and required significantly more political coordination given their longer-term implementation and operational period.

The split in the economic cabinet echoed that between Sayad and Dornelles in 1985, and once again Sarney opted for the politically easier option—that presented by Funaro. Regarding the wisdom of the unpopular alteration of the inflation index, Sayad stated that "you did not even have to study the situation, all you had to do was look at what had happened in July [with the Cruzadinho]."[44] This lack of attention to the drafting of the Cruzado II Plan, combined with a national sense of betrayal stemming from the de facto end of the price freeze only six days after the election, helped President Sarney's approval rate plunge from a high of 95 percent in April 1986 to a low of 54 percent ten days after the Cruzado II announcement.[45]

BEYOND THE CRUZADO PLAN: MORATORIUM

The announcement of the Cruzado II Plan provided a brief moment of activity that scarcely broke the paralysis of economic-policy making that had prevailed since August 1985. The poor reception of Cruzado II, and the government's defensive attitude, heralded a new period of policymaking paralysis. During this five-month hiatus, domestic economic policy came to a complete halt. Instead, partly to buy time domestically and partly out of necessity, the government resorted to a foreign debt gamble.

Domestically, Sayad became increasingly isolated, while Funaro managed a major public relations initiative to obtain public support for government actions. Time and again, Funaro spoke against recessionary policies and promised that Brazil would grow in 1987 at levels comparable to those of 1985 and 1986. However, the strength of the minister's rhetoric was not matched by political coordination or support. Disarray prevailed at the second echelon of the government, and many of the "fathers of the Cruzado" resigned their government positions. It was amidst this despondency and confusion that Funaro fixed on the issue of the country's foreign debt. He initiated his foreign debt crusade with an address to the U.S. congressional summit on debt and trade in early December 1986:

> After strenuous, prolonged attempts at convincing our partners through reasoning, we have now reached a point where all parties involved have to assume their responsibilities. We also have our shareholders. They are the people of Brazil and they number 135 million. The strategy of pumping unprecedented trade surpluses out of developing economies only to ensure the payment of interest has run its course. Debtor developing countries can no longer continue to be net capital exporters in these staggering amounts. If *the debt is to be paid, it will have to be serviced at a much lower cost in the years to come*. [author's emphasis] We shall be prepared to negotiate what is negotiable, and this does not include the growth of our economy.[46]

This populist line, even if economically sound, did not go over well with the international banking community. Funaro's intention to utilize a significant portion of Brazil's scheduled debt service payments—up to $6 billion in 1987—for domestic adjustment meant either an agreement with the country's creditors or a unilateral moratorium. Governor Leonel Brizola of the Democratic Labor Party (PDT) and the Workers' Party (PT) leader, Luiz Inacio "Lula" da Silva, were the two leading advocates of the latter course. Funaro, however, was not ready to call for a moratorium. Relying on foreign reserves and hoping for support from other major debtors such as Mexico, Argentina, and the Philippines (all countries that were either already negotiating substantial reschedulings or were about to do so), Funaro instead pressed the banks for concessions.

Funaro won a minor victory when the IMF notified the Paris Club that Brazil's economic adjustment program was workable. This tentative IMF endorsement was crucial not only for the Paris Club rescheduling but more important for the upcoming commercial bank rescheduling. In addition, the IMF go-ahead in the absence of an orthodox IMF austerity program was a victory for the Brazilian government, which had refused to negotiate an adjustment program with the IMF.[47] On January 21, 1987, the Paris Club agreed to reschedule $4.1 billion in official credits, but the creditor nations warned they "would reconsider their action if Brazil [did not] receive a "favorable report" from the IMF during annual consultations [in] July."[48] A brief period of deceiving calm ensued. During December 1986, Brazil had managed a meager trade surplus of $156 million, which in January 1987 fell to $129 million, while inflation in January reached 15 percent.

Faced with this evidence of returning inflation, the government finally lifted the price freeze on February 5, 1987. The gravity of Brazil's domestic and foreign economic picture was undeniable. A further element of instability was the resignation on February 10 of Fernao Bracher, the central bank president. It became known later that the major reason for Bracher's resignation was his disagreement with Funaro over the then impending unilateral suspension of debt service payments. President Sarney announced the de facto moratorium on February 20, 1987, in a brief fifteen-minute address on national television. He revealed that Brazil's reserves had shrunk to $3.9 billion and that to safeguard a minimum ability to pay for essential imports, he had decreed a suspension of interest payments on $67 billion in commercial foreign debt.[49]

Sarney and Funaro expected the moratorium to rally public support for the regime. In addition, they hoped that at least one of the other major debtors—probably Argentina—would join Brazil to force the commercial banks to accept terms more favorable to the indebted countries. Neither proved true. Popular support was negligible. Headlines were grabbed by those criticizing the moratorium because it was taken from a position of weakness—when reserves were nearly exhausted—rather than from a position of strength, as would have been the case in March 1986.[50] Internationally, Funaro engaged in a fruitless world tour of major OECD capitals in an attempt to establish government-to-government debate on the debt as a preliminary step to eventual negotiations with the banks.

On March 16, Funaro recognized the ineffectiveness of his recent efforts and the "perplexity" dominating the economic climate.[51] The following day, Planning Minister Joao Sayad resigned, which, momentarily, seemed to open the door to new and cohesive policies. Then Sarney chose a close personal friend with little economics training, Anibal Teixeira, as the new planning minister, thus giving Funaro control of economic-policy making. Funaro, however, continued to be consumed by the foreign debt debate, and, as the reform proposals Sayad had made before his resignation were also dismissed, the country was left once again without any firm policies.

During the month after Sayad's resignation, the economic outlook deteriorated further. Inflation persisted at 15 percent a month, and the trade surplus for the first quarter of 1987 totaled a mere $526 million—compared with $2.41 billion for 1986.[52] In addition, the prospects for renegotiating the foreign debt were dimmer than ever, with all of Brazil's possible debtor nation allies signing rescheduling agreements with the banks, or about to do so. Minister Funaro was the natural center of attention.

For months, and particularly since the February 20 suspension of foreign debt payments, there had been repeated calls for Funaro's dismissal, both domestically and internationally. On April 9, the three most powerful PMDB governors publicly demanded Funaro's removal.[53] However, on April 12, Ulysses Guimaraes and other PMDB leaders called for unified support of Sarney's cabinet and criticized the group of governors for attacking Funaro while he was in Washington.[54] This unexpected outburst of PMDB support for Funaro further clouded the political scene. Nonetheless, this political storm, combined with the creditors' cool reception of Funaro's economic proposals, meant that Funaro's days on Sarney's cabinet were numbered.

Funaro's fall, however, did not come as quickly or as easily as some had been predicting as early as November 1986. The delay in Funaro's removal reflected more than confusion over the future course of economic policy; it was a product of the entire economic decisionmaking process of the Sarney government. While public opinion—and in this case international public opinion as well—made itself heard loudly and clearly, the key decisions were taken by a very limited number of decisionmakers for reasons often not related to those current in the media. Indeed, Funaro's dismissal revealed the essence of high-level decisions in the Sarney government.

Sarney's indecisiveness, the PFL's difficulty in standing up to the PMDB, Ulysses's power within the PMDB, and Sao Paulo's place of honor in economic policy all conspired both to delay Funaro's exit and to determine his successor. In exchange for the removal of its once popular minister, the PMDB, on April 22, demanded the dismissal of Sarney's staunch ally and PFL leader, Marco Maciel, from his powerful position as the president's chief of staff.[55] Not only was Maciel's removal arranged, but once Funaro's resignation was announced on April 24, Ulysses publicly blocked Sarney's first choice for the new finance minister. Sarney chose family friend and businessman Tasso Jereissati, the young governor of Ceara, but Ulysses vetoed this choice and instead offered a short list of alternatives to Sarney, of which the least controversial and most palatable for the president was Sao Paulo entrepreneur-economist Luiz Carlos Bresser Pereira. This embarrassing cabinet reform—which started with Bracher's resignation in February—concluded the convoluted first two years of the Sarney government's frustrated attempts to create an economic policy for the "New Republic." Guilherme Afif Domingos, the federal deputy who received the largest number of votes in the November 1986 elections, stressed the importance of the dramatic conclusion of the Cruzado cycle: "this week will be remembered as the beginning of the fall of President Jose Sarney."[56]

POSTSCRIPT

Brazil's moratorium remained in place throughout 1987, in spite of trade sanctions worth $100 million imposed by the United States in November of that year. Bresser Pereira engaged in tough negotiations with the commercial banks in an effort to persuade them to accept some losses and lower interest rates. His efforts, known as the Bresser Plan in banking circles, were widely repudiated among creditors, and in January 1988, Brazil resumed full interest payments. In April of that year, the Finance Ministry changed hands once again: from Luiz Carlos Bresser Pereira to Mailson da Nobrega. The paralyzing political debate on the drafting of a constitution seemed close to an end, President Sarney was all but assured his goal of a five-year term, and after a tortuous detour, Brazil appeared to be returning to the pattern of debt negotiations that prevailed before the moratorium.

NOTES

1. Carlos van Doellinger et al., *A politica brasileira de comercio exterior e seus efeitos*, Relatorio de Pesquisa, 22 (Rio de Janeiro: IPEA/INPES, 1974), p. 152.

2. Luiz Carlos Bresser Pereira, *Development and Crisis in Brazil, 1930-1983* (Boulder, Colo.: Westview Press, 1984), p. 187.

3. Peter Kilborn, "Brazil Aid Plan Called 'Charade,' " *New York Times*, October 19, 1983, p. D1.

4. According to U.S. banking regulations, a loan must be declared nonperforming if interest payments are more than ninety days in arrears.

5. Two energetic and widely respected reformers, Almir Pazzianotto in the Labor Ministry and Nelson Ribeiro in the newly created Ministry of Agrarian Reform and Development, represented to some degree many of the demands of the masses.

6. Newton Rodrigues, *Brasil provisorio* (Rio de Janeiro: Editora Guanabara, 1986), p. 607.

7. For detailed Brazilian income distribution data, see the World Bank's *World Development Report*, 1992 (New York: Oxford University Press, 1992), table 30, pp. 276–277. Data for income distribution are particularly difficult to find; however, of those countries for which reasonably reliable data are available, Brazil holds the dubious distinction of having the highest income concentration.

8. Former finance minister Dornelles stated that Tancredo's first intention was that "in the first six months each ministry [take] stock of the resources available, and set priorities in order to establish an investment policy." However, Dornelles added: "Once Tancredo died and Sarney took over, he did not want to wait some six months of greater austerity in order to take inventory and establish priorities. He simply started to spend without any list without any description." Interview with Francisco Neves Dornelles, Rio de Janeiro, March 13, 1987.

9. Minister Dornelles's statement quoted in the preceding note is but one insider's view of President Sarney's lack of guidance in economic matters. The next part of this chapter discusses in greater detail Sarney's role in shaping economic policy.

10. Sayad, minister planning in the Sarney government from March 1986 to February 1987, made these remarks during an interview at the Park Lane Hotel in New York City, April 21, 1987.

11. The following three articles discuss in detail the "New Republic's" first economic measures: Celso Luiz Martone, "As novas medidas," *Informacoes FIPE*, no. 60 (April 1985), p. 3; Jose Roberto Mendonca de Barros, "As recentes medidas de politica economica e a conjuntura," *Informacoes FIPE*, no.60 (April 1985), p. 1; Instituto Brasileiro de Economia, "Primeiras medidas, ultimas instancias," *Conjuntura*, April 1985, pp. 7–10.

12. This observation appeared in an article, "Sarney toma biotonico, " in the national weekly *Veja*, November 27, 1985, p. 37.

13. Jose Sarney, "Brazil: A President's Story," *Foreign Affairs* 65, no.1 (Fall 1986), p. 103.

14. Ana Maria Lage, "Tudo se decide na guerra da economia," *Senhor*, no. 129 (May 29, 1985), pp. 31–32.

15. Interview with Francisco Neves Dornelles, Rio de Janeiro, March 13, 1987.

16. "Com o pe no freio," *Veja*, November 6, 1985, p. 93.

17. "Inflacao: no mesmo tom," *Veja*, November 6, 1985, p. 95.

18. "Com o pe no freio," *Veja*, November 6, 1985, p. 93.

19. "Sarney toma biotonico," *Veja*, November 27, 1985, p. 37.

20. "Um pacote enfeitado," *Veja*, December 4, 1985, p. 36.

21. "Um outro termometro," *Veja*, December 4, 1985, p. 45.

22. Ibid.

23. Mario Henrique Simonsen, "Um pacote bem embrulhado," *Veja*, December 4, 1985, p. 50.

24. Francisco Lopes, *O choque heterodoxo* (Rio de Janeiro: Editora Campus, 1986). Two brief, but interesting, discussions of the isssues are: "Hyperinflation: Taming the Beast," *Economist*, November 15, 1986, pp. 55–64; and Peter T. Knight, F. Desmond

McCarthy, and Sweder van Wijnbergen, "Escaping Hyperinflation," *Finance and Development,* December 1986, pp. 14–17.

25. Interview with Sayad, April 21, 1987.

26. *Economist,* November 30, 1985, p. 83.

27. Ibid. The banks that were liquidated were Comind (no. 6), Auxiliar (no. 12), and the smaller Banco Maissonave.

28. "A ultima cartada," *Veja,* December 25, 1985, p. 65.

29. Ibid.

30. Ibid., p. 66.

31. "Um PFL vale 2 1/2 PMDB," *Veja,* February 19, 1986, p. 21.

32. "A vida e a nova moeda," *Veja,* March 5, 1986, pp. 28–34.

33. "Sarney sai da retranca," *Veja,* December 10, 1986, p. 37.

34. Instituto Brasileiro de Economia, "O gigante volta as compras," *Conjuntura,* July 1986, pp. 7–9.

35. Jose Sarney, announcement of economic reforms on nationwide Brazilian television, July 23, 1986.

36. Jose R. Nassar, "Crescimento compulsorio," *Senhor,* July 29, 1986.

37. Interview with Sayad, April 21, 1987.

38. "FIPE registra pressoes no custo de vida em SP," *Folha de Sao Paulo,* August 20, 1986, p. 23.

39. "Escandalo da carne," *Senhor,* September 8, 1987, pp. 41–42.

40. "Desercoes no curzado," *Veja,* November 26, 1986, p. 50.

41. "O governo enche o bolso," *Veja,* November 26, 1986, pp. 42–47; and Roger Cohen, "Brazilian Effort to Moderate Economy, Improve Trade Surplus Draws Criticism," *Wall Street Journal,* November 24, 1986.

42. "O governo enche o bolso," p. 43.

43. Interview with Sayad, April 21, 1987.

44. Ibid.

45. "Sarney sai da retranca," p. 37.

46. Dilson Funaro, "Statement by Mr. Dilson Funaro, Minister of Finance of Brazil," U.S. congressional summit on debt and trade, Waldorf Astoria, New York City, December 5, 1986, pp. 3–5. Mimeo.

47. "IMF Agrees to Back Brazil Economic Plan," *Wall Street Journal,* December 11, 1986.

48. "Brazil Wins Rescheduling of $4.1 Billion in Payments to Its Government Creditors," *Wall Street Journal,* January 22, 1987, p. 35.

49. "Brazil to Suspend Interest Payment to Foreign Banks," *New York Times,* February 21, 1987, p. 1.

50. Governor Leonel Brizola and PT president Luiz Inacio "Lula" da Silva were among those who criticized the moratorium's timing.

51. Dilson Funaro, "Perspectivas da economia brasileira em 1987." Address delivered at "Brasil 87:0 Desafio Economico," Copacabana Palace Hotel, Rio de Janeiro, March 16, 1987.

52. "Brazil Trade Surplus Shrank to $136 Million in March," *Wall Street Journal,* April 24, 1987, p. 21.

53. John Barham, "Leaders in Brazil Demand Funaro Quit His Post," *Wall Street*

Journal, April 10, 1987, p. 10. These governors were Orestes Quercia of Sao Paulo, Wellington Moreira Franco of Rio de Janeiro, and Newton Cardoso of Minas Gerais.

54. "Brazilian Ruling Party Voices Support for Funaro," *Wall Street Journal,* April 13, 1987, p. 18.

55. Roger Cohen, "President Sarney's Staff Chief Quits: Shuffle May Ensue," *Wall Street Journal,* April 23, 1987, p. 29.

56. Roger Cohen, "In Brazil's Political Theater, Sarney Could Face an Early Exit from Stage," *Wall Street Journal,* April 30, 1987, p. 26.

GLOSSARY

Adjustment: A set of medium- to long-term policies designed to modify the structure of a country's economy to overcome chronic economic problems through increased reliance on market mechanisms. Policies of adjustment ordinarily include elimination of subsidies, privatization of publicly owned firms, tariff reduction, and generally reduced state involvement in the economy.

Agreed Minute: The document that embodies the terms agreed upon by official creditors in a Paris Club rescheduling meeting. Representatives at the meeting agree to recommend to their governments the adoption of these terms in the bilateral agreements that formally implement the debt rescheduling.

Arrears: The amount of past-due payments (interest and principal) on outstanding debt owed by any given debtor.

Baker Plan: U.S. government plan designed to ease the developing country debt crisis through continued reliance on market mechanisms. Proposed in September 1985 by Treasury Secretary James Baker, the plan called for continued structural adjustments of debtor country economies in exchange for a proposed increase in IMF and World Bank lending to provide the needed incentives for renewed private bank lending.

Balance of Payments: A summary accounting statement of a nation's international economic transactions. It is divided into the current account (balance of international trade and services; e.g., exports minus imports) and the capital account (balance of international capital movements; e.g., private foreign investment, public grants, and loan flows). Balance-of-payments difficulties in a given country mostly reflect an insufficient capital account inflow to cover a current account deficit.

Bank for International Settlements (BIS): Located in Basil, Switzerland, a clearing house for the central banks of seventeen industrialized countries. It assembles emergency loan packages for sovereign states, using reserves established by deposits from their central banks.

Brady Plan: The second U.S. government policy proposal to attenuate the international debt crisis. Announced September 1988, this plan called for debt relief (voluntary private bank reduction of developing country debt) in exchange for structural adjustment of debtor country economies.

Buffer Stock Financing Facility: IMF program to help finance a member country's contribution to an approved international buffer stock. Repurchases are made in 3.25 to 5 years.

Capital Flight: The outflow of money capital from a given country in response to perceived political-economic instability and a resulting loss of confidence in the domestic investment climate. This instability often is a consequence of an overvalued exchange rate, particularly if accompanied by the expectation of a devaluation. High rates of capital flight can deplete a country's foreign reserves, create balance-of-payments difficulties, and thereby inhibit its ability to import and/or make foreign debt payments.

Compensatory and Contingency Financing Facility: IMF program providing resources to a member country suffering an export shortfall or excess cereal imports due to factors beyond its control, and/or assistance to member countries undergoing economic adjustment programs that experience unanticipated external shocks that threaten the success of the program. Repurchases are made in 3.25 to 5 years.

Conditionality: Economic policy changes required by the IMF in exchange for authorization of loans in excess of a member country's unconditional reserve tranche. These conditions constitute the content of most IMF standby agreements and ordinarily entail a restructuring of the borrower's domestic economy. They generally include devaluation, reduced government spending, enhanced government revenues, and increased reliance on market mechanisms.

Consolidation Period: The period specified in a Paris Club Agreed Minute in which debt service payments to be consolidated (rescheduled or restructured) under the terms applicable to current maturities (principal and interest payments) have fallen or will fall due.

Cross Conditionality: The incorporation of IMF loan conditions into non-IMF loans, such as those extended by commercial banks and regional development banks. Cross conditionality effectively forces a debtor country to institute an economic adjustment program in order to obtain loans from virtually any source.

Cross Default Clauses: Clauses incorporated into a loan agreement that stipulate that a lender is in default on the loan in question if the lender defaults on any of its other outstanding loans, regardless of their source.

Currency Swaps: A technique for reducing developing country debt that involves the exchange of a given value of national debt for a business opportunity desired by the holder of debt paper. The debt paper (or debtor country IOU) is usually purchased on the secondary market at a deeply discounted price and swapped for national currency (or its equivalent) at a higher rate but still well below its face value, creating benefits for debtor and creditor alike.

Cutoff Date: The date specified in a Paris Club Agreed Minute before which loans whose debt service payments are to be covered by the rescheduling agreement must have been contracted.

Debt-for-Commodity Swaps: A type of currency swap in which debt paper is utilized to pay for commodity purchases.

Debt-for-Equity Swaps: A type of currency swap in which debt capital is traded for equity in new or existing firms located in the debtor nation.

Debt-for-Nature Swaps: A type of currency swap utilizing debt paper to purchase debtor country lands for ecological purposes or to obtain government promises to invest retired debt funds in environmental programs.

Debt Service: Total amount of principal and interest payments on external debt owed each year.

Debt-to-Export Ratio: A common measure of a country's ability to pay its foreign debt. It is the ratio of a country's total debt service payments (interest and principal) to its export earnings. Export earnings reflect the country's capacity to earn the foreign exchange needed to make debt payments.

Enhanced Structural Adjustment Facility: An IMF lending program similar to the structural adjustment facility but incorporating stricter provisions governing its operation. Participation in this program requires presentation of a policy framework paper and detailed annual program each year. Semiannual loan disbursal is conditioned on the member country's performance assessed through quarterly policy targets, semiannual performance criteria, and a midyear review, all of which are designed to enforce strong adjustment measures.

Enlarged Access Facility: An IMF lending program used to augment resources available under the upper credit tranche and extended fund facility programs. This facility's conditionality, installments, and performance criteria are the same as those under the programs it augments. Repurchase is completed in 3.5 to 7 years.

Extended Fund Facility: The medium-term (three- to four-year) IMF lending program designed to overcome structural balance-of-payments disequilibria. EFF drawings are provided in installments and receipt is conditioned on fulfillment of economic policy changes identified by the Fund to be completed during the first year of the program. Repurchase is made in 4.5 to 10 years.

International Monetary Fund (IMF): Intergovernmental financial organization designed in 1944 at the Bretton Woods conference and charged with the management of the international monetary system. It is best known for its assistance to member nations with the management of short-term balance-of-payments adjustments. Whenever a country wishes to draw a sum in excess of its unconditional reserve tranche, the IMF imposes conditions on the distribution of these funds, usually in the form of economic policy reforms.

Letter of Intent: A letter identifying the performance criteria (terms and conditions) required of a member country in exchange for authorization of a conditional drawing from the IMF. This letter forms the basis of a country's agreement with the Fund and often is a prerequisite for debt negotiations or rescheduling agreements with other international financial institutions or private creditors.

Loan Default: A bank declaration that a borrower is not expected ever to repay its debt, usually following an extended cessation of principal and interest payments by a debtor.

London Club: An informal grouping of private commercial banks that have extended credit to a country experiencing debt repayment difficulties. Although the Club is without formal structural organization, permanent staff, and a fixed location, it provides an arena for major money center banks, and the loan syndicates they have organized, to coordinate their negotiating positions in debt-rescheduling talks with individual developing countries.

London Inter-Bank Offered Rate (LIBOR): Traditional benchmark interest rate for international lending by private European banks (much like the prime rate for loans set by the Federal Reserve within the United States). It also functions as the standard base rate for international loans provided at variable interest rates.

Money Center Banks: Large international banks responsible for most private international lending. Their lending capital can be generated from their own deposit funds or from their formation of loan syndicates with smaller regional and local banks.

Moratorium: A unilateral declaration that a country intends to cease principal and interest payments to its creditors.

Multiyear Rescheduling Agreements (MYRAs): Agreements with official and/or private bank creditors in which a debtor country, unable to meet current debt service payments as well as those coming due in ensuing years, restructures its debt payments owed over several years.

Organization for Economic Cooperation and Development (OECD): An organization of the twenty major developed countries whose objective is to foster economic growth in its member economies through increased cooperation.

Paris Club: An informal grouping of official creditors, composed usually of major developed countries and often of members of the OECD. Operating out of the French Treasury (but without a permanent staff or organizational structure), the Club coordinates the negotiating position of countries that either loaned money directly or guaranteed private bank loans to a particular developing country experiencing loan repayment difficulties. In recent years, the Paris Club has been regularly invoked as a forum for the rescheduling of governmentally insured loans to individual developing countries.

Performance Criteria: Economic policy reform criteria or targets, identified in a member country's letter of intent to the IMF, which constitute prerequisites for continued IMF loan disbursals.

Repudiation: The permanent cessation of debt payments and obligations by a debtor country.

Rescheduling: The process by which a debtor country, unable to meet debt service payments, restructures these payments by extending the term over which debts must be repaid, lowering the interest rate charged on these loans, and/or obtaining a grace period before debt payments must recommence.

Secondary Market: The market where developing country debt is bought and sold, generally at deep discounts. The price for each country's debt paper, or IOUs, is set by market demand. This price reflects international confidence in the ability of any given country to pay off its debt and thus is seen as expressing the "real value" of developing country debt. Buyers in this market include banks, institutional investors, and participants in debt swaps.

Spread: Interest rate difference between LIBOR and the actual interest rate charged on an international loan. The size of the spread reflects the creditworthiness of the borrower country (the lower the spread, the higher the creditworthiness).

Stabilization: A set of short-term restrictive fiscal and monetary policies designed to reduce inflation, cut government budget deficits, and ease balance-of-payments difficulties. Stabilization is the immediate objective of IMF standby agreements.

Standby Agreement: Contents of the letter of intent from a prospective borrower to the IMF. It consists of the economic policy reforms (terms and conditions) the borrower agrees to institute in exchange for full disbursal of its IMF loan.

Structural Adjustment Facility: An IMF program providing resources on concessional terms to low-income member countries suffering protracted balance-of-payments problems and undertaking structural adjustment. Conditionality takes the form of a policy framework paper (PFP) in which the member country (with Fund assistance) outlines a three-year policy program. Disbursement of loans follows the presentation of detailed annual programs that include quarterly performance criteria. Repayments are made in 5.5 to 10 years.

Syndicated Loans: Most often organized by major money center banks, these loans incorporate funds from smaller financial institutions. This practice is common in international lending because of the typically large size of such loans.

Unconditional Reserve Tranche: The amount of funds any member country may draw from the IMF without having to meet Fund-imposed economic policy conditions. This tranche is equal to 25 percent of a member's quota.

United Nations Conference on Trade and Development (UNCTAD): A permanent organ of the UN General Assembly instituted in 1964 to promote international trade, economic development, and the needs of developing countries. As a representative for developing (debtor) country interests, UNCTAD is often invited to participate in Paris Club reschedulings.

Upper Credit Tranches: IMF programs providing funds to member countries in excess of 25 percent of their quotas. Recipients must meet Fund-imposed economic policy conditions to overcome balance-of-payments disequilibria, generally expressed in the form of a standby agreement including performance criteria and an installment plan. Repurchases are made in 3.25 to 5 years.

World Bank: The International Bank for Reconstruction and Development (IBRD), or World Bank, is an intergovernmental financial organization designed at the 1944 Bretton Woods conference to provide and manage medium- and long-term development assistance to member countries. The Bank also offers structural adjustment loans that provide medium-term financial assistance to member countries undertaking IMF adjustment programs. The World Bank has an office and official representative in many member countries to oversee Bank projects and interests within the country.

BIBLIOGRAPHY

International Financial Negotiations

Aggarwal, Vinod K. *International Debt Threat: Bargaining Among Creditors and Debtors in the 1980s.* Berkeley: Institute of International Studies, Policy Papers on International Affairs, Number 29, 1987.

Dillon, K. Burke, C. Maxwell Watson, G. Russell Kincaid, and Chanpen Puckahtikom. *Recent Developments in External Debt Restructuring.* Washington, D.C.: International Monetary Fund, 1985.

Friedman, Irving S. *The World Debt Dilemma: Managing Country Risk.* Washington, D.C.: Council for Banking Studies, 1983.

Haggard, Stephan, and Robert Kaufman. "The Politics of Stabilization and Structural Adjustment." In Jeffrey Sachs, ed., *Developing Country Debt and the World Economy: The International Financial System.* Chicago: University of Chicago Press, 1989, pp. 263–274.

Hardy, Chandra. "Rescheduling Developing Country Debts." *Banker,* July 1981.

Kahler, Miles. *The Politics of International Debt.* Ithaca, N.Y.: Cornell University Press, 1986.

Kuhn, Michael G., and Jorge P. Guzman. *Multilateral Official Debt Rescheduling: Recent Experience.* Washington, D.C.: International Monetary Fund, 1990.

Lipson, Charles. "Banker's Dilemma: Private Cooperation in Rescheduling Sovereign Debts." *World Politics* (October 1985), pp. 200–225.

_____. "The International Organization of Third World Debt." International Organization 35:4 (1981), pp. 603–631.

Nelson, Joan. "The Politics of Stabilization." In Richard Feinberg and Valeriana Kallab, eds., *Adjustment Crisis in the Third World.* Washington, D.C.: Overseas Development Council, 1984, pp. 99–118.

_____, ed. *Economic Crisis and Policy Choice: The Politics of Adjustment in the Third World.* Princeton, N.J.: Princeton University Press, 1990.

Puchala, Donald J., and Raymond F. Hopkins. "International Regimes: Lessons from Inductive Analysis." *International Organization* 36:2 (Spring 1982), pp. 245–275.

Putnam, Robert. "Diplomacy and Domestic Politics: The Logic of Two-Level Games." *International Organization* 42:3 (Summer 1988), pp. 427–460.

Remmer, Karen. "The Politics of Economic Stabilization: IMF Stand-by Programs in Latin America, 1954-1984." *Comparative Politics* 19 (October 1986): pp. 1–24.

Ruggie, John Gerard. "International Regimes, Transactions, and Change: Embedded

Liberalism in the Postwar Economic Order." *International Organization* 36:2 (Spring 1982), pp. 379–415.

Watson, Maxwell, Russell Kincaid, Caroline Atkinson, Eliot Kalter, and David Folkerts-Landau. *International Capital Markets: Developments and Prospects.* Washington, D.C.: International Monetary Fund, 1986.

The International Financial Institutions and Conditionality

Ayres, Robert L. *Banking on the Poor: The World Bank and World Poverty.* Cambridge: MIT Press, 1983.

Babai, Don. "The World Bank and the IMF: Rolling Back the State or Backing Its Role?" In Raymond Vernon, ed., *The Promise of Privatization.* New York: Council on Foreign Relations, 1988.

Baum, Warren C. *The Project Cycle.* Washington, D.C.: World Bank, 1982.

Bienen, Henry, and Mark Gersovitz. "Economic Stabilization, Conditionality, and Political Stability." *International Organization* 39:4 (Autumn 1985): pp. 729–754.

Biersteker, Thomas J. "Reducing the Role of the State in the Economy: A Conceptual Exploration of IMF and World Bank Prescriptions." *International Studies Quarterly* 34:4 (December 1990), pp. 477–492.

Carvounis, Chris C. *The Debt Dilemma of Developing Nations.* Westport, Conn.: Quorum Books, 1984.

Chandavarkar, Anand G. *The International Monetary Fund: Its Financial Organization and Activities.* Washington, D.C.: International Monetary Fund, 1984.

Cohen, Benjamin J. "Balance-of-Payments Financing: Evolution of a Regime." *International Organization* 36:2 (Spring 1982): PP. 457–478.

Dell, Sidney. "Stabilization: The Political Economy of Overkill." In John Williamson, ed., *IMF Conditionality.* Cambridge: MIT Press, 1983.

Driscoll, David D. *The IMF and the World Bank: How Do They Differ?* Washington, D.C.: International Monetary Fund, 1992.

Edwards, Sebastian. "Structural Adjustment Policies in Highly Indebted Countries." In Jeffrey D. Sachs, ed., *Developing Country Debt and Economic Performance: The International Financial System.* Chicago: University of Chicago Press, 1989.

Garritsen de Vries, Margaret. *The IMF in a Changing World, 1945–85.* Washington, D.C.: International Monetary Fund, 1986.

Gold, Joseph. *The IMF and the World Bank.* Washington, D.C.: International Monetary Fund, 1982.

Guitian, Manuel. *Fund Conditionality: Evolution of Principles and Practices.* Washington, D.C.: International Monetary Fund, 1981.

Hazlitt, Henry. *From Bretton Woods to World Inflation.* Chicago: Regnery Gateway Press, 1984.

Helleiner, Gerald K. *Africa and the International Monetary Fund.* Washington, D.C.: International Monetary Fund, 1986.

_____. "The Question of Conditionality." In Carol Lancaster and John Williamson, eds., *African Debt Financing.* Washington, D.C.: Institute for International Economics, 1986.

Killick, Tony. *The IMF and Stabilisation: Developing Country Experiences.* London: Gower, 1984.

Killick, Tony, Graham Bird, Jennifer Sharpley, and Mary Sutton. "IMF Policies in Developing Countries: The Case for a Change." *Banker,* April 1984.
————. "The IMF: Case for a Change in Emphasis." In Richard Feinberg and Valeriana Kallab, eds., *Adjustment Crisis in the Third World.* Washington, D.C.: Overseas Development Council, 1984, 59-81.

Moseley, Paul, Jane Harrigan, and John Toye. *Aid and Power: The World Bank and Policy-Based Lending.* London: Routledge, 1991.

Pastor, Manuel, Jr. *The International Monetary Fund and Latin America: Economic Stabilization and Class Conflict.* Boulder, Colo.: Westview Press, 1987.

Please, Stanley. *The Hobbled Giant: Essays on the World Bank.* Boulder, Colo: Westview Press, 1984.

Ribe, Helena, et al. *How Adjustment Programs Can Help the Poor.* Washington, D.C.: World Bank, 1990.

Rieffel, Alexis. *The Role of the Paris Club in Managing Debt Problems.* Princeton, N.J.: Princeton University, Essays in International Finance, Number 161, 1985.

Roberts, Paul Craig. "World Debt: The IMF Solution Has Become the Problem." *Business Week,* July 9, 1984.

Rotberg, Eugene H. *The World Bank: A Financial Appraisal.* Washington, D.C.: World Bank, 1981.

Ruggie, John Gerard. "International Regimes, Transactions, and Change: Embedded Liberalism in the Postwar Economic Order." *International Organization* 36:2 (Spring 1982): pp. 379–415.

Taylor, Lance. *Varieties of Stabilization Experience: Towards Sensible Macroeconomics in the Third World.* Oxford: Clarendon Press, 1988.

Williamson, John. *IMF Conditionality.* Cambridge: MIT Press, 1983.
————. "On Seeking to Improve IMF Conditionality." *American Economic Review,* May 1983.
————. *The Lending Policies of the International Monetary Fund.* Washington, D.C.: Institute for International Economics, 1982.

World Bank. *Adjustment Lending: An Evaluation of Ten Years of Experience.* Washington, D.C.: World Bank, Policy and Research Series, Number 1, 1988.
————. *Annual Report.* Washington, D.C.: World Bank, 1985, 1986, 1990, 1991.

Adjustment Bargaining and Economic Performance

Biersteker, Thomas J. "The 'Triumph' of Neoclassical Economics in the Developing World: Policy Convergence and the Bases of Governance in the International Economic Order." In James N. Rosenau, ed., *Governance Without Government: Order and Change in World Politics.* Cambridge: Cambridge University Press, 1992.

Cornia, Giovanni, Richard Jolly, and Frances Stewart, eds. *Adjustment with a Human Face.* Oxford: Clarendon Press, 1987.

Edwards, Sebastian. "Structural Adjustment Policies in Highly Indebted Countries." In Jeffrey D. Sachs, ed., *Developing Country Debt and Economic Performance: The International Financial System.* Chicago: University of Chicago Press, 1989.

Feinberg, Richard E., and Valeriana Kallab, eds. *Adjustment Crisis in the Third World.* Washington, D.C.: Overseas Development Council, 1984.

Foxley, Alejandro. *Latin American Experiments in Neoconservative Economics.*

Berkeley: University of California Press, 1983.

Frieden, Jeffry A. *Debt, Development, and Democracy: Modern Political Economy and Latin America, 1965–1985.* Princeton, N.J.: Princeton University Press, 1991.

Haggard, Stephan, and Robert R. Kaufman, eds. *The Politics of Economic Adjustment.* Princeton, N.J.: Princeton University Press, 1992.

Nelson, Joan M., ed. *Economic Crisis and Policy Choice: The Politics of Adjustment in the Third World.* Princeton, N.J.: Princeton University Press, 1990.

Sachs, Jeffrey D., ed. *Developing Country Debt and Economic Performance: The International Financial System.* Chicago: University of Chicago Press, 1989.

Williamson, John. *The Progress of Policy Reform in Latin America.* Washington, D.C.: Institute for International Economics, 1990.

_____. *Prospects for Adjustment in Argentina, Brazil, and Mexico: Responding to the Debt Crisis.* Washington, D.C.: Institute for International Economics, 1983.

The Origins and Character of International Debt Crises

Amuzegar, Jahangir. "Dealing with Debt." *Foreign Policy* 68 (Fall 1987): pp. 140–158.

Devlin, Robert. *Debt and Crisis in Latin America: The Supply Side of the Story.* Princeton, N.J.: Princeton University Press, 1989.

Diaz-Alejandro, Carlos. *"Latin American Debt: I Don't Think We're in Kansas Anymore."* Brookings Papers on Economic Activity, Number 2.

Eichengree, Barry, and Peter H. Lindert, eds. *The International Debt in Historical Perspective.* Cambridge: MIT Press, 1989.

Eskridge, William. "Les Jeux Sont Faits: Structural Origins of the International Debt Problem." *Virginia Journal of International Law* 25:2 (Winter 1985): pp. 281–400.

Frieden, Jeffrey. "Third World Indebted Industrialization: International Finance and State Capitalism in Mexico, Brazil, Algeria, and South Korea." *International Organization* 35:3 (Summer 1981): pp. 407–431.

Griffith-Jones, Stephany, and Osvaldo Sunkel. *Debt and Development Crisis in Latin America: The End of an Illusion.* Oxford: Clarendon Press, 1986.

Kuczynski, Pedro-Pablo. *The Latin American Debt.* Baltimore: Johns Hopkins University Press, 1988.

Lancaster, Carol, and John Williamson, eds. *African Debt and Financing.* Washington, D.C.: Institute for International Economics, 1986.

Lindert, Peter H., and Peter J. Morton. "How Sovereign Debt Has Worked." In Jeffrey D. Sachs, ed., *Developing Country Debt and Economic Performance: The International Financial System.* Chicago: University of Chicago Press, 1989.

Marichal, Carlos. *A Century of Debt Crises in Latin America: From Independence to the Great Depression, 1820-1930.* Princeton, N.J.: Princeton University Press, 1989.

Sachs, Jeffrey, ed. *Developing Country Debt and the World Economy.* Chicago: University of Chicago Press, 1989.

Stallings, Barbara. *Banker to the Third World: U.S. Portfolio Investment in Latin America, 1900-1986.* Berkeley: University of California Press, 1987.

Wellons, Philip A. *Borrowing by Developing Countries on the Euro-Currency Market.* Paris: OECD, 1977.

_____. *World Money and Credit: The Crisis and Its Causes.* Boston: Harvard Business School, 1983.

World Bank. *World Development Report.* Oxford: Oxford University Press, 1987.

Alternative Approaches to the Debt Crisis

Cline, William. *Mobilizing Bank Lending to Developing Countries.* Washington, D.C.: Institute for International Economics, 1987.

Cornia, Giovanni, Richard Jolly, and Frances Stewart, eds. *Adjustment with a Human Face.* Oxford: Clarendon Press, 1987.

Kaletsky, Anatole. *The Costs of Default.* New York: Twentieth Century Fund, 1985.

O'Donnell, Guillermo. "External Debt: Why Don't Our Governments Do the Obvious?" *CEPAL Review* 27 (1986), pp. 27–33.

Schydlowski, Daniel. "The Tragedy of Lost Opportunity in Peru." In Jonathan Hartlyn and Samuel Morley, eds., *Latin American Political Economy.* Boulder, Colo.: Westview Press, 1986: pp. 217–242.

Williamson, John. *Voluntary Approaches to Debt Relief.* Washington, D.C.: Institute for International Economics, 1989.

Mexico

Bailey, Norman, and Richard Cohen. *The Mexican Time Bomb.* New York: Twentieth Century Fund, 1987.

Evans, John. "Few Regard Mexican Accord as a Model." *American Banker,* July 25, 1989.

Harvard Business School. *Mexico's Adjustment Program.* Cambridge: Harvard Business School, 1983.

Islam, Shafiqal. "It's a Bad Deal for the Model Debtor." *New York Times,* August 6, 1989.

Kaufman, Robert. *The Politics of Debt in Argentina, Brazil, and Mexico: Economic Stabilization in the 1980s.* Berkeley: Institute of International Studies, 1988.

Kraft, Joseph. *The Mexican Rescue.* New York: Group of Thirty, 1984.

Newell, Roberto, and Luis Rubio. *Mexico's Dilemma: The Political Origins of Economic Crisis.* Boulder, Colo: Westview Press, 1984.

Rubio, Luis, and Francisco Gil-Diaz. *A Mexican Response.* New York: Twentieth Century Fund, 1987.

U.S. Congress. House of Representatives. Subcommittee on International Trade, Investment, and Monetary Policy of the Committee on Banking, Finance, and Urban Affairs. *The Mexican Economic Crisis: Policy Implications for the United States.* 98th Congress, Second Session, 1984.

U.S. Congress. Senate. Subcommittee on International Finance and Monetary Policy of the Committee on Banking, Housing, and Urban Affairs. *International Debt.* 98th Congress, First Session, 1983.

Zaire

Adelman, Kenneth. "Zaire's Year of Crisis." *African Affairs* 77 (1978).
Callaghy, Thomas M. *The State-Society Struggle: Zaire in Comparative Perspective.* New York: Columbia University Press, 1984.
Garten, Jeffrey E. "Rescheduling Third World Debt: The Case of Zaire." Ph.D. dissertation, School of Advanced International Studies, Johns Hopkins University, 1981.
Kalb, Madeline G. *The Congo Cables: The Cold War in Africa from Eisenhower to Kennedy.* New York: Macmillan, 1982.
Karl-i-Bond, Nguza. *Mobutu ou l'incarnation du mal zairois.* London: Rex Collings, 1982.
MacGaffey, Janet. *Entrepreneurs and Parasites: The Struggle for Indigenous Capitalism in Zaire.* Cambridge: Cambridge University Press, 1987.
Mahoney, Richard D. *JFK: Ordeal in Africa.* Oxford: Oxford University Press, 1983.
Stockwell, John. *In Search of Enemies: A CIA Story.* New York: W. W. Norton, 1978.
Young, Crawford. "Zaire: The Unending Crisis." *Foreign Affairs* 57: 1 (1978).
Young, Crawford, and Thomas Turner. *The Rise and Decline of the Zairian State.* Madison: University of Wisconsin Press, 1985.

Nigeria

Bangura, Yusuf. "Structural Adjustment and the Political Question." *Review of African Political Economy* 37 (December 1986).
Biersteker, Thomas J. *Multinationals, the State, and Control of the Nigerian Economy.* Princeton, N.J.: Princeton University Press, 1987.
_____. "The Relationship Between Economic and Political Reforms: Structural Adjustment and the Democratic Transition in Nigeria." Forthcoming in Biersteker, ed., *Economic Crisis, Structural Adjustment, and the Political Transition in Nigeria.*
Callaghy, Thomas. "Lost Between State and Market: The Politics of Economic Adjustment in Ghana, Zambia and Nigeria." In Joan Nelson, ed., *Economic Crisis and Policy Change.* Princeton, N.J.: Princeton University Press, 1990, 257-319.
Diamond, Larry. "Nigeria Between Dictatorship and Democracy." *Current History* 86:520 (May 1987).
_____. "Nigeria in Search of Democracy." *Foreign Affairs* 62:4 (Spring 1984).
Olukoshi, Adebayo. *Crisis and Adjustment in the Nigerian Economy.* Lagos: JAD Publishers, 1991.

Philippines

Bello, Walden, et al. *Development Debacle.* San Francisco: Institute for Food and Development Policy, 1982.
Bonner, Raymond. *Waltzing with a Dictator: The Marcoses and the Making of American Policy.* New York: Vintage Books, 1988.
Broad, Robin. *Unequal Alliance: The World Bank, The International Monetary Fund, and the Philippines.* Berkeley: University of California Press, 1988.

Galang, Jose. "More Than Sympathy." *Far Eastern Economic Review,* August 14, 1986.
Haggard, Stephan. "The Political Economy of the Philippine Debt Crisis." In Joan
  Nelson, ed., *Economic Crisis and Policy Choice: The Politics of Adjustment in the
  Third World.* Princeton, N.J.: Princeton University Press, 1990: pp. 215–255.
Karnow, Stanley. *In Our Image: America's Empire in the Philippines.* New York:
  Random House, 1989.
Kessler, Richard. "Politics Philippine Style Circa 1984." *Asia Survey* 24:12 (December
  1984).
Lindsey, Charles. "Economic Crisis in the Philippines." *Asia Survey* 24:12 (December
  1984).
Sacerdoti, Guy. "Marcos' Countdown." *Far Eastern Economic Review,* February 27,
  1986.

Brazil

Bacha, Edmar, and Pedro Malan. "Brazil's Debt: From the Miracle to the Fund." In
  Alfred Stepan, ed., *Democratizing Brazil: Problems of Transition and Consolidation.*
  New York: Oxford University Press, 1989: pp.120–140.
Bresser Pereira, Luiz Carlos. *Development and Crisis in Brazil, 1930-1983.* Boulder,
  Colo.: Westview Press, 1984.
Frieden, Jeffrey. "The Brazilian Borrowing Experience: From Miracle to Debacle and
  Back." *Latin American Research Review* 22:1 (1987): pp. 95–131.
Kaufman, Robert. *The Politics of Debt in Argentina, Brazil, and Mexico: Economic
  Stabilization in the 1980s.* Berkeley: Institute of International Studies, 1988.
Knight, Peter T., F. Desmond McCarthy, and Sweder van Wijnbergen. "Escaping
  Hyperinflation." *Finance and Development* 23: 4 (December 1986).
Lamounier, Bolivar, and Alkimar Moura. "Economic Policy and Political Opening in
  Brazil." In Jonathan Hartlyn and Samuel A. Morley, eds., *Latin American Political
  Economy: Financial Crisis and Political Change.* Boulder, Colo.: Westview Press,
  1986: pp.165–196.
Lopes, Francisco. *O choque heterdoxo.* Rio de Janeiro: Editora Campus, 1986.
Marques Moreira, Marcilio. *The Brazilian Quandary.* New York: Twentieth Century
  Fund, 1986.
Sarney, Jose. "Brazil: A President's Story." *Foreign Affairs* 65: 1 (Fall 1986).
van Doellinger, Carlos, et al. *A politica brasileira de comercio exterior e seus efeitos.* Rio
  de Janeiro: IPEA/INPES, 1974.

ABOUT THE CONTRIBUTORS

Thomas J. Biersteker is the Henry R. Luce Professor of International Relations at Brown University.

Melissa H. Birch is an associate professor at the Darden Graduate School of Business Administration at the University of Virginia.

Thomas M. Callaghy is an associate professor of political science at the University of Pennsylvania.

Hugo Presgrave de A. Faria is an investment banker in New York City.

Christine A. Kearney is a Ph.D. candidate in the Department of Political Science at Brown University.

Pamela K. Starr is a Ph.D. candidate in the School of International Relations at the University of Southern California.

Penelope A. Walker is a Ph.D. candidate in the Department of Political Science at Yale University.

ABOUT THE BOOK

The global debt burden has proven to be a bad bargain for developed and developing countries alike. This selection of case studies illustrates the complexity of international financial negotiations and the difficulty of reaching international agreements satisfactory to both creditors and debtors. The key aspects of debtor country bargaining power are explored—size, strategic significance, internal cohesion, and political stability—as we read of creditors flexing their financial muscles to produce domestic economic reform without significant international debt relief.

This volume brings together a theoretical overview of the subject, cases describing the principal institutional actors, carefully excerpted cases of bilateral financial negotiations, sugggestions for further reading, and a helpful glossary of technical terms. It illuminates how complex international financial negotiations are conducted and what their impact is on both the domestic political economy and the international relations of the countries involved.